D0421907

ROYAL HISTORICAL SOCIETY
STUDIES IN HISTORY 53

WALES IN THE REIGN OF JAMES I

WALES IN THE REIGN OF JAMES I

G. Dyfnallt Owen

THE ROYAL HISTORICAL SOCIETY

THE BOYDELL PRESS

© G. Dyfnallt Owen 1988

First published 1988

A Royal Historical Society publication
published by The Boydell Press
an imprint of Boydell & Brewer Ltd
PO Box 9   Woodbridge   Suffolk IP12 3DF
and of Boydell & Brewer Inc.
Wolfeboro   New Hampshire 03894–2069   USA

ISBN 0 86193 210 2

ISSN 0269–2244

British Library Cataloguing in Publication Data
Owen, Geraint Dyfnallt
    Wales in the reign of James I.—(Royal
    Historical Society studies in history,
    ISSN 0269–2244; 53).
    1. Wales—History 2. Great Britain—
    History—James I, 1603–1625
    I. Title   II. Royal Historical Society
    III. Series
    942.9′06′1   DA720
    ISBN 0–86193–210–2

Library of Congress Cataloging-in-Publication Data
Owen, Geraint Dyfnallt.
    Wales in the reign of James I / G. Dyfnallt Owen.
    p. cm. — (Royal Historical Society studies in history, ISSN
    0269–2244 ; 53)
    Bibliography: p.
    Includes index.
    ISBN 0–86193–210–2 (Boydell Press) :
    1. Wales—History.   2. Great Britain—History—James 1,
    1603–1625.   3. James I, King of England, 1566–1625.   I. Title.
    II. Series: Royal Historical Society studies in history ; no. 53.
    DA720.094 1988
    942.9′061—dc19   87–32631
                                                       CIP

Printed in Great Britain by
St Edmundsbury Press, Bury St Edmunds, Suffolk

FOR MY GRANDCHILDREN

Contents

The Society records its gratitude to the following whose generosity made possible the initiation of this series: The British Academy; The Pilgrim Trust; The Twenty-Seven Foundation; The United States Embassy's Bicentennial funds; The Wolfson Trust; several private donors.

Introduction

It is likely that King James of Scotland knew little about Wales when he crossed the English border to be crowned in London, and there is no indication that he showed any particular interest in its people during the ensuing twenty-three years of his reign. Contacts between the Principality and the northern kingdom had been, and still were, fortuitous and it was unfortunate that an eminent Welshman, who was admirably qualified to enlighten the King on the distinctive national and cultural features of Welsh society, should have incurred his distrust. In 1589 John Penry, the Puritan reformer and author, a native of Breconshire, had eluded his enemies in England by fleeing to Scotland, where he had friends amongst the Presbyterian ministers in Edinburgh, some of them with influence at the Scottish Court. In normal circumstances James might have had no objection to his presence, and might conceivably have been willing to meet the redoubtable reformer associated with the notorious Marprelate Tracts. To pit his theological expertise against persons of differing religious convictions exhilarated the King almost as much as did his favourite pastime of hunting. But a word of warning from Elizabeth of England that Penry was propagating subversive doctrines, destructive of State and Church government alike, was enough to pronounce him as a person unfit for royal company. Despite the exertions of his friends Penry was banished from Scotland, and one possible link with Wales irreparably broken.[1]

From now on, whatever the King learned about life and manners beyond the rivers Severn and Dee was desultorily picked up in the course of his personal or official dealings with ministers and courtiers. It was inevitable that some sources of

---

[1] *Calendar of Scottish Papers*, vol. X (1589–93), pp. 280, 295, 368, 383. *See also* Register of the Privy Council of Scotland, vol. IV, pp. 518–19, n. 1.

information should be tendentious or suspect. There is no evidence that James, who had no hesitation in dismissing his Gaelic-speaking subjects in the Highlands and the Western Isles as wolves and wild boars, held such contemptuous opinions of his Welsh-speaking subjects.[2] But his occasional reference to their language could appear at times to be somewhat disparaging. Commenting on a book which he had written many years previously, and which had been lavishly praised by Sir Robert Cecil, the principal English Secretary of State, he protested to the latter that:

> The language is extremely bad, for although it was first written all with my own hand it was marred in the orthography by Geddes copying it... in very rude Scottish spelling; and, next, it was copied by Sir Peter Young's son who pressing to English both marred it quite and made it neither, so as it is now good Britaine language or rather Welsh.[3]

Some of the distinguished company who formed his intimate circle at the English Court could have taught James a few elementary facts about the inhabitants of Wales and their mother tongue. William Herbert, Earl of Pembroke, who entertained the King at his country house of Wilton in Wiltshire, was certainly competent to do so. His father, the second Earl, whose patronage of the language and its literature had won extravagant praise from Welsh bards, could not have failed to communicate some portion of his knowledge and enthusiasm to his son. Sir John Herbert, the junior Secretary of State, could have rendered a similar service. His fluency in Welsh and his attachment to his native land remained unimpaired, even after forty years or so of diplomatic assignment all over western Europe, of acquiring foreign languages and of collaboration with his superior, Sir Robert Cecil; and even, one ventures to

---

[2] Wilson, *King James I and VI*, p. 119. The King of Scotland, however, was not content to confine his hostility to words. His treatment of the McGregor clan, for instance, was savage in the extreme and amounted to a policy of virtual extermination, which almost rivals the massacre of Glencoe in its inhumanity. *See* Register of the Privy Council of Scotland, vol. VI, 1599–1604, Index p. 99P under McGregor. *See also* Browne, *History of the Highland Clans*, pp. 23–35 and Skrene, *The Highlanders of Scotland*, pp. 335–8.

[3] HMC *Salisbury (Cecil) MSS*, vol. XXI, p. 83. King James to the Earl of Salisbury, dated 8 July 1609.

think, after the unpleasant experience of having the sycamore and fruit trees, which he had conveyed from London to plant on his estate near Abergavenny, wilfully destroyed by local hooligans.[4]

But if ever the King turned to his chief Secretary of State for clarification of certain oddities of Welsh character, it is doubtful whether he would be much enlightened. Despite his Welsh antecedents, Sir Robert Cecil chose to ignore them or, at least, to minimise them as having little bearing on the paramountcy of his family in the political life of the kingdom. He showed little patience with a Welshman, William George, obviously one of the self-employed Welsh genealogists of the time, who wrote to inform him that he had discovered Cecil's pedigree which he claimed to be able to trace to an ancient Prince of Wales. In fact, he had come across it fifteen years previously, had taken the trouble to travel to London and had acquainted Cecil's father, Lord Burghley, with the fruits of his research. He had, however, been arrested and imprisoned on some charges unconnected with the impalement of coats of arms and other heraldic devices. Despite the intervening years of detention, he was still ready to serve Cecil with his genealogical expertise, but the Secretary of State dismissed him with little pretence of courtesy. 'I desire none of these vain toys', he noted on George's letter, 'nor to hear of such absurdities.'[5]

But in the year that he voiced his deprecation of pedigree hunting, he was to discover that whereas it was possible to disregard the fanciful creations of enthusiastic genealogists, it was another and more hazardous matter deliberately to distort or mutilate a family patronymic. This, it seems, is what Cecil's father, Lord Burghley, had done and his two sons had to suffer the consequences.

In November 1605, the elder of the two, Thomas Cecil, Earl of Exeter, disclosed in a letter that he was most distressed by offensive remarks directed against his brother, the Secretary of State, by some of his enemies. One observation was to the effect that 'it was a straunge thyng that such a one as he [the Secretary], whose grandfather was a syvemaker, shold rule the whole state of England'. The Earl of Exeter, shocked that the family should be associated in any way with such a humble

---

[4] PRO Star Chamber 8 James I 125/19.
[5] HMC *Salisbury (Cecil) MSS* vol. XVII, p. 595. William George to the Earl of Salisbury, dated 1605.

craft as sievemaking, thought it imperative that the record should be put right and evidence produced to confirm that his grandfather and great grandfather had been sheriffs of Northamptonshire.[6] But he conceded that it was Lord Burghley who had started the trouble.

> My lord, my father, alteryng the wrytyng of his name maketh many that are not well affectyd to our house, to dowbt whyther we ryghtly discended of that howse of Walles, because they wryte their names Sitsilt and our name is wrytten Cecyll. My grandfather write yt Syssell, and so I mervayle what moved my lord, my father, to alter it.

Whatever accounted for Lord Burghley's reformist urge in the spelling of the family name, even his son, the Secretary of State, must have realized that Welsh antecedents could contribute to the illustrious descent of the Cecils, for he agreed wholeheartedly with the sentiments expressed by his brother in this letter.[7]

Moreover, those in Wales who claimed kinship with the all-powerful Secretary of State, did not allow him to forget that fact or that they considered consanguinity to be a good enough reason to extract all sorts of favour from him. His relationship with the members of the Cecil family who still lived on in the ancestral home at Allt-yr-ynys in Walterstone, Herefordshire, remained close, and it is to his credit that amidst all his exacting duties he found time to respond to their appeals for his protection, advice and patronage.[8] For the rest, he held the Principality at arm's length, and there is little to suggest that he displayed greater warmth of feeling towards it and its people than did his sovereign.

A reciprocal attitude of indifference was evident in Wales when he died in 1612. But one Welshman, at least, refused to allow this event to pass without offering a personal opinion on its significance to some people. He was Richard Edward John, native of that part of Shropshire which contained a Welsh-speaking

---

[6] For the descent and status of the Cecil family see Bridges, History and Antiquities of Northamptonshire, pp. 588–9 and PRO Lists and Indexes, no.IX, List of Sheriffs for England and Wales, p. 94.

[7] BM Harleian MSS 324, fols 32–32b. Thomas Cecil, Earl of Exeter to Thomas Allington, dated 13 November 1605.

[8] HMC Salisbury (Cecil) MSS, vol. XXII, 1612–28, p. 210; vol. XXIII, 1592–1605 (Addenda), p. 75; vol. XXIV, 1605–68 (Addenda) pp. 12, 13, 218, 275.

element in this period, and a member of the local bardic fraternity whose verses sometimes violated the accepted standard of defamation whenever some notable or other in the land stirred their indignation or hostility. On this occasion, John singled out the late Secretary of State as a subject worthy of his poetic vituperation at its crudest, and did so in English.

> Heare lise intombed, wormes meate,
> Little Robin, while he lived the greate;
> Neither Robin Red breast nor Robin Hood
> But Robin that was borne never to doe good.
> But now I think we have earthed the fox,
> Who stunke while he lived and died of the pox.[9]

Derision at the expense of individuals or people, in which James himself was inclined to indulge too often,[10] was not, however, a royal monopoly. The King may have assumed too readily that the majesty with which he tried to clothe his unprepossessing figure, as well as the authority which he arrogated to himself, and claimed to be of divine provenance, would be too sacrosanct in his subjects' eyes to be ridiculed in the slightest manner.

He was much mistaken. There was, in certain localities in Wales, no disposition to hide contempt for the King and his courtly institutions. The motive may have sometimes been irrepressible political or religious feelings, as when the Council of Wales was appalled to learn that an unknown and, apparently, unidentifiable person in Monmouthshire had called James a juggler.[11]

In Carmarthenshire, it may have been a personal pique that activated a gentleman of Trimsaran, Maurice Gwyn, to treat with derision an institution which the King was known to esteem very highly. The report went that;

> Whereas your Ma[tie] had bestowed on certain gentlemen
> of very great estate and regard in that countrie the honour
> of knighthood, the said Maurice Gwyn, not loving those

---

[9] PRO Star Chamber 8 James I 205/21 and 22.

[10] One of the victims of James's lack of sensitivity in this respect was Cecil himself, who inwardly fumed but dared not resent too openly the King's half affectionate half mocking address to him as 'my little beagle'.

[11] HMC *Salisbury (Cecil) MSS*, vol. XVI, p. 14. Thomas Morgan to Lord Zouche, dated 31 January 1603–4.

gentlemen but repining at your Maties favour bestowed on them, did endeavour most contemtously (so much as in him lay) to bringe the honour and degrees of the said knights into scorn, contempt and derision. To which end the said Maurice Gwyn shortly after, being at an alehouse in the parish of Llanedy in the said county of Carmarthen in or about the tenth day of January in the first yeare of your Majestys said raigne, and being then accompanied with Robert Jones alias Dolbren, Thomas Griffiths and divers other like dissolute and unknowne persons, did in a scornfull imytation of your Matie in makinge knights, cause the said Robert Dolbren, Thomas Griffiths and divers others that were then present, to kneele downe before him; and thereuppon drawing owt his sword, lay the same on their shoulders and calling every one of them by their severall names of baptisme, using the like woordes as your Matie doth in the creatinge of this honourable order of knights, commanded every one of his said riotous companyons to arise as knights; and after-wards in common speech called every one of his said dissolute companyons by the name and title of knight, saying and often tymes swearing that they were knights as good as others then made by your Matie.[12]

An open act of deliberate mockery like this was equally an open invitation for retaliation from those who had been mocked, particularly in an age when class distinctions were reinforced by sartorial privileges and the wearing of a sword to denote the gulf between gentry and commonalty. The bestowal of a knighthood was still an honour coveted by the ambitious and the rich,[13] and it had not yet fallen in public estimation as it did later, when it was exploited to raise money for the Crown. What is somewhat surprising in this case is that Maurice Gwyn made no attempt to deny the charge, but simply pleaded that what he had done was to create 'alehouse knights' in an atmosphere of innocent jollity, and that there had been no intention of bringing the King and his knighthood

[12] PRO Star Chamber 8 James I 287/17.

[13] These were the days when a knighthood could cost £100 or more, and when people, offering large sums of money for the honour, did not always succeed in being knighted by the King. See *Calendar of Wynn Papers*, p. 97, under date 3 February 1612–13.

ceremonies into disrepute. He may have reckoned on the fact that a monarch, known to forget himself between his cups, might be more ready to pardon one of his subjects who confessed that he too could be disorientated by unrestrained tippling.

1

The Council of Wales, its presidents and problems

Upon his arrival in London James had wisely decided not to disrupt the continuity of government by a change of ministers and officials, both central and local.[1] To have done so would have been a poor return for the promptitude with which they had accepted his accession. In any case, the English political stage was as yet too unfamilar for the King to meddle with those who played the leading roles on it; and the administrative and legal institutions of the southern kingdom required a closer inspection before being subjected to royal approbation or disapproval. In the case of Wales, this meant that the Council of Wales or Court of the Welsh Marches at Ludlow could continue its current policies and activities without interruption.

What the King expected from the Council was the strict and undeviating application of whatever measures were devised by him and his ministers for the effectual administration of the Principality. In his eyes, the Council was primarily a council of state dependent on, and accountable to, him and his Privy Council, and in no way subordinate to Parliament or any court of common law. It was the paramount instrument of government established to enforce the authority of the Crown, and invested with the prerogative powers of the King or of as much of them as he chose to delegate to it, to execute that function. But it could only do so with efficacy and success, and with disregard of sectional interests and social and religious barriers

---

[1] At the height of the controversy concerning the jurisdiction of the Council of Wales over the four English border shires, the King used this as an argument in defence of his prerogative powers and claimed that in view of his 'contynewing of particular persons in their services... all our lovinge subjects are the more our debtors and should consequently not presume to make innovations at the expense of the Crowns prerogative'. PRO State Papers Domestic, James I 1603–10, vol. 37, fols 113–16. Proclamation touching the Marches, 1606.

and distinctions, as long as the validity and force of the King's prerogative powers remained unquestioned and the overriding authority of the Crown was not challenged from any quarter. That challenge was to come within a short time of James's accession, but in the meantime the Council carried on with its day to day proceedings in Ludlow Castle, and with the exigent and often frustrating task of disciplining Welshmen of all classes to acquire the virtue of civic responsibility.

On the face of it, the authority wielded by the Council of Wales seemed quite adequate, for it was far-reaching, intrusive and compelling. There was practically no activity which could escape the close attention of its members, if they chose at any time to assert their all-embracing jurisdiction. For instance, all military matters affecting the Principality were the special province of the Lord President of the Council. It was he who assumed the supreme command of all the trained bands within the shires; and it fell to him, in accordance with instructions from the Privy Council, to organize their regular musters, the inspection and improvement of their weapons,[2] and the periodic levying of soldiers to serve in garrisons or expeditionary forces abroad. In this way, both domestic and foreign military service was subject to constant supervision, as was also the provision of arms, which made it easier for the Privy Council to maintain its grip on the internal security of Wales and circumvent any attempt to tamper with it. Mustering, for instance, had uses besides reviewing able-bodied men for military service. It was an effective and easy way of administering the Oath of Allegiance to the Crown to all males between the ages of sixteen and sixty who were assembled.[3]

The list of felonies and misdemeanours which, if detected, could bring retribution from Ludlow, especially in the form of fines, was long and varied enough to show how far the Council controlled and interfered with the daily pursuits and the behaviour of Welsh society. Unlawful, and often fatal, affrays and assaults were condemned and punished because of the need to curb violence amongst a people inured to it. Perjury, the intimidation of juries and the belated acquittal of criminals

---

[2] By 1618, for instance, the calivers formerly used by trained bands were no longer considered serviceable, and had in some cases been replaced with muskets. Jones-Pierce, *Clenennau Letters and Papers*, p. 99, no. 348 under date of 25 April 1618.

[3] BM Add. MSS 10609, fol. 40.

in the face of incontrovertible evidence of their guilt, were severely dealt with to prove that the Council did, indeed, exist to see that the King's laws were dutifully observed. The *Comortha* and other forms of extortion were proceeded against to demonstrate now and again that the Crown, by means of the Council, had not entirely forgotten its immemorial obligation to protect the weak against the strong. An examination of the fines inflicted on an assortment of transgressors during the reign of James I makes it quite evident that the Council's inquisitorial and penalizing powers encroached on the lives of Welshmen to an extraordinary degree.[4]

Recusants, of course, were fair game for pin-pricking harassment by officials. And so Robert Wyn, of Hafodymynydd in Denbighshire, finally caught after five years of discreet conduct, was fined £60 for 'the unlawfull buryeing the body of Jane his daughter in the church of Kerrig y Dridion, contrary to the direction of the Lord Bishop of St Assaph'. And Rees ap Einion, of Cilgwyn, was mulcted of £10 'for suffring his three daughters, being yong girles, and his maidservant to goe out of his house in the night tyme in superstitious manner to Wenefrids well'. Any such vestige of traditional Catholic practices was abhorrent to the Council and called for thorough eradication, however innocuous it might appear. But the Council was no less insistent that His Majesty's Protestant subjects in Wales should likewise be admonished and any moral aberrations in their behaviour corrected by fine. A clergyman of Marloes, in Pembrokeshire, who had created a great deal of public agitation by kissing women 'in uncivil manner', uttering blasphemous oaths and assaulting a constable had to pay £10, a heavy fine in those days when clerical stipends could be extremely low. Katherine Parry, of Llanfihangel y Creuddyn in Cardiganshire, was more fortunate. Being, perhaps, a woman of limited means but certainly not illiterate, she was only fined £3 for 'devising, publishing and singing scandalous libells in Welsh rymes'.

Adultery and kindred sexual deviations would seem to have been endemic, and not even the combined efforts of the Council and the spiritual courts of the Church, in the imposition of

---

[4] The examples which follow have been taken from BM Harleian MSS 4220, a volume consisting of the fines imposed by the Council of Wales during the reigns of James I and Charles I. Those relating to James's reign end on fol. 174.

fines and penances, were able to produce reasonable restraint in what was a general predisposition to incontinence.[5] It guaranteed, however, a regular flow of revenue to the Council and furnished it with a valid excuse – the preservation of public morals – to intervene in the personal affairs of individuals, an excuse often invoked by officialdom in the interests of public tranquillity. Moreover, in the case of this particular impropriety, the Council could inflict penalties without regard to the degree of social status or influence enjoyed or lacked by the guilty parties, and without the prospect of arousing opposition or antagonism. Sexual adventures presupposed equality of opportunity for all classes and orders; to be discovered or denounced was a risk inseparable from them, to be accepted as such and paid for without complaint. It was only when women

[5] It was doubtful, for instance, whether the incidence of adultery would be significantly reduced by the kind of light sentence imposed by the Consistory Courts on the adulterer. In one case, it was simply that, in order to cleanse himself from this offence, he should put his head in the font of his parish church and dedicate himself to a life of continence thereafter. PRO C 21 D 10/1. To counterbalance this somewhat endurable penalty, the Court of High Commission could make the guilty party wince in more than one way. Thomas Prys, of Plas Iolyn in Denbighshire, probably the son of the poet of that name, learned to his cost that cohabitation with a neighbour's daughter could bring retribution as well as enjoyment. He was not only fined £500, but imprisoned in the Fleet and sentenced to do public penance in the local parish church and the nearest market place. PRO Star Chamber 8 James I 235/11.

The unenviable reputation of the Principality in this alleged lack of resistance to carnality was even used by Crown lawyers to justify the extraordinary powers of the Council of Wales. To the charge by the Council's critics that, whereas incontinence in other parts of the kingdom was punishable only in Bishops' and Chancellors' Courts, the Council of Wales could penalize the guilty parties, without warrant of any law, by imprisonment and fines, the legal experts of the Crown replied without any pretence of verbal delicacy that:

Many tymes faultes of this nature in these partes (Wales and the four English border shires) are so fowle, so frequent as they deserve great fynes... If this vice did as much exceed in other partes of the land as in these, it were necessary to be punished in the same sorte elsewhere, but here reformation can hardly be wrought though the spirituall Court and temporal Court both do joyne in punishment, and this was inserted in the instructions many yeres since at the instance of a Bishops vice-president that found the Church censures not sufficient to repress the excessiveness of this vice there, and that in the fowlest manner and nearest degrees.

PRO State Papers Domestic, James I 1603–10, vol. 32, fol. 22.

were abducted, and sometimes indecently assaulted to force them into marriage, that the Council reacted vigorously and treated the matter as a criminal act. But only too often the Council was not actuated by the thought of the outrage done to the lady's honour, so much as by the realization that rights of ownership and inheritance could be involved, and that the injured party might seek revenge and disturb the peace of the town or countryside.

With such supervisory and punitive powers in its hands and backed by the superior authority of the Privy Council, the Council of Wales was outwardly a most formidable adversary to any restless or fractious spirit in the Principality. But, as its member well knew, this facade of strength was deceptive, and beyond the walls of Ludlow the paths along which the Council's decrees and messengers travelled were perilous as well as stony. The task of the Council was made more difficult by the hostility and contempt shown towards the law by the very people upon whom it relied to enforce its decisions. In this respect, the Welsh gentry were not much different from some of their English counterparts, and there was also a general impression that whereas crime increased the further one went from London, Wales seemed to be beyond the frontiers of legality and civic order. Sir Henry Wallop, writing of the border shires, noted that 'the neighbourhood of Wales and remoteness from London giveth more opportunity to disorder in these parts then elsewhere, and the same remoteness giveth way to the oppression of the meaner sort'. He was referring to the gentry as the principal culprits in the deliberate flouting of the law, and as a member of the Council of Wales he was in a position to know what he was talking about.[6] And, in fact, some Welsh squires behaved as if the courts of law in Ludlow and London could be ignored and their officers roughly handled with impunity.

When Edward Matthew, of Radyr in Glamorgan, received an order from the Court of Chancery to surrender his house and property to a creditor, his answer was neither compliant nor respectful. On the contrary, he was reported to have summoned his friends to his aid, bought a quantity of gunpowder in London and fortified his mansion. He was eventually arrested and committed to the Tower of London. His son George

[6] PRO State Papers Domestic, James I 1603–10, vol. 15, fol. 55. Sir Henry Wallop to the Earl of Salisbury, dated 22 August 1605.

showed greater obstinacy. He apparently strengthened the house at Radyr with stone walls and earthen ramparts, and when the representatives of the law approached the house they were met with a volley of stones and the threat of shots from calivers with which the place was well stocked. From the father in the Tower came cries of encouragement which were meant for George's ears only, but which were loud enough to reach those of the Privy Council. The King's advisors smelt treason at Radyr, the *posse comitatus* or local trained bands were ordered to batter young Matthew into submission, with cannon if necessary. This sufficed to persuade him to abandon the house without further ado.[7]

The Privy Council, however, was not always at hand to overawe refractory gentry, and the Council of Wales was reminded of its own impotence on more than one occasion. There was little it could do against such contempt for its authority as that said to be shown by Sir George Devereux. When David Gwyn, of Llanbadarn Odyn in Cardiganshire was arrested by bailiffs on orders from Ludlow for certain misdemeanours, Sir George and a group of friends allegedly rescued the man from their hands and 'took away the warrant from the said bailiffs and tore it in pieces, and in great despite threwe the same into the dirt and trod it under their ffeete'.[8] These bailiffs could count themselves lucky, for they might have suffered the barbarous treatment complained of by the misguided person who allowed himself to be hired to serve writs upon witnesses in a case involving John Price, of Strata Florida, in the same shire. Price with others cornered him in a lonely country lane and, with a razor, was said to have cut off the end of his nose and slit one of his ears.[9]

For that matter, the Council of Wales was hard put to it at times to control some of its own members, who could not always resist giving priority to their personal interests when these happened to conflict with the law or even with directives from London. It had, on one occasion, to reprimand Sir Richard Bulkeley for refusing to co-operate with the commissioner appointed to survey the King's forests in North Wales. Sir Richard claimed a title to the wood called Kingswood in Anglesey. So did the Crown, and with greater justification, if

[7] PRO Star Chamber 8 James I 54/5.
[8] *Ibid*, 291/17.
[9] *Ibid*, 30/13.

the name meant anything at all. Sir Richard, however, had as little patience with the expostulations of the commissioner as he had with the censorious observations addressed to him by his fellow members of the Council.[10]

If their betters so arrogantly ignored the authority of the law and its custodians, it was hardly surprising that the common people of Wales should be tempted from time to time to emulate them. Their attitude was dictated, at least in minor infringements of the law, by the fact that any penalty exacted would not involve loss of life or limb. As one group of impenitent transgressors was reported to have said before evicting some unfortunate tenant from his home: 'What riott or misdemeanour soever should be done touching the premises, the same was but a matter of payinge a fine, and they would discharge the same.'[11]

As for homicide, it was still difficult to convince some Welshmen that it was too heinous a crime to be compounded for money, as had been the practice, where it had not been avenged in a reciprocal manner, for many centuries. A fatal quarrel in Monmouthshire was quickly patched up when the murdered man's brother was offered £100 to acquit the guilty party of the crime, an offer accepted with alacrity to avoid further bloodshed,[12] In Radnorshire, where money was, perhaps, scarcer, compensation could apparently be paid to the bereaved kinsmen of the victim in the form of a piece of land.[13] But even this ostensible atonement for murder done could offer an opportunity for double-dealing, as happened in Merionethshire, where money was paid to the grieving relatives. Contrary to the agreement, no sooner had the murderers returned to their homes in anticipation of a quiet life, than they were denounced and indicted for their crime.[14]

In dealing with people of this mentality, the Council of Wales and the other courts of law could only fulminate and issue proclamations, which they knew could be circumvented or derided. When the Council decreed, for instance, that a notoriously illegal cattle market called Marchnad y Waun near Merthyr, in Glamorgan, should be suppressed without delay

[10] BM Lansdowne MSS 167, fol. 192.
[11] PRO Star Chamber 8 James I 168/6.
[12] PRO Requests 2 303/61.
[13] PRO Star Chamber 8 James I 202/28.
[14] PRO C21 I 7/5.

or excuse, its numerous patrons and customers were said to have cocked a snook in the direction of Ludlow and revived it in order:

> To provide cattell there at lowe prices and rates to serve other fayers and marketts nearer towardes England, and there to sell them at higher rates and prises, by which meanes stollen cattell are sould and shifted awaye, for as never or seldom the stealer thereof can be taken or found out for reformation and redress.[15]

At Presteigne, in Radnorshire, there was a more hilarious demonstration of how the lower classes viewed the law. Apparently a group of local people led by Barbara Lyde, 'late servant to a laundresse in the Low Countryes attending the camp', abducted a young man, heir to a property in Herefordshire, occupied his house and prepared to defy anyone who challenged their possession of it with guns, bows and boiling water.

> In scorne and derision of lawe and justice [so the report went, they] stiled one Phillip Sloughe, one of the said rioters with the name of Sir Ffrances Vere[16] and appointed him capteyne of the drunkards of Priesteigne aforesaid, and publishinge and charging that all the drunkards of Presteigne that did not followe the coullers of there [sic] capteyne, and at all times after were not assistant in keepinge his fort (meaninge in the holdinge of the possession of the messuage forceblie entered into as aforesaid) were forsworne in theire oathe in beinge true and obedient drunkeards.

What was more amusing, although it may not have seemed so to the town authorities at the time, was the fact that one of the leaders of the rioters tried to encourage his followers by declaring that he was a legal expert and could protect them against the consequences of their disorderly behaviour. 'He tould them he was esteemed for his knowledge and experience

[15] PRO Star Chamber 8 James I 241/18.
[16] Sir Francis Vere (d. 1609) was commander of the English troops in the service of the Dutch Republic.

in your Highnes lawes of England.' In fact, he had the superlative effrontery to call himself the 'Plowden of Presteigne'.[17]

With the King of Scotland safely on the throne of England, the Lord President of the Council of Wales, Edward, Lord Zouche, might have started to count the days before he would be removed from his office. It was not only that he had alienated many people within and outside the Council by his arrogant manners, and had challenged the ascendancy of the lawyers who were members of the Council.[18] There was also that little matter of his tactlessness as English Ambassador to Scotland in 1594, where he had been assigned by Queen Elizabeth to counteract the influence and intrigues of the pro-Spanish faction at the Scottish Court. Zouche had entered somewhat intemperately into negotiations with the Earl of Bothwell,[19] with the idea of forming a party against them, and had given him money. However, the transaction leaked out, the Queen of England calmly repudiated it, and Lord Zouche had been involved in acrimonious exchanges with King James.[20]

If the King, remembering this incident,[21] entertained any resentment, his diplomatic sense, of which he seemed inordinately proud, told him to forget the past and secure Zouche's loyalty. He certainly had good reasons for doing so. In the first place, there were strong links of affection and good will between Sir Robert Cecil, the Secretary of State, and Lord Zouche, for the latter had been the ward of his brother, Sir Thomas Cecil, later Earl of Exeter. Because of rivalries at the English Court and the presence there of not a few adversaries, it was imperative for Cecil, now created Earl of Salisbury, to have a reliable friend and ally in charge of the supreme office of power in Wales, and he was determined to keep Zouche at Ludlow. James owed too much to Cecil to overrule him on this

---

[17] Edmund Plowden (d. 1585) had been a jurist of some eminence, a member of the Council of Wales, a Catholic and the author of treatises on legal subjects.

[18] Williams, *The Council of the Marches of Wales under Elizabeth I*, pp. 299–311.

[19] He was Francis Stewart Hepburn, 5th Earl of Bothwell. After the failure of his conspiracies against James, he fled abroad and died at Naples in 1614.

[20] Stafford, *James VI of Scotland and the throne of England*, pp. 100–7.

[21] It seems to have rankled with him for some time. After Lord Zouche's recall from Scotland, James brought up the subject during a conversation with Nicolson, the English Agent at the Scottish Court, and used language that testified to his abiding dislike of Zouche. *Calendar of the State Papers of Scotland* (1547–1603), vol. III, pt 11, p. 1121.

issue, even if he had wanted to. But there was a second consideration of importance with the King. The Lord President was noted for his lack of patience with Catholics, and he had just given further proof of his zeal in recusant hunting while Elizabeth lay dying. On this occasion it was the well known Catholic Robert Pugh, of Penrhyn in Denbighshire, who had attracted the unwelcome attention of the Lord President. Trapped by his pursuers in the house of Cadwalader Wyn, of Foelas, the latter, although a Justice of the Peace, had combined with his household to help Pugh to escape.[22] Zouche was not put out of countenance by his failure. In a report on the English Court compiled by Catholic observers in 1603, he was described as being a great heretic and openly hostile to any proposal for ending the war with Spain.[23] In the circumstances, as there were rumours of Catholic unrest in the border shires, James thought it prudent to leave a dedicated anti-Papist like Zouche to deal with any recusant turbulence there.

At the time, Zouche was not certain in his mind whether, after all, he would like to remain as Lord President. He wrote to Cecil that his position was most unsatisfactory. Because of the late Queen's death, his commission was no longer valid, the Catholics were busily strengthening themselves by all means, many people had been offended by his manner of administering justice, he had no friends, was short of armour and munition and, of course, of money. All this was accompanied by a threnody that was to increase in volume in his correspondence with Cecil, that he would be a far happier man if he were allowed to serve the King in some other capacity. But that form of personal felicity was to elude him for several years. In the meantime he requested that the Government should take immediate steps to re-define his duties and enable him to perform them.[24]

James wasted no time. In August 1603 he officially confirmed Lord Zouche in his office and nominated the members of the Council of Wales. There were more than fifty of them, mostly English, since the jurisdiction of the Council extended as well over the shires of Gloucester, Salop, Hereford and Worcester. But the Principality was well represented by the Bishops of the

[22] NLW Wales 4 Gaol Files, Denbighshire, 13/1.
[23] Loomie, 'Spain and the Jacobean Catholics', 7.
[24] HMC *Salisbury (Cecil) MSS*, vol. XV, p. 17. Lord Zouche to Sir Robert Cecil, dated 30 March 1603.

four Welsh dioceses and by prominent public figures like the Earl of Pembroke, Sir John Herbert, second Secretary of State, Sir Richard Bulkeley, Sir John Wynn of Gwydir and others. They were expected to attend the meetings of the Council whenever they could, but to ensure the continuity of the administration of justice four persons, all Justices of Assize, were appointed to be constantly present with the Lord President to see that the laws were observed, a quartet known as the Quaternity.

It may have been on the advice of those of his advisors, who knew something of the congenital misdemeanours of Welshmen, that the King specified two bad habits which the Council was to suppress without delay, one being the illegal extortion of money by way of the notorious *comortha* and like practices, and the other the irreverent but precautionary wearing of weapons while assisting at divine service, a practice equally evident and provocative wherever Welshmen were gathered together in more worldly places like markets and fairs. And to cope with any extraordinary difficulty in extracting confessions from uncommunicative criminals, the King authorized the Council of Wales to use torture, although this was later to be discontinued.[25]

Lord Zouche remained in office for five years, but they must, at times, have appeared interminable to him. He was fortunate enough not to have to deal with any serious crisis. The Catholic conspiracies, however disturbing, had relatively little impact on the Principality, and they may have afforded the Lord President a further opportunity to display his Protestant sympathies. Exploiting his official position to influence church appointments, he was able to recommend and secure the election of Dr Richard Parry as Bishop of St Asaph – an eminent churchman who combined literary gifts with a faculty for accumulating ecclesiastical livings.[26] It is possible that Zouche also seized the chance to reduce the number and influence of Catholics within the immediate radius of the Council of Wales. It was during his tenure of office that John Lloyd, a practising lawyer at the Court of the Marches,

[25] BM Cottonian Collection, Vatillius C 1, fols 116–131.
[26] PRO State Papers Domestic, James I 1619–23, vol. 104, fol. 157. Instances produced to support the claims of the Lord President of Wales to approve and recommend fit persons to be appointed judges and bishops in Wales.

was forbidden to take on more legal work because 'he was not of sound and pure religion, and for refusinge to receive the hollie Sacraments'.[27]

But all these were minor successes, and they did little to reassure Lord Zouche that his authority and person were respected by his subordinates and by the country at large. His anxiety apparently was not only occasioned by the often intractable problem of implementing the directives that served to reaffirm the predominance and exclusiveness of the Crown's powers as exercised by the Council. It also stemmed from his own disinclination to use his right to enforce obedience with moderation and tact, two qualities which he rarely allowed to guide his actions. That he had already, in the previous reign, showed that he could be as imperious as the proverbial *Milord d'Angleterre*[28] was not a happy augury for his future relations with his subordinates, and with the passage of time he found it increasingly difficult to accommodate himself to any restrictions on, or criticism of, his administration of justice and imposition of penalties.

One of the earliest indications of dissent within the Council of Wales came to light before the end of 1603, when the President wrote to Cecil to the effect that his presence in Ludlow was not exactly a source of pleasure to some members of the Council, and that they were circulating rumours to discredit him with the general public. Who they were he did not specify, but the Secretary of State knew enough about the insidious influences of Court factions to appreciate how precarious Zouche's position could become. He did what he could to dismiss Zouche's apprehensions, but even Cecil may have been irritated by the President's querulous complaint that he was not being given first knowledge of political and diplomatic developments, which he claimed had been the privilege of his predecessors in Ludlow.[29]

Neither did his hostility towards the Lord Chancellor, Sir Thomas Egerton, whom the King admired very much, help Zouche to avoid becoming irascible through the cares of office. And when Egerton succeeded in abrogating the old custom

---

[27] HMC *Salisbury (Cecil) MSS* vol. XVI, pp. 11–12. Lord Zouche to Cecil, dated 22 January 1603–4.

[28] McClure, *Letters of John Chamberlain*, vol. 1, p. 166. Chamberlain to Dudley Norton, dated 15 October 1602.

[29] HMC *Salisbury (Cecil) MSS*, vol. XV, p. 252. Lord Zouche to Lord Cecil, dated 30 September 1603.

recognizing the traditional right of the President and the Council to have directed to them all warrants for taking the oaths of sheriffs in Wales, Zouche told Cecil that he considered this to be another attempt to bring him into disrepute, and that he would prefer to serve the King elsewhere than at Ludlow. He mentioned Guernsey where, presumably, he thought he would be more secure against gratuitous indignities.[30]

Hardly had the President ventilated this particular grievance than he had cause to be conscious of another. The endemic lawlessness within the Principality had long convinced him that severity rather than indulgence was the only way to reduce the incidence of crime, especially homicide. And so when Sir John Salisbury, of Llewenni in Denbighshire, notified him that a kinsman of his, John Lewis Gwyn, had been murdered by Fulk Lloyd, and that the latter and his accomplices, far from showing fear and contrition, were openly boasting that they would stop the course of justice against them by procuring a pardon, Zouche could conceive of no reason why Lloyd should not, indeed, repent of his misdeed but with the statutory rope round his neck.

To his mortification he learnt that his views on the propriety of the punishment he intended for Lloyd were not shared by others of higher rank and authority. The Earl of Pembroke, a favourite with the King, who might have claimed that as a Welshman he knew much more about the capricious moods and wayward habits of his countrymen than an imported English President like Zouche, for some reason set his face against the extreme penalty. Even Cecil proved irresolute and hedged on the matter when appealed to, despite additional information which claimed that the murderer was also a recusant who welcomed Jesuits and seminary priests to his home. Zouche may have been somewhat baffled when the all-powerful Secretary of State showed an unexpected vacillation in his attitude by suggesting that where factions existed, as in Wales, extra care was needed not to believe the worst of any accused person, and that judgment should be tempered with discretion. In Cecil's own words, which the President may have had to reread in order to fully understand their meaning:

Whensoever I hear of any such violent courses in these countries where faction so abounds, though I doubt not

[30] *Ibid*, p. 336. Lord Zouche to Lord Cecil, dated 23 December 1603.

but extraordinary care must be had to find out offenders, or else justice will fall to the ground, yet I confess in doubtfull cases, my course ever is rather to be inclinable to believe the best rather than the worst, for fear of touching innocent blood.[31]

Zouche had no doubt that the innocent blood spilt in this particular case was that of Sir John Salisbury's kinsman. He presented a report, based on the testimony of witnesses which revealed, to his satisfaction at least, that Fulk Lloyd was guilty of premeditated murder. To demonstrate his impartiality he accorded Lloyd an interview, which only reinforced his feeling that he was right in his judgment of the man's capacity to commit such a crime. However, his proposal that an example should be made of him to counteract the current prevalence of crime and violence in Wales was rejected by Cecil, the Earl of Pembroke and the Lord Chancellor who all disagreed with the President's reading of the situation and advocated a pardon, particularly as the King was in favour of one too.[32]

It was a disappointment that was not made less unpalatable by Zouche's failure to obtain something more rewarding from the King than occasional verbal commendations of his service, a few pieces of land of small value and a parsonage or two.[33] He had hoped, he told Cecil, that James would have seen fit to bestow on him a substantial gift for the amount of work he had put in at Ludlow. Instead he had received a demand from the Privy Council for a contribution to ease the King's acute shortage of funds. No sum had been specified, but the President may have been as aware of the piquant speculation of the Privy Council as to how much he would give, as he was of his own massive debts of £6,000. In the end he ventured to send £2,000 to the Exchequer, and this he thoughtfully followed up with a list of gentry in six Welsh shires who, he opined, could very well afford to lend James between £40 and £100 each. It was a gesture that may have suggested to the gentry concerned that the President could not always be relied upon to show sound judgment.[34]

An attack of measles laid Zouche low in 1605, and he was

[31] *Ibid*, vol. XVI, p. 288. Lord Cecil to Lord Zouche, dated August 1604.

[32] *Ibid*, p. 301. Sir John Salisbury to Viscount Cranborne, dated 3 September 1604.

[33] PRO State Papers Domestic, James I 1603–10, pp. 137, 142, 214 and 220

[34] HMC *Salisbury (Cecil) MSS*, vol. XVI, p. 175. Lord Zouche to Viscount Cranborne, dated 17 July [1604].

probably still recovering from it when he finally realized that his position was becoming untenable. Opposition towards him within the Council of Wales was hardening rather than slackening with the passage of years. The fault lay partly with him, for Zouche did not consider it incompatible with his duties to absent himself from Ludlow to attend to his private affairs or go down to Bath for the sake of his health, the ague giving him as much trouble as any critical adversary of his in the Council. However much his conscience chose to disregard his lack of attendance, some members of the Council, not least those of the legal fraternity, found it intolerable, for it meant that they were tied to Ludlow and so precluded from carrying on their private practice as lawyers. What fomented their indignation still more was Zouche's aversion to the Quaternity. He had given proof of his attitude towards it by deciding to dock the fees of its members, nominally £100 a year, and discipline them to live within a limit of 6/8d a day. One of the four Justices of Assize, Sir Henry Townshend, complained to the Secretary of State that the new arrangement would entail an appreciable loss of income for him, since he was often absent from Ludlow and was not permitted to practise by the conditions of his office. In the circumstances, he pleaded that the fixed fee of £100 should be retained.[35] Zouche was perfectly aware of this resentment and admitted to Cecil that certain members of the Council of Wales 'take little delight in my being here', and were devising ways and means 'to draw the affections of the country from me'.[36] He added that he was getting to loathe his office, but Cecil chose not to interpret this as a hint that he would be glad to leave it.

In any case, this was not the moment to alter the complexion or the structure of the Council in any form or manner. More ominous than these internal dissensions and animosities, which Zouche himself tried to moderate by using his influence with Cecil to have Townshend knighted by the King, was the open threat of public insubordination and hostility directed against the Council and its jurisdiction. For some time there had been indisputable evidence that people of all classes in Shropshire, Gloucestershire, Herefordshire and Worcestershire

---

[35] *Ibid*, vol. XV, p. 137. Justice [Sir Henry] Townshend to Lord Cecil, dated 17 June 1603.

[36] *Ibid*, p. 252. Lord Zouche to Lord Cecil, dated 30 September 1603.

resented the fact that they were subject to the authority of the
Council and treated in the same way as the inhabitants of
Wales. Egality of status, in the eyes of the Council, and no
discrimination in punishment and penalties, made no appeal to
them, and their desire to be freed from control by the Council
of Wales and to be governed by the common laws of England –
their birthright, as they termed it, became more vocal and
insistent as the years passed.

The issue had been well publicised in 1603 and 1604 when a
widow had sued a John Farlie or Farley of Herefordshire for a
copyhold which she claimed by the custom of a manor in that
shire. The case came before the Court of the Marches, which
ordered Farlie to allow the possession of the property until the
court of the manor had tried the rights of the respective
parties. Farlie had ignored the order and had been detained in
the Porter's Lodge of Ludlow castle by the Deputy-Porter,
Honyng. He had complained to the Court of the King's Bench
in London and obtained a writ of Habeas Corpus for his release
and the removal of his case. This had never happened before
in the history of the Council of Wales and Honyng had, with a
clear conscience, ignored the writ although Farlie was eventually given his liberty.

Zouche became apprehensive of the inconvenience and
tension that might be caused by the ensuing contention
between the courts in Ludlow and London, and concluded that
it was a matter for the King to decide since, in his opinion, it
was 'primarily a pointe of government and not of law'.[37] In the
meantime Farlie had aggravated the business by bringing a suit
against the Deputy-Porter, Honyng, for alleged false imprisonment and bad treatment. A William Witherley, who had
likewise known detention in the Porter's Lodge, joined him in
these proceedings, and a third complainant, Hugh Powell of
Shropshire, allowed himself to be persuaded by them to sue
Honyng at the Court of Common Pleas in London and claim
£40 damages.[38] For his part Honyng confined his defence to
the innocent plea that he had acted on the authority of the
Council of Wales, as defined by the Crown's instructions.

[37] PRO State Papers Domestic, James I 1603–10, vol. 10A, fols 201–8.
Differences between Kinges Bench and the Council in the Marches,
December 1603.
[38] PRO C 3 274/73.

Inevitably drawn into a legal conflict which intimately affected his ultimate authority, the King ordered the judges not to proceed further until he had considered the matter. When he had done so and heard both parties to the dispute, James roundly declared that no justifiable exception could be taken against Zouche and the manner in which the Court of the Marches had conducted itself. At the same time he tried to mollify the judges by referring the issue to the Privy Council, so that the rights of both courts should be respected and maintained. In a subsequent hearing the judges did not deny that the order of the Council of Wales regarding the widow's suit was just , and recognized that the Court of the Marches was 'an absolute Coort'. But since the Council of Wales's conduct and decision were warranted by the instructions given to it by the King, the judges tried to justify their writ by arguing that 'the fowre sheeres of Salop, Hereford, Worcester and Gloucester were not contained in the Act of Parliament by which that Councell was establisht, and howsoever they were expresst in the Commissions of our Kinges, yet the regall prerogative by law did not extend so far as to erecte a Coort of equitie for triall of sutes', and that 'therefore the causes of those sheeres must returne to Westminster and the coorse of common law'. Upon this assumption and contrary to the King's commandment, and without formal judgment from the Privy Council, the judges proceeded on their own initiative to order the arrest of the Deputy-Porter who had had charge of Farlie. He was brought to London and fined, and even the lawyer who had undertaken the suit of the widow in the Court of the Marches was similarly fined. Following up their success, the judges showered the Council of Wales with prohibitions, forbidding all suits of the four shires which were ready to be tried in Ludlow.

And heereuppon it came to pass that without any cryme or justifiable complainte and at the sute of one clamarous person, the Lord President of Wales, a pier of the realme and Councellor of State, was publiquelie disgraced, the Coorte of the Marches being the Kings Councell, was broughte in contempte, and his Ma^{ts} prerogatyve, the cheife jewell of his crowne, was laide open to more exception then in former tymes it had byn.

What had begun as a piece of arrogance and temerity – one observer doubted 'whether Farlie were a worthie Sampson to shake at once so manie pillars of this state' – now threatened to develop into a dispute both disturbing and perplexing to the King, who realized that the issue touched him deeply in his immutable belief that he possessed prerogative powers derived directly from God. These, he was firmly convinced, he could employ entirely at his own discretion, without being accountable to any person or court of law, to construct a system of government both beneficial to all his subjects and conducive to domestic peace. Consequently, any attempt to call in question and depreciate the supremacy of those powers was, in effect, detrimental to the stability of state and society, and a challenge to the overriding authority of the Crown.

> The state whose proper dutie is to the generall good, and, in that regarde, to the ballancing of all degrees, is in danger of becoming an Aristocracy when prerogatives are made envious or subject to the constructions of laws; for by the first, the King is made accountable and brought under the law, and by the second, the law is overruled and inspired by the Judge.[39]

These words suggest that two sources of anxiety were weighing on James's mind when considering the full implications of the campaign to reduce the dependence of the four English shires on the jurisdiction of the Council of Wales. One was the degree to which the aristocracy, in the shape of the local gentry of those shires, were involved in it, their motives in supporting it, and to what extent they reflected the attitude of the ordinary people. It was upon the gentry, after all, that the King and his ministers relied for the due and proper execution of their decisions. Any opposition on their part, however disguised, was capable in the long run of dislocating the whole machinery of local government, and engendering unhealthy thoughts of treating the central government in the same way. There is some evidence that recollections of the Barons' War of the reign of Henry III obtruded themselves into the deliberations of James's ministers. However exaggerated as well as pessimistic the comparison may have appeared, the King was only too aware

---

[39] PRO State Papers Domestic, James I 1603–10, vol. 10A, fols 201–8.

of the contemporary belief in the doctrine of regicide, and of the vulnerability of royal autocracy to the pressures of aristocratic pretensions, as was happening in France at the time, where the powers of government were more concentrated in the hands of the monarch than almost anywhere else in Europe.

The other threat that disturbed the King's peace of mind came from the quarter that was responsible, in the first place, for challenging the jurisdiction of the Court of the Marches to an open contest of legality. The Judges of England, headed by the Chief Justice of the King's Bench, were gradually becoming more conscious of the looming constitutional issue as to whether the source of sovereign power lay with the Crown or with Parliament, and had already decided in their minds that the ancient Parliamentary tradition of the kingdom had first call on their loyalties and obedience, rather than the alien principle of divine right promulgated and practised by the Scottish House of Stuart. However much they instinctively recoiled from the notion of confronting the Crown on fundamental issues such as the final repository of authority in the land, which was slowly but perceptibly being claimed by Parliament, they could not, without abandoning their essential role as custodians of the common law of the kingdom, acknowledge such unconventional and unpalatable formulas as that 'uppon pretence of liberties or laws, government should have any head but the Kinge', or more boldly that 'by the ordinance of God the King has power to establish a court of equity' like the Court of the Marches, where principles of justice were used to correct and supplement the law of the land, 'since it is the King who has been divinely entrusted to administer justice and judgment to the people'. And the patience and allegiance of the judges may have been strained to the utmost by the proposition of the King that he 'hath powre to stay sutes of the Common Law, yea *pro bono publico* to temper, change and controll the same. Nay, our Acts of Parliament by his sole authoritie may be mitigated or suspended uppon causes to him knowne. And this inherent power of his and what participateth thereof is therefore exempt from controllment of any court of law'.[40] Rarely has a claim to exclusive control of every constitutional and legal institution within a kingdom been so baldly, confidently and minatorily stated, and the warning to the legal profession to steer clear of any controversy on the issue was unmistakable.

[40] *Ibid.*

But for the moment James was more concerned about the activities of the anti-Council-of-Wales-movement in the four English shires. There was little doubt in the minds of the Council officials themselves that it was being conducted and encouraged by some of the most prominent gentlemen in those counties and that, although there was no indication of its taking an insurrectionary form, there was no reluctance among its leaders to organize some kind of passive resistance to the control exercised by the Council in Ludlow. The genuinely uncompromising element amongst them were the sheriffs of the four shires, who categorically refused to carry out the orders directed to them to arrest persons for indictable offences, levy amercements due to the Crown, and serve writs issued in the King's name by the Council of Wales. Zouche wasted no time in reminding them that their temerity was far less rewarding than dutiful compliance with the requirements of their office. Sir Roger Owen, sheriff of Shropshire, was fined £10 in 1604 for not detaining a suspect, and a year later his successor, Humphrey Briggs, was fined double that sum for dereliction of shrieval duties.[41]

The next manoeuvre of the advocates of the liberation of the four English shires was a more serious one, for it threatened to transfer the dispute to the floor of the House of Commons, a move that displeased the King immensely since he did not relish the idea of involving Parliament in any conflict with his prerogative.

It will be both a great dishonor and inconvenient unto me [he wrote to Cecil] that the parliament should bandy that matter amongst them before I be first at my wits end into it. This far only I recommend to your [the Privy Council's] considerations, that a king's old prerogative in continual possession may be in as great security as a private subject's old possession, that the common law be not made to fight against the king's authority, that the abuse of a king's predecessor be not a ground to deprive his successor of his lawful and rightly used privilege, and that the country of Wales be not too justly grieved by dismembering from them their ancient neighbours.[42]

---

41 PRO E 101 Bundle 124, no. 1.
42 HMC *Salisbury (Cecil) MSS*, vol. XVI, p. 325. King James to Viscount Cranborne, dated 7 October 1604.

It was now that two of the border gentry, Sir Herbert Croft of Herefordshire, and Sir Roger Owen of Shropshire, emerged as the leading protagonists of the unqualified release of the English shires from the Council of Wales's control, despite the fact that they were actually members of that Council. As MPs of their respective shires they commanded wide influence and respect, and were typical of the self-confident, occasionally presumptuous, country gentlemen who were beginning to assert themselves in the House of Commons, and were indifferent to the resentment which their behaviour generated in Court circles. Of the two, Croft was, perhaps, the more persistent and experienced campaigner, but before he could concentrate his energies on an organized course of persuasive propaganda, his main opponent had retired from the scene.

In 1603, Lord Zouche had been nominated member of the Privy Council, and this elevation to the dignity of a Privy Councillor, with a seat at the centre of royal authority, may have stirred ambition in him to exchange the tense atmosphere and tiresome dissensions at Ludlow for the more exhilarating, if slightly unsavoury, environment of Whitehall. As early as January 1605, there was a rumour in North Wales that he was not likely to remain President for long, since the four English shires were to be removed from his jurisdiction.[43] But it was at the end of March in that year that Zouche wrote to Cecil that he was indisposed and added the dull and familiar moan: 'I desyre only eythyr to lyve in that place with that honor the preceading presidents have done, or with favor or punishment to leave the place to some other in the same honor I fownd it. Howe contemptuous it is nowe my eares glowe to heer and my harte lamenteth to thincke of.' His final appeal to the Secretary of State was that an end should be put to 'these unhappy accidents', by which he presumably meant the current offensive against the authority of the Council of Wales.[44] Cecil was in no hurry to act, and it was not until late summer in 1606 that a courtier like Sir Dudley Carleton could reliably report that 'Sir George Carie being to be made President of Wales in place of my Lord Souche, who for his indisposition (as they

[43] *Calendar of Wynn Papers*, p. 58. John Wynn to his father, Sir John Wynn, under date of January 1604–5.
[44] PRO State Papers Domestic, James I 1603–10, vol. 13, fol. 85. Lord Zouche to Viscount Cranborne, dated 29 March 1605.

say) hath a disposition to give it over'.[45]

However, the post did not go to Sir George Carey. Cecil had need of a resolute man at Ludlow, and one who could legitimately claim that he was not easily intimidated by border factions or pretensions. In addition, of course, he had to give proof that he would not lightly disregard the patronage or favours conferred on him by the Secretary of State. Casting around, Cecil thought that he had discovered the right man in Ralph, Lord Eure. There were a number of factors in his favour. His father, grandfather and great grandfather had all been Lord Wardens of the Middle March, the most difficult to govern of the three wardenries on the Anglo-Scottish border, since it was the wildest and most mountainous region between the two kingdoms and the most vulnerable to raids. In 1593, he himself had been appointed Lord Warden, but had failed to find a solution to the problem of how to restrain the English border families from allying with the Scots for the sake of plunder or revenge. He had also fallen foul of the Woodrington or Witherington family of Northumberland, a devious set of squires who had interests on both sides of the border. Such was the hostility between them that on the occasion of a visit to London, Eure and his brother were assaulted by their opponents in one of the capital's streets and wounded. Eure, however, showed a strange ineptitude in feuds of this kind by trying to ambush the Woodringtons in retaliation and making a muddle of his dispositions.[46]

Cecil was convinced, however, that a man who had been brought up in the rough and tumble of border politics and forays had the necessary stamina to deal with similar situations in a region which, to all appearances, was beginning to become restless, just as the Scottish border was showing signs of decreasing violence after James's succession. Moreover, he felt that although the indocility of the border families had proved too much for Eure, the latter had been the victim of his own good nature as well as of the hostility of his adversaries. Later Sir Robert Carey, who succeeded Eure as Lord Warden and ended his career as Earl of Monmouth, confirmed this impression by recording in his memoirs that Eure's administration in the Middle March was a failure because he was 'trusting to men

---

[45] *Ibid*, vol. 23, fol. 14b. Dudley Carleton to John Chamberlain, dated 20 August 1606.
[46] Sisson, *Thomas Lodge and other Elizabethans*, pp. 192–210.

that hee thought honest and faithful to him'.[47] This propensity in a soldier and official of high position was one that would naturally attract Cecil, always on the look out for men in whom he could have complete confidence. Eure had declared his allegiance to him in a letter,[48] and henceforth the correspondence between the two was conducted in terms of reciprocal friendship and alliance.

By August 1607 Eure was presiding over the Council meetings in Ludlow,[49] and was soon made aware that he had inherited Lord Zouche's position as the target of vituperation and criticism from the dissidents in the four English shires. They were not resigned to the decision of the King, after his intervention in the Farlie case, that they were not immune from the jurisdiction of the Council of Wales, despite the few concessions he had made to propitiate their outraged sentiments of provincial patriotism. When taking up his duties, Eure informed Cecil, he had made it perfectly clear that the King had not granted exemption but that he, as the new President, hoped that the inhabitants of the English shires would be satisfied with the manner in which the Court of the Marches would dispense justice to them in conformity with the King's latest instructions. Despite this conciliatory gesture, some individuals in Herefordshire were anxious to misinterpret it 'pretending (that by the syrenes songs of the now President) dangers might fall to their libertie and native freedome as they termed it'.[50]

What had happened was that the Justices of the Peace in Herefordshire had to all intents and purposes revolted against the authority of the Council of Wales, as defined in the King's instructions.

> At the Quarter Sessions holden at Hereford next after Michaelmas last, divers of the Justices of the peace of that countie, by the instigation and motion of Sir Herbert Croft, knight, beinge then noe Justice of the peace and therewith discontented (as yt seemed) had combyned themselves together with resolution to withstande and

---

[47] Carey, *Memoirs*, p. 107.
[48] HMC *Salisbury (Cecil) MSS* vol. XVII, p. 60. Lord Eure to Viscount Cranborne, dated 18 February 1605.
[49] He had assumed the Presidentship before the end of July 1607.
[50] PRO State Papers Domestic, James I 1603–10, vol. 31, fol. 93. Lord Eure to the Earl of Salisbury, dated 6 February 1607–8.

disobey all processes and proceedings of this Coorte for any cause or matter arisinge within the countie of Hereford. Yet in hope of their better conformitie, we spared to relate the same by way of complaynte.

So ran the official report of the Council of Wales,[51] but their policy of letting bygones be bygones elicited no response. On the contrary:

Now understanding by like credible information and matter apparant that Sir John Pakington, knight, now Shirief of the countie of Worcester and divers of the Justices of the peace of the same county, upon occasion of an ordinary process of proclamation sent from this Courte (of the Marches) to the said Shirief in a cause here dependinge betwine partie and partie concerning a debt of fower pounds, have very lately upon a speciall assemblie and meetinge appoynted for that purpose and procured by the Shirief likewise resolved and combyned together to withstande and disobey all processes and proceedings of this Courte for any cause or matter arysinge within that countie of Worcester.

Eure had sharply rebuked the sheriff for his contumacy in not dealing severely with his under-sheriff, who had ignored the Court of the Marches's order, and had received in return a brusque note of acknowledgment and an impenitent defence of his attitude and that of the inhabitants of Worcestershire. 'This countie, by the generall consent of the Judges of the Lawe, hath bynne resolved and determyned to be out of the jurisdiction of that Courte (of the Marches); the inhabitants of this countie are resolved to challenge the benefitt of the lawe, being their birthright.'[52]

The association of the name of Sir Herbert Croft with this organized protest presaged some awkward dilemma or other for Lord Eure, and it did not take long to materialize. Upon a complaint that a Justice of the Peace of Herefordshire had refused to grant the protection of the law to a group of defendants, who happened to be Sir Herbert Croft's tenants

[51] *Ibid*, vol. 31, fol. 74. The Council of Wales to the Earl of Salisbury, dated 26 January 1607–8
[52] *Ibid*, fol. 76. Sir John Packington to Lord Eure, dated 17 January 1607–8.

the Lord President summoned the two parties to appear at Ludlow. Croft, however, had solicited the judges in London to prohibit the case from being tried by the Court of the Marches, an action 'which gave great triumph to the followers of the sayd Sir Herbert, and gave occasion to dissipate many gent[lemen] who held newtrally yet well inclined to the jurisdiction of this Courte'.[53]

Lord Eure may have hoped that his censure of Sir Herbert Croft would have gained Cecil's approbation. To build up still further a formidable list of grievances against that squire, he informed the Secretary of State that Croft, in his capacity as Steward of the Queen of England's manors in Herefordshire, was treating the tenants in a shameful way by oppressing them with extra work, exacting extraordinary fines for his own use, and intimidating them with threats. The reply from Cecil may have stupified him as much as had the Secretary of State's letter of non-collusion to Lord Zouche, after he had expressed his unalterable conviction that the penalty for murder should be hanging. Eure was courteously but firmly warned not to handle such complaints against Croft, since it was the Secretary of State alone who was authorized to investigate matters arising from the Queen's manors, whatever they were. It was particularly exasperating in this case that other members of the Privy Council had heard of Eure's interference, whereas Cecil had been ignorant of it.[54]

A chastened Lord Eure readily acknowledged his error of judgment and had the satisfaction of learning some months later that the egregious Croft and his ally, Sir Roger Owen, had been dismissed from the Council of Wales, although their expulsion had been 'a matter of much consultation at the [Privy] Counsell table and went not so current but had some contradiction, though at last it was so determined'.[55]

As was predictable in the case of an obdurate opponent like Croft, his arbitary dismissal hardened his resolution to continue the struggle against the President and to seek supporters from all quarters, thus widening the field of action. He had already, at the beginning of 1607, set on foot a new plan of campaign with the help of the gentry of the four shires.

---

[53] *Ibid*, fol. 93. Lord Eure to the Earl of Salisbury, dated 6 February 1607–8.

[54] *Ibid*. fol. 86. The Earl of Salisbury to Lord Eure, dated 2 February 1607–8.

[55] *Ibid*, vol. 28, fol. 87. Dudley Carleton to John Chamberlain, dated 16 September 1607.

The gentlemen of Herefordshire and Worcestershire, Lord Eure complained to Cecil, were trying by all means 'to strengthen themselvs in the eares and hartes of the people that they were neerelie exempted from the jurisdiction of this Cort, even in the least causes of sut whatsoever'. And he enclosed a copy of a letter written by a number of Herefordshire gentry to Croft, expressing their gratitude for his endeavours on their behalf to be freed from the control of the Council of Wales and promising 'any further assistaunce that our powers may lawfully affoorde for the publique cause of our countrey'.

The Secretary of State may have been relieved that they had stressed their intention of proceeding lawfully in the matter, but the President had no reason to be entirely satisfied with the letter. For though the signatories agreed that since the King's latest instructions, 'we and all his Ma^{ts} subjects of this countrey have found great peace and quiet in respect of former tymes, for which we rest as farre thanckfull to his Matie as may be possibly testified', yet, 'now upon the coming of the right honorable Ralph Lord Eure to the presedencie, not onely great rumours being given out of the regayning of our subjection to that Cort but divers processes being awarded...not onelye summoning diverse of our countreymen to appeare there, but to the sheriefs themselves signifying fynes imposed and threatning further fynes to be imposed for not executing the proces of that Cort'. The letter was signed by twenty-seven gentlemen, some with Welsh surnames, and including many from the prominent Scudamore family.[56] One man, however, refused adamantly to subscribe his name. Sir Thomas Cromwell had no hesitation in announcing that:

Since I must be subject to any [law] at all, then had I rather bee unto this of the Principalitie then any other, being fedd thereunto as well for neernes of the place as also for that I know it to be his Ma^{ts} pleasure as also the noble Prince.... Besides this, my father and myself have heretofore subscribed to the necessary government of the fowre English shires to be within the jurisdiction of the Council in the principalitie and Marches of Wales.[57]

---

[56] *Ibid*, vol. 31, fol. 84. Lord Eure and the Council of Wales to the Earl of Salisbury, dated 13 January 1607–8.

[57] *Ibid*, fol. 83. Sir Thomas Cromwell to James Scudamore, dated 23 January 1607–8.

One lone voice raised in opposition did not deter Croft from his next manoeuvre, which the King had wished to avoid since the beginning of the dispute, and that was to enlist the sympathy and support of the House of Commons. He did so at a most auspicious moment, when the crushing weight of his debts was forcing James to consider trimming certain of his prerogative powers in exchange for a substantial grant of money. Realizing that this was a unique opportunity to force him to redress some of the pecuniary burdens afflicting the kingdom, the House of Commons conceived the idea of a bargain or Contract whereby, in return for £200,000 the Crown would make a number of concessions, surrendering, for instance, the emoluments which it had reaped from wardships and other customs associated with feudal tenures now considered antiquated.[58]

While James and the House were arguing over the terms, Sir Herbert Croft showed his sense of expediency by inserting the protest of the four shires against their subjection to the Council of Wales as yet another grievance long due for rectification by the Crown. The House did not particularly like his emotional disparagment of the Court of the Marches which, it was objected, conduced to the derogation of the King and his authority, but before the debate ended Croft managed to get his pet grievance referred to a committee.[59] Eventually the House submitted a petition, amongst its other complaints, that the four shires should have a trial by law concerning their inheritance of the common law of England, and, so, win exemption. And with their eyes on the Great Contract, the MPs further petitioned that such exemption was highly desirable for it would enable the inhabitants 'the better to perform their part of the Contract by easing them of much causeless vexation and charges which in trifling suits they now bear and endure'.[60]

In the event, the haggling between the necessitous King and his faithful but obstinate Commons proved inconclusive, and the Contract was dropped. Parliament was prorogued, but Sir Herbert Croft, Sir Roger Owen and those MPs who negated the legality and force of the royal prerogative powers could

---

[58] Gardiner, *History of England*, vol. II, pp. 68–9.
[59] *Journals of the House of Commons*, vol. 1, 1547–1628, p. 451.
[60] *Journals of the House of Lords*, vol. 2, 1578–1614, p. 661, under date of 18 July 1610.

congratulate themselves that they had not agitated and argued in vain. For in his answer to the petition of grievances, before the members of both Houses of Parliament dispersed to their homes, the King, despite his uncompromising rejection of the plea for the exemption of the four shires, had not only undertaken to re-examine the question, but had gone one step further than anyone anticipated. He was unwilling to alter the present system, but was prepared to abide by a voluntary engagement on his part 'never to erect in any other parte of the Realme any like Courts or Provincial Councils except it be by assent of Parliament'.[61] In itself, this was a concession of perhaps greater value and consequence than any monetary transaction or remedial agreement that might have resulted from the proposed Contract.

In the midst of this controversy Lord Eure allowed himself to be distracted for a while by another problem which, although of marginal importance, nevertheless threatened to add to the multiplicity of difficulties facing the Council of Wales. In April 1612, he received a letter from the Receiver for North Wales, Thomas Trafford, giving him ample notice that he and the Council of Wales could no longer expect money from him to defray the expenses of their diet and the fees of their judges, since all receipts were henceforth to be allocated to the Prince of Wales. A similar disagreeable warning came from Sir Edward Carne, the Receiver for South Wales, but in his case, apparently, the reason was an economic one. He explained that 'by the sale of landes made in South Wales, together with his other payments, he doubteth he shall not have sufficient to make payment of the proportion due for his parte for the diett as hath bene heretofore accustomed'.

This information posed an awkward problem for the President, since the household at Ludlow was already indebted to him and other members of the Council, who had paid out of their own pockets for provisions and other necessities. Lord Eure saw no reason why he should conceal what he considered to be one incontestable factor that had a bearing on the straightened circumstances of the household. He recommended to Cecil that some:

---

[61] *Ibid*, p. 659, under date of 23 July 1610.

Strickter course be held with the adversarie to this
jurisdiction, who not only force us to a greater chardge
for the maintenance of suites in defence of the jurisdiction, but also doe dissipate the affections of diverse for
repayring to the cort, whereby ffynes might encrease to
the king, which is an honor to the Cort for the better
maintenance of this place. We having had one suite lately
for the defence of the English shires in Madoc his name,
which did cost us two hundred marks, stayed at the last
assizes holden in Shropshire by an injunction out of the
Chancery.

Because of this and other legal charges, which were impover-
ishing the Council of Wales, Lord Eure urged that money
should be provided by some other receiver or by state funds.[62]
He was gratified by the Secretary of State's immediate
response to his appeal, and for a year or so the charges for the
council's diet were borne by the Exchequer.[63] Then, possibly
because the resources of the Treasury were too attenuated even
to support this relatively light burden, it was decided to throw
it back on the shoulders of the Receiver for South Wales, and
Sir Edward Carne, helpless but loyal, was directed to squeeze
out of his annual receipt the fairly sizeable sum of £1106.13s.4d
to furnish the council with provisions.[64] From then onwards,
the amenities of life seemed to have multiplied and ramified at
Ludlow. Certainly the kitchens and larders of the castle
suffered from no deficiencies of sustenance. The slaughtermen
and caterers of the household regularly attended markets and
fairs over a wide area, purchasing ewes and lambs at Keynton,
wethers at Welshpool and Bishop's Castle, and driving them
all the way back to Ludlow, not without danger, however,
from the foxes that lurked in ambush at the side of the roads.
Oxen and heifers were bought at Tenbury fair, wheat at
Leominster, olives and cheeses at Worcester and butter at
Kingsland. More expensive or selective items like fish were
transported to Ludlow from London.[65]

[62] PRO State Papers Domestic, James I 1603–10, vol. 63, fol. 64. Lord Eure to
the Earl of Salisbury, dated 24 April 1611.
[63] *Ibid*, fol. 31. Warrant dated 13 May 1611
[64] HMC *Salisbury (Cecil) MSS*, vol. XXI, p. 388. Warrant to Edward Carne, dated
7 March 1611–12.
[65] PRO E 101. Bundle 613, no. 13 under date of November 1615.

Relieved of the dilemma of feeding his staff and his Council, the President could turn his thoughts, occasionally, to the more agreeable task of providing them with entertainment and diversions. Lord Eure was well qualified to do this, for he was one of the group of English aristocrats who had the interest and the means to maintain companies of actors. He had formed his own company of players as far back as 1600, and for some years it had been touring the provinces. In 1607, still under his patronage and calling itself the 'Lord President's Company', it travelled extensively throughout the kingdom, performing in many provincial towns like Coventry, Leicester, Ipswich and Ludlow, but relying upon the liberality of the President for its upkeep. Lord Eure's cultural interests also included music and he extended his support to a company of musicians who, like the players, led an itinerant life and performed in various towns.[66] On special occasions, however, the President allowed himself to be dictated to by considerations of prestige and ceremony. On the evening of 5 November 1615, for instance, he invited the Queen's Company of players to stage a show for his guests, and took care also to hire a reputable cook from Ludlow town to prepare the pastry for them in the banquet that followed.

Social distinctions and aristocratic valuations were never far from Lord Eure's thoughts, and he was given another opportunity to express them when his son was involved in a quarrel over dogs with a Yorkshire squire named Wharton, during a hunt organized in Lincolnshire. Wharton challenged young Eure to a duel and the President, well aware of the King's aversion to that violent and often lethal method of resolving disputes, wrote immediately to the Earl of Northampton, entreating him to intervene by punishing Wharton for his insolence and for exceeding the limited privileges of his inferior status. 'Your lordship seethe', he commented in his letter, 'howe inferior persons intrude themselves into the sportes and pastymes of the greateste, and how insolently they beare themselves, seekinge to enable their reputation by quarellinge with the beste.'[67]

It would have demanded exceptional political prescience to

---

[66] Murray, *English Dramatic Companies*, pp. 44–5 and 245.
[67] BM Add. MSS 12514, p. 132. Lord Eure to Henry Howard, Earl of Northampton, dated 8 December 1609.

foresee the eventual extinction of the Crown's prerogative powers at the hands of Parliament, and Sir Herbert Croft did not possess it. But neither was he inclined to give credence to royal declarations which did not exactly correspond to his expectations. That the King had bound himself not to exercise his overriding authority to establish more prerogative courts was besides the point. The real issue, to Croft, was the emancipation of the four English shires, and if this could not be bought from the Crown by negotiating a mutually beneficial Contract, then other measures had to be tried. And Lord Eure soon heard of some of them.

A reappraisal of his former campaign led Croft to the conclusion that it had not been altogether wise to equate the movement for exemption with the almost exclusive support of the gentry, and that it needed a broader basis of popular approval, which he set out to engineer without delay. Within a short time, Lord Eure was able to warn Cecil that the adversaries of the Council of Wales intended to undermine its jurisdiction by:

> Procuring a generall subscription under the handes of them in Herefordshire of the greevance they find by this jurisdiction, whereby they labour not only to satesfy his Matie that it is rather a generall inconvenience whereof the whole countie desireth to be eased then the private distaste of any particular men; but also hope that his Matie will be hereupon induced to grant them a free exemption. And this project I conceave is occasioned through some of their wilfull misinterpretation of his Ma^{ts} last gratious speech in Parliament to this pointe, that his Highnes would take tyme to be informed of this business. And this their project they have in this manner seconded.

The President alleged that at the last Quarter Sessions in Leominster:

> The Grand Jurie (selected no doubt of purpose) treating verie litle of any ordinary or usuall busnes of the countie, presented by way of petycon to the Justices the greevance the whole countie (as they conceave) finde by being subject to this jurisdiction of the Court of the Marches – how prejudiciall an example and presumpteous a part it is

for Grand Jurie men to intermeddle in matters of state or make inquiries in businesse of this nature, I leave it to your Lordships wisedome – with a request unto the Justices that they would recommend it to the Knights of the Sheire that, in love and zeale unto theire countrey by whom they were putt in trust, they would be earnest both unto his Matie and the High Court of Parliament for theire freedom and exemption. Yett, for that it should seame to proceed meerely from the freeholders and commons of the country, without the direction of those who are knowne and professed prosecutors of the busines, the Knights themselves were absent from this assemblie as being ignorant and not partaking of that action.

Lord Eure assured the Secretary of State that if the King granted commissions to impartial persons of worth 'to examine and trie the affections of the inhabitants within these counties, I well hope it would plainely appeare they generally stand otherwise affected then these gentlemen make shew of'. The President did not develop this embryonic conception of a referendum but added: 'Assuring your Lordship that since my comming downe within these three yeares, notwithstanding the great opposition that hath been and the devises to withdraw, and even to terrifie the subjects hence, there hath been out of those 4 English counties more suitors then out of halfe Wales, as may appeare by the records of the Court [of the Marches].'[68]

Lord Eure was not making an empty claim. He was able to produce figures that testified that from October 1608 to October 1609, there had been a total of 1350 suits which, by October 1610, had climbed to 3376. Even Sir Herbert Croft's own county of Hereford showed a startling increase in the number of suitors which had jumped from 228 in 1608 to 810 two years later.[69] In 1607, Sir Henry Townshend had stressed in a letter to Cecil that the people of the English shires and not least 'the general sort' were satisfied with the Council of Wales's authority[70] and

[68] PRO State Papers Domestic, James I 1603–10, vol. 57, fol. 218. Lord Eure to the Earl of Salisbury, dated 10 October 1610.

[69] *ibid*, vol. 58, fol. 152. 'The number of the severall causes before the Lord President and Councell in the Marches of Wales out of the fowre English shires for two severall yeeres past.'

[70] HMC *Salisbury (Cecil) MSS*, vol. XIX, p. 348. Sir Henry Townshend to the Earl of Salisbury, dated 30 November 1607.

neither the King nor his Secretary of State could give any serious consideration to the thought of introducing changes which might prove superfluous and unproductive.

Their attitude may have hardened after reading another letter from the President, describing a somewhat desperate attempt to discredit him and the council's jurisdiction.

> As for the Council of Wales, though it have some few opposors, yet it hath no such notorious and malicitous (sic) contemners as one John Cole of Shropshire who being lately sued in this court for a misdemeanour procured by him and committed by his servants, and both himselfe and his servants by his direction (according to their own confessions) disobeying all the processes of this Court, at lenght (sic) Peers Madox, the messinger or pursuerant attending this place, by warrant from hence, attached his sayd servants, whereupon the sayd Cole was heard openly to say that Spooneley (being one of his servants so attached) was a cowardly knave that he did not kill the pursuerant when he did arrest him. And that if he had, he would have borne him out therein, if it had cost him £500. And shortly after procured an Habeas Corpus for removing his servants out of the Porters Lodge to the Kings Bench, where the writt is yet depending.

This was reminiscent of the Farlie case of 1603 which had inaugurated the dispute over the jurisdiction of the Council of Wales, but worse was to follow.

> In the meantyme Spooneley hath brought an action of trespass or false imprisonment against the said pursuerant for his former apprehension; and one Edward Cole (sonne unto John Cole) with the assistance of one John Corbyn have by vertue thereof arrested the said pursuerant neere Shrewsbury (refusing to show him any warrant or make knowne at whose suite) as he was then carrying the bookes and commissions of subsidie to the Commissioners appointed for that service in that countie; which his Ma[ties] service, though the pursuerant then made known unto them and shewed both the bookes and the seales annexed to the commissions, yet they without any respect thereof forced him back agayne to Shrewsbury

to the sheriffes office there, and in disgracefull manner
leading him through that towne; being advised to be wary
in that action otherwise they would be scarce able to
answere it, the sayd Edward Cole replyed he would carry
him thither in despight of whomsoever should say nay;
and so have ever sithence the 13 day of this August
deteyned him prisoner.[71]

Lord Eure was certain in his mind that Cole was the instrument of high-ranking individuals dedicated to the destruction
of the dignity and credibility of the Council of Wales, and may
have thought that by reporting the outrage at full length he
would convince Cecil that more severe measures were necessary
to deter men like Sir Herbert Croft and Sir Roger Owen from
manipulating people's emotions for their own ends.

There was, however, one last arrow in Croft's quiver which,
if aimed selectively and accurately, might even induce the King
to review the matter of the Council of Wales. It was generally
believed in court and parliamentary circles that the influence of
Robert Carr, Earl of Somerset, over James could only be
terminated by the unpredictable disgrace or death of that
favourite. Why Croft should have assumed that the Earl would
find any personal interest or profit in promoting a cause that
was distasteful to his royal patron and prejudicial to the
Crown's authority, is not clear. Nevertheless, he decided to try
and enlist his support, and the death of Cecil in 1612 removed
the only person who might have restrained Carr from lending
his support to Croft. But the prospects of any fruitful co-operation
between the two men were hardly encouraging. James showed
his opinion of Croft and his manoeuvres inside and outside the
House of Commons by refusing to knight his son. Sir Herbert
dutifully resigned himself to the rebuff, but this did not
prevent him from pressing the Earl to deliver a communication
to the King, in which he again recapitulated his views on the
right of the four shires to demand exemption.

Privately, Croft intimated to the Earl that, if he did not
obtain satisfaction in the matter, he would not be able to 'yelde
noe good accompte to those that have chosen mee nowe to
serve for them, of my consentinge to geeve their money to the
Kinge from whome the Parliament cannot obtayne for them so

[71] State Papers Domestic, James I 1603–10, vol. 57, fol. 45. Lord Eure to the Earl
of Salisbury, dated 20 August 1610.

just a desyre of their birthright to the lawes of the kingdome'.[72]
So indelicate a hint that he was only prepared to vote in favour
of money supplies to the King – much of which, in fact, went
towards granting pensions and gifts to favoured courtiers like
the Earl – in return for a specific concession, could not have
pleased the Earl very much. On the other hand, he may have
been flattered by a letter signed by fifty or so gentlemen from
the counties of Hereford, Salop and Worcester, thanking him
for his services as liaison between them and the King, urging
him to further exertions on their behalf, and reminding him of
the exemplary pertinacity of another favourite, Robert Dudley,
Earl of Leicester, who had won the heart of Queen Elizabeth
and an immunity for an English border county, Cheshire, from
the oppressive jurisdiction of the Court of the Marches.[73]

This tampering with his favourite may have been one of a
number of factors which incited James to strike back at the
critics of the Council of Wales. He demolished the arguments
of Sir Herbert Croft, and then counter-attacked the phalanx of
the common law judges, whom he rightly calculated to be the
most dangerous opponents of his prerogative powers.

On 6 June 1616 an open contestation of his right to grant
commendams gave him the excuse to assemble all the judges at
Whitehall, and confront them with the charge that they were
instrumental in challenging the Crown's legitimate authority.
He had called them together, he asserted, concerning a
question that had relation to no private person but concerned
God and the King, the power of the Crown and the state of his
church. By insisting on his royal authority and 'reminding
them that he was the head and fountain of justice under God
in his dominions', he waved all their observations aside and
castigated them for allowing the royal prerogative to be
questioned and debated by barristers and other legal persons.
His detestation of some members of the legal profession was
evident in his comment that 'ever since his comeinge to the
Crown the popular sorte of lawyers have ben the men that
most affrontedly in all Parliaments have trodden upon his
Prerogative'. And he wound up his scathing remarks on their
shortcomings with the bitter complaint that the courts of the
common law, under their guidance 'are growne so vaste and

[72] *Ibid*, vol. 77, fol. 22. Sir Herbert Croft to the Earl of Somerset, dated 9 May 1614.
[73] *Ibid*, vol. 78, fol. 129. The Gentry of Herefordshire to the Earl of Somerset,
dated 19 December 1614.

transcendant as they did both meddle with the Kings Prerogative and had incroached upon all other Courts of Justice as the High Commission, the Courtes established in Wales and at Yorke, the Court of Requests'. The irascibility of the King was such that the judges, with the notable exception of Sir Edward Coke, found it advisable to confess their errors on their knees before James, implore his pardon and agree unreservedly with his dictum that 'any disputing of the Kings authority in public was both dangerous and dishonourable to his Majesty'.[74]

Having disposed of any overt opposition from the Westminster Hall legal fraternity, James could afford to pay less attention to the fractiousness of his critics in the House of Commons. But in fact the fortunes of Sir Herbert Croft, Sir Roger Owen and their confederates were declining in more than one sense. They could, at times, behave like political mavericks, as when Croft implicitly criticised the Speaker for bringing messages from the King to the members, which Croft maintained he should not do except when he had been sent by the House of Commons to the King. And Sir Roger Owen could hardly have commended himself to James by warning his fellow members that, if the King accepted the sum of £200,000 stipulated in the Great Contract, they should ensure that the money was not wasted on courtiers and the like. There was a modicum of political wisdom, too, in his admonition that care should be taken not to give the Crown too much money, in case the King should take it into his head that he could do without Parliament.[75]

But these interjections became less noticeable, and, in the case of Sir Roger Owen, there were certain alarming symptoms of incipient insanity. In May 1617, he 'was noted to be crasie and distempered'. 'The physicians have him in hand', John Chamberlain wrote to Sir Dudley Carleton, 'and were not without hope to recover him'.[76] Whatever seventeenth century doctors could do, or thought they ought to do, in cases of mental affliction, they probably did, but Sir Roger did not respond to their treatment. A little later the report circulated in London:

> Of a strange accident that befell Sir Roger Owen, the great Parliament man yesterday, who soddainly fell into a

---

[74] Ibid, vol. 87, fols 93–102. See also Acts of the Privy Council, 1615–1616, pp. 595–609.

[75] Notestein, Relf and Simpson, Commons Debates, 1621, pp. 311, 328 and 405.

[76] McClure, Letters of John Chamberlain, vol. II, p. 76. Chamberlain to Sir Dudley Carleton, dated 24 May 1617.

fit of desperate madness; first as hee was passing from Westminster Hall to London, where he would have drowned himself; and then being com on land, would have beaten his own head against the pavement of the streets; but being brought into a house and induced to eat and sleep, hee is somewhat amended.[77]

Sir Herbert Croft's departure from public life was less traumatic, but no less embarrassing for him personally. It is suggested that, because of the prodigious extravagance of his wife and other reasons, his estate became so 'weakened and wasted' and encumbered with debts that to avoid his creditors he fled to France. Later, he renounced the world and whatever meagre portion of its wealth remained to him, became converted to the Catholic faith and retired to the monastery of St Gregory in Douai, where he died in 1622. Commenting on his change of religion and mode of life, John Chamberlain wrote that it should cause no surprise since 'desperation hath made more moncks than him'. James would have probably concurred with that opinion. In any case, he was convinced that a good number of the gentry of the four English shires were Catholics masquerading under the guise of loyal Protestant subjects.[78]

The muted revolt of the four shires did not only constitute a challenge to, and indirectly a hesitant repudiation of the authority of the Council of Wales, which was a component and an important one of the Crown's prerogative powers. It also occurred at a most unpropitious moment for the King, when he was exerting all his efforts and influence to promote his great scheme of the union of England and Scotland. Few of his ministers, Cecil not excepted, shared his opinion that the time

---

[77] HMC *Downshire MSS*, vol. VI. John More to William Trumbull, dated 18 May 1617.

[78] McClure, *Letters of John Chamberlain*, vol. 11, p. 106. Chamberlain to Sir Dudley Carleton, dated 18 October 1617. For an assessment of Croft's career and role in the four shires controversy *see* Ham, 'The Four Shires Controversy', 381–99. It was the firm belief of the King and his ministers that as regards the Catholics in the four shires, 'there are in those 4 counties and some parts of Wales adjoyning about XX thousand persons become recusants, most of them suspected to be reconcyled to the Pope'. PRO State Papers Domestic, James I, 1603–10 vol. 19, fol. 72. 'An Examination of the Byll passed in the Lower House of Parliament for explaining the Statute of 34 H.8 touching the government of the Lord President and Counsell in the Marches of Wales.'

was ripe for a political amalgam of the two kingdoms which would eventually result in uniformity of government and law. James urged it on the House of Commons who chose to temporize. He argued unconvincingly with the Secretary of State, for Cecil emphasized the necessity for caution and an empirical approach to the whole matter. Eventually, he persuaded the King to reduce his inordinate demands to the more practical proposition that commissioners should be appointed in both countries to determine how far it was feasible, in the circumstances, to remove certain barriers separating the two countries.[79]

One obstacle, naturally enough, was the inveterate hostility and suspicions between the two peoples over the centuries, which no amount of friendly words and generous gestures could dissipate at a stroke. The only possibility of generating a new spirit of affinity amongst them was by creating equality of status and freedom of opportunity which might gradually eradicate, or, at least, attenuate the more virulent forms of nationalist and separatist feelings north and south of the border. James's first plan of cajoling the Scots into a more co-operative mood by advancing some of them to high positions in England, reminiscent, in some degree, of Henry VII's desire to promote the fortunes of his Welsh countrymen, did little to recommend it to his English subjects. The supercilious attitude of many of the latter towards their northern neighbours was expressed in verses designed to remind them, and the King indirectly, that they were a poor lot before they crossed the border to batten on the wealth of England, a sentiment emphasized in the refrain with which the verses ended:

> The Bonny Scott well witness can,
> Twas England that made thee a gentleman.[80]

The King's Scottish susceptibilities were, no doubt, exacerbated by popular lampoons of this kind, but they did not distract him from attempting to force through the union. At the same time, they may have convinced him that what was particularly needed to overcome ingrained prejudices and ancient enmities was a practical demonstration that peaceful existence, with the consequent blurring of national distinctions,

[79] Gardiner, *History of England*, vol. 1, p. 176.
[80] PRO State Papers Domestic, James I 1603–10, vol. 191, fol. 7.

could become a political reality with the passage of the years. In James's view such indisputable evidence lay at hand in Ludlow, where the Council of Wales had laboured for more than a century to reconcile two antagonistic peoples in the spirit of law and mutual material benefits.

In the belief that unimpeachable evidence in this respect could be furnished by Welshmen, who had had experience of Council administration, two Welsh members of the House of Commons, Sir Richard Bulkeley and Sir Robert Mansel, were assigned to the commission set up to discuss the issue with the Scots. Certainly, there were other Welsh members who enthusiastically endorsed the scheme of a union, no one more so than Sir William Maurice, of Clenennau, MP for Caernarvonshire, who, in fact, was obsessed by the idea that the union would become more of a reality and more acceptable if James were to assume the title of King of Great Britain. He obstinately refused to be deflected by the arguments of some English MPs who, animated by an eruption of nationalist feeling, talked at great length about the glory and superiority of England, and expressed fears that their nation might be called upon to sacrifice these and other irreplaceable qualities – 'the adder shall tread upon his heel that breaketh down the hedge', as one of them crystallized his emotions in the idiomatic imagery that embellished Parliamentary oratory in those days. 'Let us proceed with a leaden foot' was the advice of another apprehensive English MP. But slow motion of that kind had no appeal whatsoever to the squire of Clenennau. On 10 February 1609, it was recorded that Sir William Maurice, 'best speaking when none speaks', addressed the House of Commons again on the advisability of promoting the union. After greatly extolling the laws of England as being ancient, godly, just and equal he made the point, which does not appear to have stirred any historical emotions in him, that Edward I had united Wales and England by his own authority. There might have been a hint here that, by using his prerogative powers, James could conceivably do the same in the case of England and Scotland. If other MPs detected it, they gave no sign of their reaction, but Sir William, had the satisfaction of being invited to prepare a bill for the union and the title of King of Great Britain, which he presented to the House in due course.[81]

---

[81] *Journals of the House of Commons*, vol. 1, pp. 160, 178, 179, 183 and 392.

Personal motives, of course, were never far from an MPs mind when recommending a course of action to the House of Commons, and Sir William, no doubt, shared the general conviction that the floor of the House was an excellent echoing board for the transmission of opinions to certain quarters where they were likely to be appreciated, and later, perhaps, remunerated. To gain the King's ear and favour was a desirable objective, and a privilege and advantage which no one under-estimated, from the Lord Chancellor down to the humblest state official and the most self-effacing Member of Parliament. In his case, Sir William had shown admirable parliamentary tactics. In his opening speech to his first Parliament, James had announced quite unambivalently that one of his reasons for convening the two Houses was to pass legislation for the union of the two kingdoms, and he had followed this up with the contentious statement that those who opposed the union were either ignorant or malicious or preferred a divided to a united Commonwealth. Sir William had judiciously taken the lead in advertising his support for the King and, by constant repetition, hoped to convince him that at least one Welshman was as dedicated as James himself to the achievement of the union.

What Sir William hoped to gain by this partisanship is, perhaps, revealed in a letter written to him by his sister, in which she urged him to prosecute his personal affairs in London as energetically as possible, since at home they lacked success. His servants had been heavily fined by the Council of Wales and little favour was shown to them in Caernarvonshire itself. She advised him to complain to the King and ask him to intervene with the Lord Chancellor and the President of the Council of Wales in his favour. There was no reason why the King should not do so, she argued, considering the services that Sir William had rendered as MP, but, above all 'by reason alsoe that you intiteled his highnes Kinge of Great Britain'.[82] Sir William, incidentally, had also tried to ingratiate himself with the King by assuring him that certain ancient Welsh prophecies had foretold his accession to the English throne. James may have been pleased that even the vaticinatory utterances of the Welsh had endorsed their allegiance to him, although some of Sir William's countrymen might have maintained that his behaviour, at times, laid him open to the

---

[82] Jones-Pierce, *Clenennau Letters and Papers*, p. 61. Anne Wen Brynkir to her brother Sir William Maurice, under date of 6 February 1603–4.

charge of superstitious beliefs. As apparently happened on one occasion when a fuller renting a mill from him near Clenennau had a piece of cloth stolen. He complained to Sir William, whereupon the squire of Clenennau, so it was said:

> Did send for one Jane Bulkley to his house at Clenenney aforesaid to tell him, the said Sir William Morris, by sorcery who did steale the said cloath. And the said Jane came unto the said Sir William Morris and after, by the commandement and in the presence of the said Sir William Morris, about a yeare sythence at Clenenney aforesaid, the said Jane Bulkley did cutte tenne severall pieces or bitts of cheese and uppon each bitte of the said cheese one William ap William, servant of the said Sir William Morris, did write such charmes as the said Jane did speake. And the said Jane did give the said tenne bitts so written upon to be eaten of tenne persons suspected for the stealinge of the said peece of cloth there then present who did eate the said bitts.[83]

The King's mind was firmly made up on one issue. Any significant surrender or diminution of the authority of the Council of Wales would not only derogate from the Crown's prerogative; it would have the further disastrous effect of undermining the relationship between the Welsh and English communities on the borders, which the Council had laboriously improved by its policy of pacification and impartial judicial administration. And, consequently, it would hardly be plausible to exploit it as a precedent to be acted upon to vindicate a similar policy of unification between the English and the Scots. All possible arguments were now employed by James, his Privy Councillors and ministers, and, in particular, those reasons which envisaged a threat to the coalescence of the Welsh and English peoples. Where time and considerable erudition had hitherto been spent on debating over-subtle and academic points as to whether the four English shires had ever been part and parcel of the 'Marches' of Wales, or whether

---

[83] PRO Star Chamber 8 James I 136/15. Unfortunately, no explanation was offered as to how this particular piece of sorcery succeeded in identifying the thief. In any case, Sir William Maurice denied the whole business and declared that even if it had happened, the matter would have been one of witchcraft and, consequently, outside the competence of the Star Chamber.

the Council of Wales had been either constituted or confirmed by the Act of Union of 1536, the King and his advisors now claimed unequivocally that, if a hair of the Council's power was arbitrarily touched, then:

It will cast a general skorne and contempt upon the remainder of authoritie left in that Court for hereafter and make the Welshmen despised by the English, who are now by their common governement holden in termes of love; and so will ere longe revive the ancient enmytie betweene these two people and bring all to the old confusion againe, which as nothing could redresse at first but that Court, so it is not probable anie thing can better prevent than the continuance of the same.[84]

Even the Welsh language was recruited to subserve the King's purpose, for it was maintained that the four shires were intrinsically a part of the Welsh Marches since 'in many of them the Welsh tongue, even to this day, is as frequent and usuall as in other shires in Wales'.[85] On the other hand, the opponents of the Council, especially those in Gloucestershire, were able to quote with glee from another reputable Welsh source:

Divers other unanswerable reasons may be collected out of Mr [David] Powells Chronicle in his Discription of Wales, who sheweth that when the principallyty of Wales was in lymits most extended, no parte theirof did ever reach or come on this syde Severne; noe, not powes land which was the third parte of that dominion.[86]

Francis Bacon, the Solicitor-General, argued that one of the intentions of the establishment of the Council of Wales 'was to make a better equality of commerce and entercourse in contracts and dealings betweene the subjects of Wales and the subjects of England'.[87] Mindful of how fundamental this

[84] PRO State Papers Domestic, James I 1603–10, vol. 19, fol. 53b. A Breviat of the cause in Parliament touching the governement of the Lord President and Counsell in the Marches of Wales.

[85] *Ibid*, vol. 37, fols 107–112. Draft of Declaration concerning the four shires, 1606.

[86] PRO State Papers Domestic Supplementary (SP 46/127) fol. 18. Proofs that the counties of Hereford, Gloucester, Worcester and Salop are not in the Marches of Wales, 1605.

[87] BM Add. MSS 25244, fols 5–8.

equality of commerce would be in any negotiations for an Anglo-Scottish union, the King's concern about any adverse commercial effects of the interruption of the Council of Wales's authority was obvious.

> All traffique and commerce betweene the English and Welsh will cease, whiles the one cannot have equall remedie against thother as they have had, the Welsh being subject to answere the English at the Counsell, but not being able to implead the English but in the courts of Westminster. This will open a gapp for all suits of vexation which are the greatest reproches and scandalls in the institution of our lawes.[88] [And]...whereas now uppon confidence of this readie justice the English of theis sheeres send yeerlie greate herds of catle to be summered in Wales, and buy there greate store of cattle, sheepe, wools, frizes and cottons for exchange of corne, fruite and merchandize of all sorts, now all this traffique (the maine grounde of the present wealth of them both) must necessarilie decay; and so both must retorne to that povertie, rudnes and disorder which was amongst them before this Coort made them quiet and rich.[89]

To demonstrate that equality of commerce was practicable and already in full operation on the Welsh border, the King hoped, would help to remove one source of non-collaboration when the English and Scottish commissioners met to discuss the union.

Two other reasons, which revealed James's unappeasable sense of insecurity regarding the real attitude of the Welsh towards him, despite their public acclamations of loyalty and the praises of some of their poets[90] were:

> If Wales, upon any concept of bondage by beeing continued under this governement [at Ludlow] when the English shires are freed of it, or upon anie other ill homor, shall breake out into disorder, where shall the President and Councell have meanes to suppress the

---

[88] PRO State Papers Domestic, James I 1603–10, vol. 19, fol. 53b.
[89] *Ibid.*
[90] One being John Owen the Epigrammatist [d. ?1628]. *See* Davies, *Writers of Wales*, p. 41.

same in the beginnings of mischief so soone as were fitt
and safe for the State, if the 4 shires shall be exempted?[91]

A piece of reasoning which confirmed the official point of view
that the shires had, from the initial establishment of the Council
of Wales, been put under its control for military and security
reasons – 'the Welsh who by situation and nature beinge ever
prone to ryotts and rebellions doe therfore need to be bridled
with the strength of theis sheeres'.[92] What was, perhaps, more
dangerous was that tampering with the Council of Wales:

Will prove but a deseigne for the Welshmen to free
themselves also from the same governement, and a
manifest overture to abridge or dissolve the like authoritie
of the Lord President and Council in the north; especiallie
now, when the happie union of England and Scotland
maie happilie admitt more pretenses for the same than
hereto fore.[93]

The project of the union suffered the same fate as the Great
Contract. It hardly got off the floor of the House of Commons
before the prorogation of Parliament; and later parliaments did
very little to reanimate it. The King himself soon realized that
to dissolve the identities of the two nations demanded more
than negotiations and legislation, and this was brought home
to him by religious rather than by commercial or other
susceptibilities which he may have overlooked.

Invited to send delegates to represent the Church of England
at the Synod of Dort in Holland in 1618 James nominated four
divines whose polymathy and ability could compare with any
other international deputies at the Synod, one of the four being
George Carleton, Bishop of Llandaff. The King may have
congratulated himself on his choice of representatives, but was,
perhaps, slightly disconcerted when he received a despatch
from his ambassador at the Hague reporting that many Dutch
and other churchmen were surprised that the Church of
Scotland had sent no delegates to the Synod. He was requested to
rectify the omission without delay, in case 'those of that nation
should take it ill that they were not thought of, as Geneva hath

[91] PRO State Papers Domestic, James I 1603–10, vol. 19, fol. 53b.
[92] *Ibid*, vol. 31, fol. 115b.
[93] *Ibid*, vol. 19, fol. 53b.

much stomaked that they were so long forgotten'. James was not slow in realizing that he had made a blunder in selecting only English divines to go to Dort, that to ignore his country-men might be interpreted as a gratuitous offence to them, and that it was imperative to remove any misconception on that point so as to 'avoyde the dislike which they (the Dutch) suspect may be conceaved in Scotland'.[94]

On behalf of the King, Secretary of State Naunton, having fabricated a number of excuses, instructed the ambassador to tell the Dutch that it had been initially proposed to send some Scottish divines to the Synod, but that because of the shortness of time and atrocious weather conditions, they had not been ready to travel. The situation was to be amended immediately, and the Scots amply compensated for the inadvertent omission. One of their leading divines, Walter Balcanqhual, Professor of Divinity, was being dispatched to Holland, and the Dutch were to be requested to extend all care and courtesy to him 'that so the Scottish nation may receive that satisfaction to have the same respect with them as others have'. In addition, the ambassador was to recommend that Balcanqhual 'may be conveniently accommodated for his lodging and other intertainments as near our English as may be, if he cannot be consorted with them in the same company'.[95] When it came to the point, James's own innate and irrepressible consciousness of his Scottish descent and his pride in it, could override his idealistic conceptions of political union and equality.

It was not that James renounced them, but circumstances and the realities of his political environment made him more aware of the futility of forcing the pace of the union, and of the limitations imposed on the combining of disparate and nationalist emotions and aspirations. Examining the situation more carefully he had, however reluctantly, to agree with the more mature and empirical views of Cecil, who had died some years before this event, that 'the union must be left to the maturity of time, which must piece and piece take away the distinctions of nations, as it hath already done here between England and Wales'.[96]

---

[94] PRO State Papers Foreign, Holland (SP 84), vol. 86, fol. 116. Sir Dudley Carleton to Sir Robert Naunton dated 29 September 1618.

[95] *Ibid*, vol. 87. Sir Robert Naunton to Sir Dudley Carleton, dated 25 November 1618.

[96] HMC *Salisbury (Cecil) MSS*, vol. XVI, p. 363. James I to Lord Cranborne, dated 22 November 1604.

Lord Eure's last years as President, unlike those of his predecessor, were comparatively restful. The even tenor of duties at Ludlow was occasionally punctuated by nervous messages from London and elsewhere that State enemies and declared traitors might be tempted to seek refuge in the Principality, and that alarm bells should accordingly be set ringing in towns and countryside. In the year that he took up office, Sir John Salisbury had sent him the improbable news that Hugh O'Neill, Earl of Tyrone and sworn enemy of the English establishment in Dublin, had paid a flying visit to Wales.[97] A few months later another notable Irish rebel, Lord Delvin, who had escaped from Dublin Castle, was the cause of alarm in Whitehall, where it was thought that he might possibly find a hide-out in Wales.[98] Then five years elapsed before the President was notified that defective security measures in the kingdom had concentrated the mind of the Privy Council wonderfully on the prospects of the Principality as a haven for traitors. This time it was Lord Maxwell, a Scottish nobleman, who had been reported as embarking at Bordeaux in the hope of making his way home via Ireland. The Privy Councillors had as little trust in him as they had in English weather, for they feared that storms might force Maxwell to land somewhere in Wales instead, and Eure was instructed to organize a diligent watch along the coast.[99]

At the same time the President had a sharp eye for the pursuit of objects other than the political and religious opponents of the State. Like Lord Zouche and his class in general, Eure did not believe that his social status precluded him from dabbling in property or industrial transactions, wherever the prospects appeared promising. Moreover, during the last years at Ludlow, he had reason to apprehend some decline in his financial position because of the loss of revenue to the Council of Wales, and the consequent difficulty of funding the remuneration of its officials and legal functionaries.[100] To

---

[97] *Ibid*, vol. XIX, p. 267. Lord Eure to the Earl of Salisbury, dated 5 October 1607. This was shortly after the famous Flight of the Earls of Tyrone and Tyrconnell from Ulster to the continent.

[98] Jones-Pierce, *Clenennau Lettters and Papers*, p. 69. Lord Eure to Sir William Maurice, under date of 18 December 1607.

[99] *Ibid*, p. 77. The Privy Council to Lord Eure, under date of 4 April 1612.

[100] The revenues of the Court of the Marches had declined from £2311 in 1602–3 to £683 in 1606–7. Williams 'The Attack on the Council of the Marches', 5.

investigate other possible sources of income, while he was still in a position to wield influence and exploit patronage, was the natural thing to do.

He had, in fact, done some preliminary prospecting along these lines very soon after his appointment, when he had been granted the Constableship of Harlech Castle with its yard and green for the duration of his authority as Lord President.[101] The possibility of turning this sinecure to his profit must have occurred to him, for he wrote to Cecil shortly afterwards that the castle was a formidable stronghold in a strategic as well as sensitive area on the Welsh coast, and might appeal to the King's enemies as a place to be seized and retained: consequently, it should never be entrusted to the hand of a stranger, but its custody and annual fee of £30 be reserved for the Lord President of the Council of Wales, and made disposable by him as he thought advisable and proper.[102]

Eure's perception of the self-serving advantages of his office was considerably sharpened when to his rank of Constable of the castle he added that of Mayor of Harlech. The corporation of Harlech had long been seized of certain lands within the commote of Ardudwy, and Eure shared the views of the bailiffs and burgesses, and of the occupiers, too, that the income produced by these properties hardly reflected their potential economic value, which could be raised if they were properly exploited. In fact, bailiffs, burgesses and occupiers appeared ready to show their appreciation 'if the said Lord Eure could make them anie better estate in their said lands than formerly they had, and to purchase his good will withall'.[103]

Lord Eure had no objection to converting his good will into solid English or Welsh silver or some other form of recognition. The problem was to justify the confidence which the people of Harlech were willing to repose in him. An opportunity to do so came early in 1608, when he received two petitions from them that raised his hope. The one complained that the townspeople had neither trade nor commerce to enable them to make a decent living, and that in recent years they had experienced much poverty:

---

[101] PRO State Papers Domestic, James I 1603–10, vol. 44, p. 495. The grant is dated 2 March 1609.

[102] HMC *Salisbury (Cecil) MSS* vol. XX, p. 295. Lord Eure to the Earl of Salisbury, endorsed 1608.

[103] PRO E 134 20 James I, Easter 20.

By reason that the Greate Sessions houlden for the sayd country [of Merioneth], which were usually heretofore kept within the sayd towne, be nowe of late yeres kept in other places of the sayd shire, to the greate and utter undoing of us who lived only thereby, and allsoe to the greate annoyance and ruyne of his Ma^{ts} castle within the said towne which is from tyme to tyme, at such tymes only as the said Sessions be kept at the sayd towne, repayred without any charge to his Matie, for the Judges, Sherif and prenotharie to lye therein.[104]

The second petition reiterated the general complaint of penury, and was signed by many of the Merioneth gentry. It added one or two interesting details to the previous petition.

Whereas the poore county of Merioneth hath not any towne within ytself that may affoorde any good and convenient lodginge for gent[lemen] or for any great assembly of people, especially at tymes of the great Sessions and Quarter Sessions, there our service and attendance is nowe more requyred then yt hath bene ever before, at which tymes the greater number of the gent[lemen] and freehoulders of the shire have bene enforced to absent themselves and make deffault of attendance for want of lodgings. And such as doe come are so disquieted and pestered in respect of the smallnes and scarsitye of the roomes and the multitude of the people that they are fayne to lye in heapes together; and where the same inconvenients may not be helpen or redressed unelesse the great Sessions and Quarter Sessions may be allwaies tyed to one towne or locall place within the said county, where the gent[lemen] in deffault of buildings and lodgings to be made and prepared by the inhabitants and dwellers of the same, would provide and buyld lodgings for themselves rather than be pestered and disquieted as aforesaid.

At the same time, the President's attention was drawn to the fact that the Crown stood to lose almost as much as the inhabitants of Harlech by allowing the castle to fall into a ruinous condition. It was pointed out that it was the sole royal

[104] PRO State Papers Domestic, James I 1603–10, vol. 43, fol. 79. Justices of the Peace of Merionethshire to Lord Eure, dated 3 February 1608–9.

fortress on that part of the coast, and had hitherto been maintained in a better state of repair and habitability than any other castle in North Wales, thanks primarily to the conscientious efforts of the people of Harlech; for when the Great Sessions were held in the town the castle was 'ayred, scoured and clensed, and some voluntary chardges bestowed by every sherif towardes the reparation thereof'. Then followed the warning that the fortress would inevitably be reduced to ruins if the Sessions were not held there, or if the King no longer defrayed the costs of repairs. It was absolutely imperative, so the argument in the petition ran, to preserve the castle not only to defend the coast against possible foreign invasion, but also 'to keape the countrey in awe from any insurrection or rebellion'. It was a point calculated to impress the President, and through him the Crown, obsessed at the time by the vague dangers of rebellion in the border shires if the Council of Wales was stripped of its authority, and to spur them to spare a thought for Merionethshire. It could, conceivably, have a greater effect on the King than the exaggerated self-respect of the townsfolk who deplored the fact that the Great Sessions had been transferred from Harlech to Bala – 'a very vilthy dyrtye towne without any lodginges fytte for gentlemen to lye, and a place farre remote'.[105]

The thirty-one persons, who subscribed to the first petition, were of one mind that Harlech was the only town that qualified for the distinction of accommodating the Sessions, and Lord Eure agreed with them. The petitions had placed him in the fortunate position of rendering a service to the town that would place its inhabitants under an obligation to him. They had also provided him with two cogent arguments that, in his opinion, should help him to win the King's approval; the one being the undertaking by the town to assume financial responsibility for the regular upkeep of the castle – an irresistible bait to a monarch cornered by his debts; the other being the equally imperative demand for action to be taken to repair a serious omission in local government facilities in Merionethshire, which James and his ministers could not afford to ignore. But what may also have impelled the President to act as effectually as he could in the matter, was the realization that one of the signatories to the second petition was Sir William Maurice of Clenennau, who was

---

[105] *Ibid*, fols 80–1. Burgesses and inhabitants of Harlech to the Lord President, dated 4 February 1608–9.

sheriff of the shire where he had property and, what was more pertinent, was also being pressurized by the inhabitants to approach the King on their behalf by means of his contacts at the Court as Member of Parliament.[106]

Sir William had been solicited by the bailiffs and burgesses, as far back as 1604, to promote their interests in the House of Commons and, in particular, to procure for the shire the right to elect a burgess Member of Parliament, as well as to secure the lasting attachment of the Great and Quarter Sessions to Harlech. Other facts about Sir William Maurice's dealings with the corporation were likewise known to Lord Eure; for example, that he had been entrusted with its charters and writings and, more to the point, that there was a project on foot to enclose Harlech Marsh between Llandannog and Llanfihangel y Traethau or Llanfihangell in the Marsh, in which the squire of Clenennau was personally interested.

The President had to act speedily if he was to anticipate Sir William and derive some benefit to himself from the situation, and he did so on two fronts. In London, he arranged for the petition of the burgesses to reach the King's hands, and was gratified to understand that James was sufficiently influenced by it to authorize him, as Lord President, to canvass the opinions of the gentry of Merionethshire on the advisability of fixing the location of both Sessions in Harlech. Their affirmation was hearty and unanimous, and Lord Eure wrote to Sir Daniel Donne, Master of the Requests, that if the King granted them by charter the annual keeping of the Great and Quarter Sessions, the inhabitants of Harlech intended 'to make such preparation and provision at theire owne charge as shalbe fitting both for the receipt of the Judges and for the ease of the whole countie'.[107]

At the same time, the President took steps to secure some public recognition of his services to the people of Harlech. Realizing that Sir William Maurice had not been wasting his time but, having got himself chosen as one of the town's bailiffs, was possessed of an influential post to prosecute his interests, Lord Eure first ordered him to bring the documentary

[106] Jones-Pierce, *Clenennau Letters and Papers*, p. 73, no. 252. Draft of letter from Sir William Maurice to Sir Patrick Mooney, one of the King's Privy Chamber, under date of 28 August 1609.
[107] PRO State Papers Domestic, James I 1603–10, vol. 44, fol. 94. Lord Eure to Sir Daniel Donne, dated 18 March 1608–9.

evidence deposited with him by the corporation to Ludlow, so that he could study their contents before further consulting the bailiffs of Harlech on how best to promote the welfare of the townspeople.[108] It transpired, however, or so later evidence suggested, that the President:

> Did promise and beare the town in hand that he would procure the Great Sessions and Quarter Sessions of the said county to be contynnualie kept in the said town and to be tyde to be all wayes kept there. And thereupon did cause some kind of deed to be ready drawn to be sealed by som of the said corporation unto one Eaton and Harrys (being his men) to his use upon present condition and not other weise.

The condition being that some of the property in the possession of the corporation would be transferred to Lord Eure in exchange for his active intervention in securing both Sessions for Harlech. It would appear, too, that a second deed, similar in content and intent, was drawn up and that one of the burgesses invited to sign it had second thoughts on the matter and refused to do so 'for that he would not wronge himself and the poor countrey soe farr as to seale any more writtings in that matter'.[109] It is possible that the President had allowed himself to become involved in the dispute over the division of Harlech Marsh, to a part of which Sir William Maurice also laid claim.

In any case, Lord Eure did not achieve what he had set out to do for the town and himself, so that what had initially promised to be a profitable arrangement did not materialize. What took its place, however, was a bitter quarrel between him and Sir William Maurice in 1613, when the President charged the latter with deliberately harassing another Caernarvonshire gentleman, Robert Wynn, by disturbing him in the possession of land which Wynn had recently recovered by process of law, and actually sending his servants to plough it. After administering a formal reprimand: 'I cannot but let you know that I expected a more befitting respect, if not towards him (Wynn), yet towards myself, from you,'[110] Sir William was brusquely

---

[108] Jones-Pierce, *Clenennau Letters and Papers*, p. 75, no. 257. Lord Eure to Sir William Maurice, under date of 28 March 1611.

[109] PRO E 134 20 James I, Easter 20.

[110] Jones-Pierce, *Clenennau Letters and Papers*, p. 90, no. 316. Lord Eure to Sir William Maurice, under date of 27 November 1615.

ordered to attend at Ludlow on a certain day, where the differences between him and Wynn might, by the President's mediation, be resolved. He obviously did so, but was disconcerted by the manner in which Lord Eure conducted the inquiry. For, whereas the President had indicated that he would invite certain legal officials to reach a satisfactory conclusion 'because Maurice relies on him principally to perform the office of a friend', none of them came together to discuss the case. Moreover, Sir William was prohibited from seeking any remedy by law except by having his case tried by a court in Merionethshire, besides being condemned to pay twenty marks in money.[111]

Lord Eure's incursion into another field, with a view to stabilizing his finances, was fated to end in a similar negative way; and it too detonated a mine of ill-feeling between him and another, more powerful, member of the Welsh gentry. Upon the news of the President's arrival in Ludlow, Sir John Wynn, of Gwydir, had taken the trouble to send him a courteous message of welcome and good wishes together with a piece of Welsh beef for his kitchen.[112] This amicable gesture induced Lord Eure, acting upon certain information supplied by a German mineralogist that Sir John Wynn's estates contained minerals, to put forward vague suggestions that a profitable partnership might conceivably be established between them and some other friends, if trials proved that exploitable minerals really did exist on the Gwydir lands. Sir John responded to the hint with an ecstatic assurance that the place abounded with copperas and brimstone, and that technical skill was the only component lacking in a happy combination of factors – the accessibility of a navigable river capable of taking ships of twenty tons; an inexhaustible supply of peat and turf as fuel – which, if properly handled, could make their fortune. However, he discounted the exploitation of copperas and recommended the production of alum, which was a commodity much needed for the dyeing of cloth in England which had, for the moment, to be imported at considerable cost from Italy.[113] There was also, of course, the transmutation of iron into copper by a certain process, which Sir John had witnessed in Anglesey,

---

[111] *Ibid*, p. 93, no. 327. Sir William Maurice to the Chief Justice in the Marches of Wales, under date of 28 August 1616.

[112] *Calendar of Wynn Papers*, p. 74, no. 453. Sir John Wynn to Lord Eure, dated 30 October 1607.

[113] *Ibid*.

and of which he reluctantly conceded some details to the Lord President.[114]

Any alternative to the manufacture of alum was laid aside when Sir John received an offer from Gerard Malines, a German industrial immigrant who was hunting around for a chance to display his knowledge and experience. He asked for a lease of the mine on the Gwydir estate and offered the eighth part of all the profits in exchange. Sir John, usually quick-witted in these speculations, appeared to be puzzled by the proposal, or he may have decided that it was expedient to throw the onus of any resolution on the Lord President, and let him shoulder the responsibility for any lack of success in the enterprise. But he was alert enough to inform Malines that if the transaction were approved, he would be able to provide him with all the equipment he needed at a reasonable price; and, for that matter, Malines would have no reason to look further than the squire of Gwydir if he required a careful and industrious overseer for the mine.[115]

There was no correspondence, or so it would appear, between the parties until 1615 when, towards the end of that year, Lord Eure summoned Sir John Wynn to appear before the Court of the Marches. Sir John replied that it would be hazardous for a man of his age – he was sixty-two at the time – to journey all the way to Ludlow. Not only was he an old man, but he had caught a severe cold. In short, he would not be able to attend the Court, but should be allowed time to make depositions to whatever charges were levied against him, and given every facility to prepare for a hearing at some later date.[116]

What had caused this revulsion of feeling and minatory attitude towards Wynn was disclosed in Lord Eure's letter to Cecil's son, the 2nd Earl of Salisbury:

His Maties Attorney here hath informed against Sir John Wynn of Gwyder, knight and baronett, for several oppressions and violences committed under colour of being a Justice of the Peace, a deputy-Lieutenant and farmour under his Matie of certayne escheate landes in

[114] *Ibid*, p. 75, no. 456 and p. 77, no. 471. Sir John Wynn to Lord Eure, dated 9 November 1607. See also *History of the Gwydir Family*, p. ix, letter no. 1.

[115] *Ibid*, p. 77, no. 407. Sir John Wynn to Gerard Malines, dated 21 December 1607.

[116] *Ibid*, p. 111, no. 705. Sir John Wynn to Lord Eure, dated 30 October 1615 and p. 112, no. 714, dated November 1615.

the countie of Carnarvon. In the examination of which cause, the proofes have been so apparant and the offences so foule and monstrous by imprisoning and manicling some upon feyned causes and putting out whole families, some of them being young children and naked, by 3 a clocke in the morning, only because they would not turne tenants unto him.

Sir John had been fined a thousand marks by the Court of the Marches, though 'both his abilitie might have endured, and his offences deserved, a farre greater summe'. He had also been declared unworthy, 'to hold any place of authority in the county', since he exploited it, 'too much to his owne benefitt and the countryes prejudice'. The Earl of Salisbury was requested to ask the King to authorize the President to discharge Sir John as member of the Council of Wales, and to recommend to the Lord Chancellor, in addition, that he should be removed from the office of Deputy-Lieutenant of Caernarvonshire. In almost the identical words that Lord Zouche had used before him, Lord Eure added that any irresolution in inflicting this severe disgrace on the squire of Gwydir would only serve to stimulate other Welsh gentlemen to follow his discreditable example.[117] This condemnatory exposure was followed by similar letters denouncing Wynn for his callous behaviour, and calling for reprisals along the lines proposed by Lord Eure.

Sir John Wynn, however, had his friends, not least amongst lawyers and courtiers. Sir William Jones, Justice of the King's Bench, advised him to counteract the call for his removal from the Commission of Peace by stating his case in writing to the Lord Chancellor. Even the President's brother, Sir Francis Eure, wrote to Ludlow that Sir John should be given a fresh hearing so that he could clear himself from the charges of which, so the writer averred, Sir John stood unjustly condemned.[118] But then, Sir Francis Eure had in mind to be a candidate for the post of Justice of North Wales, and a favourable word from an obligated gentleman like Sir John at the right moment would not come amiss. Finally, Evan Lloyd, Attorney of the Common

---

[117] PRO State Papers Domestic, James I 1611–18, vol. 84, fol. 25. Lord Eure to the Earl of Salisbury, dated 5 December 1615.

[118] *Calendar of Wynn Papers*, p. 114, no. 720. Sir Francis Eure to his brother, the Lord President, dated 12 December 1615.

Pleas, advised Wynn to come to London to see the Lord Chancellor, Lord Ellesmere, personally, or to send him an explanatory and self-exculpatory letter.

Sir John had found it impossible to travel as far as Ludlow, but the tedious journey which he undertook to London does not seem to have impaired his health or aggravated his old age. He may have seen the Lord Chancellor, but he also took the wise step of submitting a petition to the King. Some manoeuvring went on in the corridors of Whitehall, for in the New Year directions were issued to the Lord Chancellor to review the sentence passed on Sir John by the Council of the Marches. Two months later, no doubt after further airing of his grievances, Wynn was persuaded to submit to the President and Council of Wales. As the Lord Chancellor and other interested officials rather euphemistically explained to Lord Eure, the squire of Gwydir 'in coulde bloud upon better advisement finding his errors', thought it incumbent upon him to submit. He also stood to gain by being so amenable 'since it is therefore advisable to follow the course of grace and favour practised by the Star Chamber where, upon humble submission, the time of imprisonment and the fine are abridged and abated'. Moreover, so Lord Eure was encouraged to believe, the voluntary submission of Sir John 'so strongly allyed in his countery and supported with soe powerful freends in Court, will add more grace and lustre to the authority' of the President himself. In the light of the threat to that authority from the antipathy and insidious conspiracy of the gentry of the four English shires and their friends in high places, Lord Eure could be counted on to perceive and judge correctly the import of that statement.[119]

Having earned only resentment by his entry into the sphere of property and industrial speculation at Harlech and Gwydir, the Lord President eventually realized that there was, at least, one asset in his possession convertible into cash, and that was his own office of authority and trust. As soon as it was put on the market, there was no lack of bidders for it.

Here is a competition between the Lord Chandos and the Lord Gerrard for the Presidentship of the Marches of Wales. The Lord Eures, who maryed the Lord Chandos

---

[119] *Ibid*, p. 121, no. 749. The Lord Chancellor, Secretary Ralph Winwood and Sir Fulke Greville to Lord Eure, dated March 1615–16.

wifes aunt is willing to part with yt to him; but by meanes of Sir G. Villars, [the Earl of Buckingham] and the Lord Ffenton, who have stood for the other, the question is difficult who shall bee. But I heare of some breach betwixt my Lord Chandos and the Master of the Horse [the Earl of Worcester] about yt which, if it be true, will loose him many frendes. Seldome ffavorites continue theyr frindes.[120]

Another who had his eye on the post was Sir Thomas Egerton, the Lord Chancellor's son, and his interposition may have conduced to a quick settlement of the business.

My Lord Chancellor is very ill and conceaved to be partly out of discontent for that he staies so long without an Earldome and partly by reason that his sonne, Sir Thomas Egerton, hath failed of his expectation (which was earnestly followed by his father) for the Lord Presidentship of Wales, the same being now conferred upon the Lord Gerrad by his composition with the Lord Ewre.[121]

By a tragic vicissitude, neither Lord Eure nor Lord Gerrard was able to enjoy the fruits of their transaction. The former died in April 1617, and seven months later Gerrard followed him to the grave, having barely had time to implement a directive from the King that, in view of the demise of so many members of the Council of Wales, the new President should replace them with Crown nominees, who included some eminent Welsh gentry like Sir John Stradling, Sir Roger Mostyn and others.[122] Within a short time, the King appointed William Compton, the Earl of Northampton, to take Gerrard's place, and there began that slow but steady process of attrition whereby the authority of the Council of Wales was gradually undermined by increasing disrespect, sometimes by downright challenge and defiance, until it finally expired at the hands of the Long Parliament.[123]

---

[120] PRO State Papers Domestic, James I 1611–18, vol. 87, fol. 117. John Chamberlain to Sir Dudley Carleton, dated 4 June 1616.

[121] Ibid, vol. 90, fol. 155. Edward Sherburne to Sir Dudley Carleton, dated 23 February 1616–17.

[122] Ibid, vol. 93. Cope (sic) of his Majestys letter for making Councillors in the Marches, dated 12 August 1617.

[123] Williams 'The Attack on the Council of the Marches', 1–22.

2

The Catholics and their fortunes

It was with relief that the overwhelming majority of the English people saw James VI of Scotland established on the throne as James I of England. Later this title was to be expanded into King of Great Britain, but, for the moment, his coronation did not symbolize the removal of the ancient frontier between the two kingdoms so much as the elimination of any dispute over the succession to the throne.

> All men [wrote Sir Henry Carew to Sir Robert Cecil, the Secretary of State] are exceedingly satisfied and praise God who of his goodness hath so miraculously provided for us, contrary to the opinions of the wisest who for many years past trembled to think of her Majestys Queen Elizabeths decease, as if instantly upon it the kingdom would have been torn in suner.[1]

Sir Robert may have privately thought the praise slightly disproportionate, in view of the fact that he had been more instrumental than any agency, celestial or otherwise, in engineering the smooth transfer of the crown to the head of the King of Scotland. But he passionately believed, and in this he shared the conviction of his countrymen, that the unity of the kingdom and the lives and property of its citizens had been preserved by the peaceful accession of the new King.

It was to be expected that these sentiments would be expressed also by the people of Wales. The most influential class within the Principality, the landed gentry, and the spiritual mentors of the nation, the clergy, were sufficiently loyal to the Crown to welcome a king who was not only a

---

[1] HMC *Salisbury (Cecil) MSS*, vol. XV, p. 8. Sir Henry Carew to Sir Robert Cecil, dated 27 March 1603.

Protestant, but had been designated as her successor by the last monarch of the beloved House of Tudor. An instinctive acceptance of the late Queen's choice, coupled with the tranquillizing feeling that things would go on very much as before, governed their attitude towards the change of dynasty. In any case, resistance was inconceivable to the majority of the Welsh landed families, although opposition was not entirely discounted by some circles in North Wales.[2] It was only two years since Sir Gelly Meyrick had forfeited his life for supporting the reckless Earl of Essex in his rebellion against the Crown, in which two brothers of the Salusbury family of Rug in Merionethshire were involved, one of them, Owen, being killed during the siege of Essex House in the Strand, and the other, John, imprisoned for his part in the affair.[3] The lesson had not been lost on the Welsh squires; moreover, the situation in Wales was being closely watched by the Council of Wales at Ludlow. Under the presidency of the late William Herbert, Earl of Pembroke, it had once again become the formidable instrument that it had formerly been for enforcing submission to the Crown and its ministers.

However, there were some dissonant notes in the general chorus of rejoicing which reverberated from Anglesey to Monmouthshire as the proclamation of the King's accession was read in one market place after another. William Dolben of Denbigh, was alleged to have publicly commented that the new monarch 'should lyve but six monethes and six daies, and that warres should contynue in England after by the space of three yeres'.[4] And when Sir Henry Danvers, who had been appointed by the Privy Council to supervize the proclamation in Wales and Ireland, arrived in Conway and ordered the bailiff of that town to announce the news, he found his instructions ignored. Upon inquiry, it was said that the bailiff was afraid of incurring 'the displeasure of John Gwyn of Gwydir, being then deputie leutenant of the countie of Caernarvon and pretending to be lineally descended from one Owen Gwynedd, sometymes prince of Wales'. The King was informed that Gwyn had actually issued a warrant for the arrest of Danvers. Moreover:

---

[2] Dodd, 'Wales and the Scottish Succession', 201–25.
[3] For the support given by North Wales to the Earl, see Dodd, 'North Wales and the Essex Revolt of 1601', 363–4.
[4] NLW Wales 4 Gaol Files, Denbighshire 13/2.

The said John Gwyn, having then the custodie of possession of your Highnes castle of Conway, where all the armour and munition of the said counties were remayninge under his keeping... then and there did retayne and take upp all the old and well experienced souldiers of the said counties under his paie, readie to attempt whatsoever he commanded to theire abilitie; being not well pleased, as it seemed, that your Highnes should be proclaymed Sovereigne, according to your undoubted right, untill he did well perceive all the gentlemen and commonaltie, with full consent in those partes, desyre and proclayme the same to their great joy and contentment.[5]

That the Crown took no action suggests that it considered the accusation to be groundless, grossly exaggerated or plain nonsense, the more so as it had been preferred against a gentleman to whom the Council of Wales had partly entrusted the responsibility of suppressing all disorders and unlawful assemblies in Caernarvonshire at the beginning of the reign. But there were other and more ominous incidents which the Government took more seriously. In Montgomeryshire, immediately upon the death of Queen Elizabeth, a certain Lewis ap John, so it was alleged:

Tooke a foolyshe concept in his head that all lawes were doen and ended, and that all offences before your Ma[ts] personall repayre into this realme were dispunishable; and did contryve in his own idle brayne to sack and spoille the whole contrey there adjoyninge to his native parish of Betws, well knowinge that by the death of the late Quene and untill newe commissions from your Majestie, the power of all sheriffs, undersheriffs, Justices of the Peace and such like was quitte determyned, and by strickt order of lawe they had no auctoritie to represse anie whatsoever malefactors.

Happy in the belief that an interregnum meant the suspension of law and order and no restriction on pillage, Lewis ap John was said to have gathered a band of ruffians from all over

---

[5] PRO Star Chamber 8 James I 311/33. For the exchange of letters between Danvers and Wynn on the latter's behaviour, see *Calendar of Wynn Papers*, p. 44, nos 246 and 247.

Wales and terrorized the countryside. His activities were reported to be 'tendinge to rebellion'. Rural society was alarmed by the rumour of a threat made by him to a lady of breeding that he would 'cutt of her hedd as they did in Ireland'. But there was greater consternation when one of his followers was said to have opposed the proclamation of the King's accession at Newtown with the presumptuous words: 'Shall we have a Scott to be our King?' Where acts of violence had hitherto failed to galvanise the local gentry into action, the first hint of sedition succeeded. The band was hunted down or dispersed by Edward Price, of Newtown, and Lewis ap John thrown into gaol.[6] It was in the same shire that another refractory Welshman, James David Lloyd, of Llanfair, was reported to have publicly professed his aversion to the King and armed a group of like-minded followers to subvert the laws of the realm. On this occasion, the Council of Wales reacted sharply against such flagrant disloyalty and inflicted a swingeing fine on the offender before he could do much damage.[7] However, these were isolated incidents, and the local officials of the Crown and the gentry could generally be relied upon to control or suppress such disturbances.

What really perturbed the Council of Wales at Ludlow and the Government in London was the possibility of resistance movements by the Catholic minority up and down the Principality. There was little credible evidence that the Welsh recusants were involved in any open insurrection or conspiracy against the new King. But there were some who behaved as if they were careless of the suspicions that they might arouse, or confident enough of their influence in local society and politics to demonstrate their adherence to the old faith at this particular time. In Monmouthshire, it was alleged that no sooner was the old Queen dead than Edward Morgan and his sons, the redoubtable Catholic family of Llantarnam, dispatched teams of oxen to transport muskets and calivers from the county armoury at Caerleon to their manor house. If true, their action was untimely, but it is improbable that it had a treasonable motive.[8]

[6] PRO Star Chamber 8 James I 122/6.
[7] PRO E 101 553/25 Unpaid Fines in Wales and the Marches.
[8] PRO Star Chamber 8 James I 207/28. It is possible that some people in Monmouthshire, who were no friends to Llantarnam, could not forget that one of Edward Morgan's sons was married to a daughter of the Catholic Earl

What added appreciably to the nervousness of the authorities was their ignorance of the actual numerical strength of the Catholics throughout Wales. That they formed a small minority was indisputable, but it is very likely that even the most sanguine amongst the ministers of the Crown hesitated to accept the diocesan returns of 1603. According to these, there were scarcely eight hundred recusants or thereabouts who were distinguishable from an estimated total of 212,000 communicants in the four Bishoprics of Bangor, St Asaph, Llandaff and St David's.[9] To have done so would have displayed a naiveté not unlike that of Roger Owen, a priest and native of Pwllheli, in Caernarvonshire, who confessed when interrogated that he firmly believed that one-third of the inhabitants of Wales (and England) were Catholics.[10]

There was, however, disquieting evidence that such speculation was far from reflecting the influence that recusants could wield in certain localities. A striking instance of this occurred at Machynlleth, in Montgomeryshire, in 1603, when John Owen was fined £40 by the Council of Wales 'for not fynding a bill of indictment for recusancy according to his evidence, he being foreman of the grand jury'. What was disturbing in this case, in the eyes of the authorities, was that eleven other members of the jury were his accomplices in flouting the law, and that they came from the widely scattered country parishes of Llanbrynmair, Llandinam, Darowen and Penegoes within the same county.[11] There was no apparent reason why other isolated and mountainous areas in Wales should not conceal similar groups of resolute and defiant recusants, as well as more discreet sympathizers.

These fears were put to the test in midsummer 1603, when the kingdom was alarmed, but soon reassured, by the discovery and

---

of Worcester, Lord Lieutenant of Monmouthshire, and may have been too ready to assume connivance on the part of the latter. Unlike them, the Government could forget this fact and had no such qualms about his loyalty to the Crown, for he was deputed shortly afterwards to go down to Wales to deal with any troubles caused by recusants and Jesuits. See HMC *Gawdy MSS*, p. 101, under date of 26 June 1603.

[9] BM Harleian MSS 280, fols 162–4.

[10] PRO State Papers Domestic, James I 1603–10, vol. 2, fols 4 and 49, under dates of 6 and 22 June 1603.

[11] PRO E 101 533/25.

prompt suppression of the double-headed conspiracy known as the Main and the Bye or Priests' Plot. The Government chose to differentiate between them, but they were concurrently organized, and the Catholic lay and religious personalities implicated in the two plots shared common aspirations and knew of each other's plans, despite the fact that they differed in their choice of means to attain their objectives. These were to seize control of the government and likewise of the King's person, if necessary replacing James on the throne by his cousin Arabella Stuart, which is what the extremists amongst them wished to do; to secure complete toleration and equality for the Catholic minority; and finally, to guide the country towards friendship with its old enemy, Spain, with whom the kingdom was still officially at war. Since the King had shown himself benevolently disposed towards his Catholic subjects when he crossed the border, and favoured the end of hostilities with Spain – he was to sign a peace treaty in the following year, there seemed to be little justification for the plots. What was more incongruous was that Sir Walter Ralegh, who embodied the persistent anti-Spanish sentiment in the country, was made privy to the conspiracy, and allowed himself to be sufficiently involved as to be charged with treason when the leaders were arrested and brought to trial.

The Main Plot passed almost unnoticed in Wales. It was true that a certain Richard Parry, a recusant in Breconshire, was detained in London and examined for possible complicity in it.[12] Moreover, it was asserted that the feasibility of landing a Spanish force at Milford Haven had been discussed by the conspirators, although Ralegh strenuously denied that he had advocated it.[13] The notion that a distant but naturally-endowed haven like Milford was admirably suitable for the disembarkation of foreign invaders was not a chimerical one. The place had been regarded as a weak link in the chain of littoral defences of the kingdom by the Elizabethan government,[14] and this fear was to lose none of its force until the middle of the seventeenth

---

[12] PRO Star Chamber 8 James I 227/8.
[13] HMC *Salisbury (Cecil) MSS* vol. XV, pp. 285–6 and 305. *See also* Edwards, *Life of Sir Walter Ralegh*, vol. 2, p. 462.
[14] PRO State Papers Domestic Addenda (SP 15) vol. 30, fol. 186. 'The opinion of the Lord Gray and others what place were most lykelie the enemy would land at, 1588' Milford was included amongst those 'which were the aptest for thenemy of Spaine to land at'.

century.[15] But the potential vulnerability of the inadequately
fortified haven was pinpointed when the rumour spread that a
number of the partisans of the Main Plot had captured Milford
and were awaiting the arrival of Spanish soldiers.[16] There was,
of course, no truth in it, and the collapse of the plot soon
afterwards nipped any expectation of active support in Wales,
even if there had been some sign of it.

The repercussions of the Bye or Priests' Plot in the Principality
were more distinctly felt. Its acknowledged leader was William
Watson, a secular priest who had, at first, advised the Catholic
priesthood and laity to acquiesce in James's accession as an
expedient step towards securing toleration, in opposition to the
Jesuits, who ridiculed the idea and advocated a policy of revolt
and foreign intervention to overthrow the Government and the
English Church. It was Watson's disillusionment with the King
and the renewed collection of fines imposed on Catholics for
not attending church services, that led him to exchange concili-
ation for conspiracy. He was a frequent visitor to Wales, and it
is possible that he made his fateful decision when he happened
to be in Carmarthenshire in July 1603. If so, he may have
allowed himself to be deluded into thinking that militancy was
rife amongst the recusants of South Wales. Later, he was to
confess that he had been assured that ten thousand Catholics
were ready to rise in arms in the border counties – a piece of
very dubious information supplied by a Mr Meredith of
Abergavenny, in Monmouthshire, who shortly afterwards was
said to have crossed into the opposing camp of the Jesuits who
held no brief for Watson.[17] Whether he believed such fantasies
or not, Watson was sufficiently hopeful of substantial support
as to hurry back to London, fortified, perhaps, by a secret
confabulation with a Welsh priest named Clennock or
Clynog, a 'cunninge man in prophesies', who predicted that
the King would be killed and that a woman, presumably

[15] HMC *Salisbury (Cecil) MSS*, vol. XXII, 1612–68, p. 219. Preparations against
invasion, dated 1626.
[16] *Ibid*, vol. XV, p. 222. William Francis *alias* Clerke to (Sir Griffin Markham)
before August 1603.
[17] PRO State Papers Domestic, James I 1603–10, vol. 3, fol. 27. Confession of
William Watson, under date of 10 August 1603. According to the Bishop of
Hereford, some Welsh recusants of Monmouthshire 'had their finger in the
late Watson's intended treason which was in part hammered here in these
parts'. *Ibid*, vol. 14, fol. 16. Bishop of Hereford to the Earl of Salisbury, dated
22 June 1605.

Arabella Stuart, would eventually rule in his place.[18]

In London, Watson summoned his adherents from amongst the Welsh and English recusants, and laid his plans for the forcible seizure of the King. These were soon revealed to the Government by the Jesuits, who allegedly took good care to intrigue against Watson amongst his supporters in the countryside. At the final rendezvous in London, Watson and his close associate, Anthony Copley, were most disconcerted by the poor response to their appeal, not least from the Principality. Captain Thomas Vaughan, brother of Sir John Vaughan, of Carmarthenshire, was there, and so were a Mr Fludd and a Mr Knight, all gentlemen, but of relatively poor estate and with very few followers. When Thomas Harries, of Pembrokeshire, joined the gloomy company with apologies for not bringing more men with him, his explanation allowed of no other interpretation but that the conspiracy was doomed. He informed Copley that 'the Jesuite party in that part of Walls had either gotten some inkling of the accon (action) and so labored to crosse it, or els had some accon of their owne on ffoote, wherein to make use of the Catholiques there'.[19]

Watson summarily dismissed his followers the same day, and left London with Harries, making his way towards Wales as rapidly as he could. But he was not fast enough to outrun or avoid the directives of the Government. The Council of Wales at Ludlow and its Lord President were forthwith instructed to arrest the fugitives, and since it was assumed that both were making for Thomas Harries's house in Pembrokeshire, and from there to Ireland, the judicial authorities in West Wales were alerted and warned to make every effort to find them.

The hunt for Watson ended near Abergavenny, where his capture was due to an absence of caution on his part, according to the description of the scene as related in the memoirs of a native of that town, who, later, became a prominent member and historian of the Benedictine community in England.

> The treason against King James...being discovered and the authors flying away severall wayes, a Catholick priest that was of it thought to have made an escape through Wales into Ireland. This was Mr Watson. He had taken for a guid of his journey a Catholick man of Wales called

[18] *Ibid*, vol. 2, fols 168–168b, under date of 21 July 1603.
[19] *Ibid*, fol. 134. Declaration of Henry Copley, dated 14 July 1603.

David Williams. They, passing through Abergavenny, did make some stay there at an inne, and Mr Baker passing by and taking notice of the guid, first entered into discourse afterwards with the stranger. But Mr Watson and his guid were gone but a little way out of the town when the guid, being again thirsty, stept aside into an alehouse to drink, leaving Mr Watson on the highway. When one Vaughan, a justice of the peace and his brother passing by and seeing a stranger there who had for his guid a Papist whom they knew, began to have a suspition that this man might be one of the traitors. And though he had little grownd to suspect more than that he was a stranger and one whom he did not know, yet he [Vaughan] seized upon him and his guid. And soon after the description of the persons who were of the treason being come down, Mr Watson came to be better known and discovered, and his guid to be much troubled and for a long time imprisoned.[20]

The complete miscarriage of the conspiracies and the obvious reluctance of his Catholic subjects to participate in them encouraged the King to exercise clemency, and only Watson, Copley and one other leader were put to death. In Wales, the authorities continued to keep a close watch on recusants, but for the next eighteen months or so, they had little reason to complain of their behaviour. Nothing they did could be construed as treasonable, but one or two Catholic gentlemen did show what was considered to be bare-faced irreverence towards the Anglican Church in Wales, as established by law. For instance, David Bowen, of Llanelli in Carmarthenshire, had apparently been harassing his weaker neighbours for some time and playing havoc with their property, when he decided, in May 1604, to offend their Protestant susceptibilities as well. He was reported to have gathered his armed followers:

And making noe conscience to prophane and abuse the said Temple of God and howse of prayer, he coulde not be satisfied onelye with causinge a most profane and scurrulous stage playe to be acted and played upon or abowte the twentieth daye of Maye last within the parishe

---

[20] *Catholic Record Society*, vol. XXXIII, p. 81. *Memorials of Father Augustine Baker.* Baker was recorder of Abergavenny at the time, but was converted to Catholicism in 1613.

church of Llanelly aforesaid, to the great dishonor of God, the prophayninge of his temple, the breeche of your Majestys lawes and the greevous offence of many trewe Christian protestants and loyal subjects.[21]

In England many Catholic squires, even members of the nobility, encouraged the presentation of plays and interludes, either in the privacy of their homes or in the public market place when opportune, as one means, and not the least effective, of propagating their faith. This was particularly true of the north of England, and Bowen would appear to have shared their views as well as the assumption that there would be little interference by the local custodians of the law. But, if true, it was uncommonly daring or arrogant of him to have staged an anti-Protestant play in a parish church.[22]

The Main and Bye Plots had badly misfired, but Catholic militancy had by no means evaporated. The more moderate recusants might still cherish the notion that the King was a Catholic at heart, but had to wear a Protestant image for dynastic reasons. 'What will not any Prince doe to gaine a kingdom?' was the thought that may have flashed through the minds of many, who could recall the conversion of the Protestant King of Navarre, Henri de Bourbon, to Catholicism to secure his grip on the throne of France.[23] The uncompromising and combative element within the Catholic community of England and Wales, however much it might share this illusion, was more inclined to believe that the King would, eventually, have to come to terms with his Catholic subjects because of evidence of their strength and influence throughout the kingdom.

The mood of the recusants within the border shires, more notably Monmouthshire and Glamorgan, was truculent enough to verge at times on downright defiance. Priests were made welcome in gentlemen's homes, mass was often celebrated in the open air, burial services performed with Catholic rites, and images and altars set up in private houses in many parishes. Public opinion affirmed that the real instigators behind this show of religious militancy were the Jesuit missionaries, who

[21] PRO Star Chamber 8 James I 287/22.
[22] HMC *Salisbury (Cecil) MSS*, vol. XXIV. Addenda 1603–68, p. ix.
[23] PRO State Papers Domestic, James I 1603–10, vol. I, fol. 18. Minutes of conversation with the Romish priests Griffin and Roberts (?) March 1603.

openly preached physical resistance to the Government, much
to the dismay of the loyal and moderate Catholics.

All theise persons [ran one report] have nothing in their
mouthes but the sworde, the sworde and warres. They saye
there is nowe no further hope for Catholicks beeing keapt
out of the fryeing panne into the fier. Nor other course to
bee taken for them but onely by force to free themselves.
And the rather to move the people, they bragg much that
they shall have assistaunce from the King of France and
the kinge of Spaine. In respect of which perswasions many
Catholicks in Wales are in greate feare and doe wishe the
Jesuites with all their adherentes out of the land.[24]

Their wishes were realized for in February 1604 the Government struck hard by issuing a proclamation which banished all
Jesuits and seminary priests from the kingdom, and made it
abundantly clear that the King had no intention of introducing
toleration or releasing Catholics from the laws which penalized
their faith and practices.

For the loyal Catholics there was no choice but to submit to
this reversal of their hopes, and attempt to win eventual relief
by not compromising their allegiance to the Crown. The
extremist Catholic element, however, reacted desperately and
in the only way conceivable to them. The conspiracy known as
the Gunpowder Plot was hatched by Catesby and a few other
English Catholic notables, who planned what would have been
the most spectacular and momentous explosion in English
history if there had not been a leak at the last moment, and
Fawkes discovered with his faggots and barrels of powder in a
cellar under Parliament House.

For reasons of security and the speedier execution of their
plan, the plotters kept it so close a secret that few Catholics
knew of its existence, and it was this that enabled the Government to isolate and destroy the conspiracy. There is little
doubt, however, that Hugh Owen was conversant with the
plot. That Welsh Catholic arch-conspirator, of the family of
Plas Du in Caernarvonshire but resident in Brussels, was as
dedicated to the overthrow of the Protestant establishment
under James as he had been to the subversion of the church

[24] PRO State Papers Domestic, vol. 14, fol. 95. A Relation of the Jesuit
proceedings.

settlement under Elizabeth. He certainly had no more objection to the physical liquidation of a Stuart King than of a Tudor Queen, which he had tried his best to achieve for some years. It was incredible to those, who were aware of his many intrigues and plots, that this most influential Welsh Jesuit should be innocent of complicity. The King and his ministers were so convinced of the contrary that they mounted an intensive campaign to urge Archduke Albert, co-Regent of the Low Countries, to surrender Owen so that he might be brought to trial in London. The Archduke refused a request for his extradition, but did agree to have the Welshman imprisoned and interrogated. However, pressure from the King of Spain soon resulted in Owen's release.[25]

There is no concrete evidence that Welsh Catholics were privy to the Gunpowder Plot. According to Guy Fawkes's own testimony, the conspirators had agreed that for the more effective execution of the arrangements to blow up King and Parliament, all other Catholic militant action was to be suspended, postponed or abandoned. This applied, in particular, to the Principality, which did not figure at all in the design except as an asylum for the plotters if their scheme should ever come to grief. That the Government was very much alive to this contingency was revealed soon after the conspiracy had failed.

A proclamation was circulated, naming the traitors and calling on all local authorities to pursue and arrest them. In some Welsh shires, there was an immediate response in the form of a hue and cry after any person who aroused suspicion by his behaviour. At the same time, very close attention was paid to strangers travelling in the direction of Ireland. This was especially the case in Pembrokeshire whose sheriff, Alban Stepneth, informed the Privy Council that while bonfires were being lit to celebrate the King's escape from violent death, the coast of that county was under constant surveillance.[26]

---

[25] PRO State Papers Foreign, Flanders (SP 77) Bundle 7, fols 119, 122 and 273. Of all Hugh Owen's schemes, the most fantastic was his projected combined operation involving Spanish troops and Irish rebels. The latter were to land in Wales and England under cover of foul weather on the pretence that they were in transit to Flanders. Once on dry land, they were to infiltrate far enough into the kingdom to seize the English fleet at Rochester, while musketeers from Flanders were to be conveyed across the Channel from Dunkirk to join them. *See* Loomie, *The Spanish Elizabethans*, pp.83–9.

[26] HMC *Salisbury (Cecil) MSS*, vol. XVII, p. 485. Alban Stepneth to the Privy Council, dated 13 November 1605.

In one or two shires, however, the inhabitants were somehow slow to believe that the Gunpowder Plot had taken place.
at all. In Monmouthshire, which was noted for the intransigence
of its numerous recusants, some Justices of the Peace were
inclined to question the need for a rigorous watch on the local
ports, havens and creeks, despite a rumour that a few of the
conspirators were hiding in the vicinity of the town of Usk.[27]
Three of the Justices wrote without hesitation to the Lord
Lieutenant, the Earl of Worcester, to affirm in the most positive
manner the loyalty of the shire in these words:

> Althoughe ther are more recusants in this sheere then in
> out hartes and conscience wee would wishe, yett we can
> nott finde by any meanes but that this newes [of the
> Gunpowder Plot] ys verie straunge generallie. Neythyr
> can we understande of any maner of preparation to the
> maintenance of soe haynouse a treason in anye place
> within this countie. And further [so they went on to
> assert] we are boulde to saye that we reste assured that yf
> ytt shoulde happen that any weare soe lewdlie bente as
> that they woulde eythyr abette or maintaine or defende
> anye of thes traytors...we make littell dowbte butt that
> the number of good subjects farre exceedinge the other
> with greate ease and safetie to the State, they shalbe
> suppressed in verie shorte space.[28]

On the other hand, the Mayor, Aldermen and bailiffs of
Caernarvon were distinctly more nervous of popular reaction
to the reading of the proclamation, and anticipated some
trouble at the fair which was due to be held in the town
towards the end of November. They accordingly announced
that any person having weapons in his possession that day
would be unceremoniously bundled into prison. The prohibition
was pointedly ignored by a group of toughs who, with the
alleged connivance of the Owen family of Bodsilyn, aggravated
the ordinary stresses of life for many inoffensive citizens
during the two days that followed. In addition to other
misdemeanours, it was said that they

---

[27] PRO Star Chamber 8 James I 167/18
[28] PRO State Papers Domestic, SP 14/216, pt 1, fol. 128. The Gunpwder
Treason Book. The Gentlemen of Monmouthshire to the Earl of Worcester,
dated 12 November 1605.

Did rioteously and unlawfully set upon and assault one Hugh Thomas ap Rees, then High Constable of your Ma^{ts} hundred of Ucha, and other persons at that tyme ayding and assisting him then in pursuing and following hue and cry after the traytours, which weare in the last horrible and damnable treason of Gunpowder entended by Sir Edward Digby, late knight, and his most wicked and vile confederates against your Matie.[29]

It is most likely that this was no demonstration of sympathy with the Gunpowder Plot, but of congenital hostility towards the appointed custodians of law and order.

A general ignorance of the plot may have helped to keep the situation in Wales quiescent, but it would not be entirely idle to speculate whether Digby and his friends would have won the active collaboration of some unappeasable Welsh recusants, if they had disclosed their intentions to them. Three years after the dramatic events of November 1605, there arose a violent altercation between John Edwards, the notorious and irrepressible Catholic of Chirk, and some of his neighbours over a mill course. Observing that a number of workmen were engaged in repairing the course, Thomas Bailly, one of Edward's servants, was said to have warned them not to proceed at the risk of their lives, and to have abused one of them for refusing to allow his master's friends to pass through the group of watchers, who had been stationed on a stone bridge near by, after the flight of the Gunpowder conspirators. And he was reported to have added these significant, if not ominous, words: 'There was a day and now it is night, but I hope to see a day againe', which, in the light of his master's undisguised defence of Catholicism, could have been considered by the authorities to be not only shamelessly seditious but a genuine expression of regret that the King and his Parliament were still in one piece.[30]

In the atmosphere of tension and doubt that inevitably followed upon the failure of the conspiracy, the suspicion of treasonable activities was a weapon that could be employed by unscrupulous elements in society to blacken the character, and even endanger the lives, of enemies and rivals. The feuding gentry did not refrain from resorting to it upon occasion. Sir John Wogan, of Boulston, in Pembrokeshire, was conceivably on

---

[29] PRO Star Chamber 8 James I 230/8.
[30] PRO Star Chamber 8 James I 135/18.

very unfriendly terms with Thomas Canon, of Haverfordwest, to accuse him bluntly of sending his servant, George Parker, to Ireland to buy weapons and armour and convey them to Milford Haven at the time of the Plot. Canon denied any complicity, and the charge was not pressed.[31] But it was taken up by a more formidable opponent of his, Sir James Perrot of Haroldston, in the same shire, who brought it to the notice of Lord Zouche, the President of the Council of Wales. Perrot did not commit himself by expressing an opinion on the alleged guilt of Canon, which he avoided by saying, somewhat unconvincingly, that he was too much the other's enemy to show impartiality in his case. However, this did not prevent him from hinting openly enough that it deserved a closer investigation, and that it would not be amiss to interrogate not only Canon's servant, but also the passengers who had crossed with him from Ireland. He added, for good measure, that Canon was intimate with the friends of the Earl of Northumberland, who was suspected of abetting the Gunpowder Plot and had been imprisoned in the Tower of London.[32] Perrot was, perhaps, unwise to do this, for it was an invitation to his own adversaries to impugn his motives in introducing Northumberland's name into the business. They might conveniently remember that Sir Thomas Perrot, legitimate son and heir of Sir John Perrot, Sir James being an illegitimate son, had married the daughter of Walter Devereux, Earl of Essex and that she, after her husband's death, had married Northumberland as his second wife, and had been granted an annual pension of £500 raised on the Haroldston estate – much to the annoyance and resentment of Sir James Perrot.[33]

The savage punishment of the leaders of the Gunpowder Plot removed the likelihood of further conspiracies against the person of the King and the security of the Government. That

---

[31] PRO Star Chamber 8 James I 113/7. It is interesting to note that many years later, when the inhabitants of Haverfordwest were pressed to contribute to the privy seal loan to Charles I in 1626, Thomas Canon figured among the few gentlemen who chose to give nothing. Whether his refusal was motivated by personal, political or religious reasons is another matter. Charles, *Calendar of Haverfordwest*, p. 58.

[32] BM Add. MSS 6178. Sir James Perrot to Lord Zouche, dated 18 December 1605. *See also* HMC *Salisbury (Cecil) MSS*, vol. XVII, p. 555.

[33] PRO State Papers Domestic, James I 1603–10, vol. 8, p. 114, no. 46. Warrant dated 29 May 1603; and vol. XIII, fol. 20. Thomas Canon to Sir Thomas Lake, dated 4 March 1605.

there should follow a more severe application of the anti-papist laws generally was something to be expected, but the gradual repudiation of militancy meant that the Catholic subjects of the Crown could hope for an eventual modification of such penal legislation, once they had shown that they were submissive to the King's rule in temporal affairs, however much they chose to remain irreconcilable to his Protestant doctrines.

There was a further reason for the growing realization that extremist action was impracticable and inimical to the best interests of the recusants. Slowly the news percolated into all ranks of the Catholic minority that the traditional maintainer of their cause and abettor of their opposition, the King of Spain, was revising his policy of hostility towards England and seeking some form of friendly coexistence. The peace treaty of 1604 showed how the political wind was blowing from Spain, and later events – the proposal of marriage between Charles, Prince of Wales and the Infanta of Spain, and the departure of Hugh Owen from his conspiratorial headquarters in Brussels to the relative obscurity of Rome, indicated the wish for better relations between London and Madrid. That the Spaniards intended to exploit this rapprochement in order to camouflage their role in the initial stages of the grand Catholic counter-offensive of 1618-48 in Germany and to nullify, if possible, any attempt by the King of England to succour the Protestant cause there, was revealed later. For the moment, it was part of the Spanish plan to eliminate any suspicion of their ulterior motives by satisfying James that his Catholic subjects could no longer rely on the Spanish Government for encouragement or tacit endorsement of any movement to overthrow him and his ministers. This was made quite clear in the King of Spain's instructions to his ambassador in London. Sarmiento d'Acuna, later Count of Gondomar, was directed to advise all recusants within the kingdom to show their loyalty to the Crown on all occasions, to obtain and deserve the King's favour by their exemplary obedience, and to eschew hostility and resistance to central and local authority. As far as the recusants were concerned, the policy of Philip III of Spain demanded their submission to the English throne and not, as his father had requested and hoped in the reign of Elizabeth, their collaboration in conspiracies to overthrow it.[34]

---

[34] PRO State Papers Foreign, Spain (SP 94), vol. 19, pt 2, fols 382–3. Philip III to Sarmiento, dated 4 March 1605

What particularly exercised the minds of the recusants now and for some time to come, was not only their survival as a spiritual force in the kingdom, but the consolidation of their influence and power in those districts where they were numerous, well-connected and quite capable of putting up an organized and coordinated opposition to any coercion or provocative interference on the part of the authorities without, of course, unduly exciting the intransigent fears of the King. To close their ranks and present a united front was, therefore, the prerequisite to their main purpose of convincing James that, although quiescent and obedient subjects, they were not subservient to him in their religious beliefs; and that a policy of repression and extreme penalization, if he permitted one, might force them to become the reluctant sympathizers with a violent Catholic reaction.

This tactical approach to the question of defining the relations between Crown and Catholics, and guaranteeing the comparative immunity of the latter from the excesses of the legislation affecting them, had as good a chance as any of succeeding in Wales, and, conceivably, a better one than in England. Whatever element of pugnacity had existed amongst Welsh recusants, it had been muted and restrained. There had been no overt act or campaign of treason and, consequently, no call for retributive justice. Where English Catholics had witnessed three abortive plots in as many years, the liquidation of their recognized leaders and the resultant spread of a feeling of impotence, fear and resignation, the strength of the Welsh recusants, however limited, had not been impaired by rash conspiratorial adventures, nor had the more prominent members of their community been removed on charges of treason. Welsh Catholics of all classes felt themselves strong or influential enough, and no less resolute, to display from time to time a cool and calculated indifference towards the sovereignty of the law and the supremacy of ministerial authority in matters of State, whenever they chose to regard them as incompatible with their religious convictions and, occasionally, with their more secular interests. And, until the end of the reign, there was no lack of evidence – not all indisputable, of course, that the Catholics in Wales found it to be demonstrably true that audacity, if not downright arrogance, could sometimes win them more respect and recognition than a feigned acquiescence in all things.

It might have been expected that the strength of Welsh recusancy would lie in the vast mountainous areas of North Wales and the more remote parts of the south-west where veneration for, and devotion to, traditional religious beliefs could be thought to have a firmer grip on people than in the more accessible and exposed lowlands. But this was not the case. The fact that the two main ports linking England with Ireland were Holyhead and Milford Haven meant that the constant passage through them to Ireland of officials, soldiers, colonizers and traders would serve to accentuate the outward and impressive signs of Protestant supremacy on both sides of the Irish sea. By the same token, it would contribute to the gradual attrition of Catholic sentiment and attachment to the old faith. This would be particularly true of those immediately affected, not least materially, by this uninterrupted intercourse between the two countries. The final affect would be to drive the Catholic religion to seek sanctuary in the Llŷn peninsula, the mountains of Merionethshire and the upper reaches of the Towy river in Carmarthenshire.

There was also the undeniable fact that the landed gentry in these two regions of Wales exhibited a partiality for the established religion of the kingdom, partly because of the advantages that they gained by their voluntary compliance with the ecclesiastical authority approved of by the King. But some of them went beyond the normal requirements of conformity, and made a point of disturbing the peace and tranquillity of recusants wherever they could unearth them. The name of Sir James Perrot of Haroldston certainly became synonymous with a hearty dislike of Catholics. Apart from his unrelenting campaign against them in the House of Commons, the manner in which he harassed a defenceless woman recusant, Anne Heyward of Haverfordwest, revealed his total unconcern for spiritual sensitivities other than his own.[35]

To show disregard for the Protestant ascendancy, which Sir James Perrot personified, was not always easy, and only a few Catholic gentlemen ventured to do so. One of them was Sir John Vaughan, of Golden Grove in Carmarthenshire, who was said to

---

[35] The Justices of the Peace of Haverfordwest were no less desirous than Perrot of making life miserable for their recusants. Acts of the Privy Council, 1619–21, p. 367; 1621–3, p. 305. See PRO State Papers Domestic, James I 1619–23, vol. 119, fol. 21, Mayor and JPs of Haverfordwest to the Privy Council, dated 21 January 1620–1; and vol. 124, fol. 199, Anne Heyward to her father, dated March 1620–2.

maintain two hundred of his tenants, all recusants. Not only had he refused to administer to them the Oath of Allegiance to the Crown, but he had allegedly dissuaded his fellow Justices of the Peace in that county from executing the anti-recusancy laws passed by Parliament.[36] If these accusations were true, Sir John may have been encouraged to show his Catholic colours by the fact that the neighbouring countryside harboured a strong community of recusants who were not Welsh, but originally came from the English border shires. Their leader was Robert Acton, of Worcestershire, who had migrated to Llandeilo with his family, and had been followed in the course of time by other Catholics from the same region. The fact that Acton's name was linked with the Gunpowder Plot made matters worse, and moved the Bishop of St David's to write to the Secretary of State that the movements of such recusants to remote places like the uplands of Carmarthenshire should be prohibited unless they had taken the Oath of Allegiance, which Acton had either omitted, or refused, to do.[37]

A few months later, Sir James Perrot, in a letter to the Secretary of State, confirmed the impression given by the Bishop of St David's that recusancy in the south-western parts of Wales was being much revitalized by the settlement of English Catholics there. 'It is treu', he wrote, 'that there are certayne Jesuites and seminary priestes that doe keepe an intercourse and holde intelligence betwixt the recusants of Worcestershier, Herefordshier, Monmouthshier and the recusantes of these partes in Southwales, norishinge theyr discontentmentes and feeding them with forayne and home-bredde hopes.' He suggested to the Secretary of State that a loyal and reliable Catholic should be sent to the border counties to investigate the haunts and activities of priests, and that this course of action was imperative 'the rather because the recusantes of the Marcher shiers adjoyninge unto Wales have of late more than in former times come to settle them-selves in these remote partes of Wales'.[38]

[36] PRO Star Chamber 8 James I 302/31.
[37] PRO State Papers Domestic, James I 1611–18, vol. 67, fol. 386. Bishop of St David's to the Earl of Salisbury, dated 2 November 1611.
[38] PRO State Papers Domestic, James I 1611–18, vol. 68, fol. 139. Sir James Perrot to the Earl of Salisbury, dated 13 March 1611–12. Professor Glanmor Williams points out that much of the tenacity shown by recusants in the diocese of St David's could be attributed to the arrival of English Catholics in that Bishopric. On the other hand, he stresses that recusancy made

But whatever pockets of Catholic opposition existed in the western extremities of the Principality, there is little doubt that the main bastions of the strength of Welsh recusants lay in south-east and north-east Wales, probably because of their proximity to the English counties where Catholicism was still a potent religious force in a society which was essentially rural and conservative, as in Herefordshire and Gloucestershire to the south, and Lancashire and Yorkshire to the north. The relations between the Welsh and English border shires had been close from medieval times, and they retained an independent attitude and showed, occasionally, a stubborn dislike of, and resistance to, political and ecclesiastical innovations imposed by the Crown. The mere existence of the Council of the North at York and the Council of Wales at Ludlow was sufficient testimony that special powers were needed to reduce these two outlying areas of the kingdom to some semblance of conformity and obedience. But where compliance with the administrative and political directives of government had been exacted, the Crown still had to reckon with the implacable antagonism of the old faith and of the many who adhered to it.

This was particularly true of Glamorgan and Monmouthshire, and it was a situation which profoundly disturbed the President of the Council of Wales.[39] Lord Eure, who conveyed his anxieties in a letter to the Secretary of State, expressed quite categorically where he thought the trouble lay. Speaking of the landed gentry of the two shires, the real repositories of power, he described them as being 'well-educated, of great livelyhood, and verie potent in the places where they inhabite', all of which could and should be conducive to good public order and stability. But he understood that, 'the countie of

---

little actual progress within the diocese because of the absence of leaders from amongst the landed gentry, who could have encouraged opposition to the established Church and protected Catholics of the lower orders. *See* his 'The Diocese of St David's from the end of the Middle Ages to the Methodist Revival', 23.

[39] The actual number of recusants in these two shires remains unascertainable as yet, but they must have been impressive. One of Sir Robert Cecil's correspondents estimated that about one thousand were to be found in the parishes adjacent to Herefordshire. HMC *Salisbury (Cecil) MSS*, vol. XVII, pp. 455–6. The most detailed study on this subject is by Frank H. Pugh. *See* his 'Glamorgan Recusants 1577–1611', 49–67; and his 'Monmouthshire Recusants in the reigns of Elizabeth and James I', 57–110.

Monmouth was wholy divided almost into factions by reason the number of those who, being addicted and misled with Poperie, are so powerfull and they so daring to professe and show themselves, as that fewe causes arise in the shire which is not made a question betwixt the Protestant and the Recusant'.[40]

One gentleman, who made no secret of his recusancy nor of his belief that he could override any hindrance arising from it, was George Langley of Caerleon, 'a person of great power and abilitie' on account of his wealth and rank, a convicted recusant and a shrewd trader. He kept a number of boats in a creek of the River Severn called Goldcliff Pill which was 'an obscure place where no shipping used to resorte or people dwell'; and it was here, far from the inquisitive eyes of the King's Customs officers, that he was said to load his craft with butter, leather, calf-skins and raw hides, which were expressly forbidden by law to be conveyed overseas. Langley treated this interdiction with the same heavy-handed contempt that he apparently showed for some Customs men, who tried to interfere with him on one occasion and whom he quickly put to flight. What distinguished him from other clandestine transporters of prohibited goods was that he sent his wares overseas, 'for the benefitt and maintenance of other recusants beyond the seas and in England and Wales'.[41] That one cargo was estimated to be worth about £500 must have afforded much relief and encouragement to his co-religionists abroad.

The most notable Catholic family in Monmouthshire was undoubtedly the Morgans of Llantarnam, without whose wealth and protection the recusants would have had to temporize and seek some accommodation with local officialdom.

[Edward Morgan] by reason of his greate livinge, power and allyance in the said county [was] accompted the chief piller and only mainteyner of the papists and recusants thereabouts, whoe, havinge bene in the tyme of our late soveraigne lady Queene Elizabeth more in nomber in them partes then in any place of England quantity for quantity, are since your Ma[ts] raigne by the countenance and protection of the said Edward Morgan more than doubled, and,

---

[40] PRO State Papers Domestic, James I 1603–10, vol. 48, fol. 163. Lord Eure to the Earl of Salisbury, dated 23 October 1609.

[41] PRO Star Chamber 8 James I 308/12.

thereby, not only upholden and soe farre encouraged in theire superstition that masse is more usually said in the house of the said Edward Morgan and the parishes of Llantarnam aforesaid, Llandenny thereunto adjoyninge and other places thereabouts then divine service in the said parishe churches.[42]

Catholic conventicles in private houses were said to be on the increase, and no effort made to conceal the fact that people were being married and buried according to Catholic rites. There was, perhaps, no stronger evidence of the dominating influence of this recusant family than that two hundred Catholics were alleged to have attended the burial of Morgan's daughter Winifred, and put the local curate to ignominious flight when he showed his face.

Along the borders of Wales, as far as Flintshire, reputable landed families and ordinary folk alike paraded their Catholic beliefs and practices. Sir William Aubrey of Brecon, the Winters of Llanfihangel Tal-y-llyn, and the wife of John Madock, the sheriff of Breconshire, shared their faith with weavers, farm servants, feltmakers, labourers and tinkers, as well as with public notaries like William Bevan of Llanthew.[43] Flintshire, possibly, had the closest knit Catholic community in North Wales, for its leading recusant families – the Mostyns of Talacre, who kept 'papisticall books' in their library, the Conways and the Pennants – had intermarried. Some of them attained high office like Sir John Conway, the sheriff of Flintshire, and could thereby avoid too close attention from the more dedicated and industrious executors of anti-Catholic legislation.[44] It was partly the concerted pressure and the infectious devotional example of these and like families that did more than stiffen the resistance of recusants. For Richard Parry, the Bishop of St Asaph, was forced to confess to the Secretary of State that, whereas in 1602 the number of Catholics in his diocese had been about 140, he was confronted by the

[42] PRO Star Chamber 8 James I 207/32.
[43] PRO State Papers Domestic James I 1623–5, vol. 162, fols 62–73. List of recusants presented at Brecon, 12 March 1623.
[44] PRO Star Chamber 8 James I 6/12. In his *Cymru a'r Hen Ffydd* Emyr Gwynne Jones examines in some detail the role played by Catholic families and other social classes in the recusancy movement during the reign of James I, and draws attention to the predominance of women in their ranks. *See* pp. 46–62.

uncomfortable fact that some three years later, there were four hundred of them.[45]

The relative success of the recusants within the Principality in exerting pressure, where this was feasible, to counteract the policy of State and Church to reduce their number as well as to circumscribe their influence was partly due to certain innate weaknesses in their main opponent, the ecclesiastical establishment, whose foundations had been laid by Henry VIII, and which had been completed by the religious settlement of Elizabeth I. Much time and effort had been expended in defining the doctrinal truths and particularizing the ceremonial practices which it was intended to perpetuate as appendages to the essentially Protestant character of the Church. And with the exception of a few peripheral sects, who were critical of its hierarchical institutions and authoritative exegetical monopoly, it had been accepted by the generality of the public, although not with any marked enthusiasm.

The reality behind the ostensibly unchallengeable paramountcy of the Church seemed to be such as might conceivably encourage many recusants to believe that their cause was not entirely lost; that if they could hold their ground, they might yet experience a change for the better in their fortunes and status; and that those who had abjured the old faith might, in time, witness the impermanence of the new. For, on looking around, there were signs that all was not well in the religious life of Wales, and that the ecclesiastical organization which claimed the power to control and guide it, could not wholly conceal the defects that invited the animadversions of its enemies and critics.

One aspect that was bound to trouble its dignitaries was the existence of a body of opinion that held no brief for the accepted doctrines of the Church nor, in some cases, for the fundamental and simplest tenets of the Christian faith itself. What was disconcerting was that this attitude of scepticism and irreverence had really nothing to do with political or religious affiliations, but reflected an inclination towards atheism or rejection of any institutionalized religion whatsoever; and that it was not confined to any particular locality in Wales. Reynold Clarke of Church Stretton, in Montgomeryshire, may

---

[45] HMC *Salisbury (Cecil) MSS*, vol. XVII, p. 374. Bishop of St Asaph to the Earl of Salisbury, dated 15 August 1605.

have horrified the more respectable members of the congregation in the parish church when he was reported to have declared that: 'Our Lord and Savioure Jesus Christe was noe more able to live in heaven without naturall foode then he the said Clerke could doe upon earthe.'[46] This, however, could be regarded as a somewhat rhetorical interjection or a debatable, and not necessarily heretical, proposition compared with the announcement alleged to have been made publicly by Miles Williams of Pendeulan, in Glamorgan, a wealthy yeoman, to the effect that: 'I had rather heare an old wives tale then to heare anie church man preach, that the gaggling of a gander is as good, and that there is noe truthe in what they saye.'[47] It was this kind of open defiance of the Church, its orthodox views and its discipline that led some people to suspect and deplore that its obvious aim was to 'advance Atheism'. And it certainly galvanized Sir John Wynn of Gwydir into meeting the Bishop of St Asaph, to confer with him on the urgency of devising counter measures, such as the translation of the Psalms into Welsh, for, to his anguish of mind, people all over Caernarvonshire seemed to be falling into atheism.[48]

Nor could Welsh recusants fail to notice that, despite the fine personalities, the remarkable erudition and, particularly, the genuine spiritual concern of many of the Welsh Bishops and lower clergy, the character and activities of some clergymen were a discredit to their calling, and called into question their professed vows of devotion and dedication to church teaching. It was not so much the pluralism and absenteeism of the higher ranks of the clergy that excited criticism, for no honest recusant could deny that these abuses were commonplace and damaging enough in the Catholic Church. It was the actual behaviour of the clerics, particularly the parish clergy, that seemed calculated at times to create the impression that the new faith, as practised at the parochial level, was no improvement on the old, and that nothing was to be gained in the matter of personal salvation by submitting to the dictates of its frocked representatives.

The parishioners of Llanarth, in Cardiganshire, including some of the local gentry, had according to a report good reason to fear the vicar, David Griffith, when he failed to have his

---

[46] PRO Star Chamber 8 James I 230/24.
[47] PRO Star Chamber 8 James I 44/6.
[48] *Calendar of Wynn Papers*, p. 87, under date of 15 August 1610.

own way. Presumably no one had protested too much at his outrageous conduct in abducting a young girl of sixteen from her mother at dead of night and marrying her, although he was twenty-four years her senior. But his attempt to filch a piece of land under the pretext that it belonged to the vicarage, and to force the tenant, David ap Ievan, to commit perjury by swearing that it was not a freehold, brought matters to a head. The tenant refused to give false testimony and the infuriated vicar retaliated, not only by excommunicating him, but by subjecting him to a most humiliating scene.

> Upon the Sundaie then next following, when he was in the pulpit and in the middest of his sermon, he did cause the said David to stand at the altar of the said church of Llanarth, and there and then the said David Griffith uttered, spake and published in disgrace of the said David ap Ievan to the parishioners there assembled to hear divine service and the said sermon: Behould the Devill is on his face: thereby intending and meaneing the said David ap Ievan, which unsemelie and reproachful words the said David Gruffith then uttered and spake because the said David ap Ievan refused to make the aforesaid oath.[49]

No less consternation would seem to have been provoked by a clergyman at Bangor, Arthur Williams, who was himself hardly a paragon of religious single-mindedness because of his alleged absenteeism from a number of livings which he held in North Wales. During a service in the Cathedral Church of Bangor, where there were two stone statues – one of Richard Vaughan, formerly Bishop of Bangor and then of London, the other of the more recent Bishop of Bangor, Henry Rowland – Williams was said to have turned towards them and, at the same time, addressed the congregation with these words:

> Marke these twoe pictures, shewinge and mentioninge the pictures aforesaid. They are the pictures of twoe cut-throats, but they did differ in the manner of it; for, sayde he, the said Arthur Williams, Richard, late Bishop of

---

[49] PRO Star Chamber 8 James I 203/11. The vicar was a Fellow of Oriel College, Oxford, but even this distinction had not prevented him from contravening the statutes of the college by selling his Fellowship for £40.

London, was like a fine barber who did first wash a man with his balles (bowls) and sweete waters, and then smoothely with a sharpe razor cutte his throate. But the other, nameinge the sayde Harri Rowland, late Bishop of Bangor, woulde butcherlike without any maner of preparation at all cutte a mans throate.[50]

If opprobrious observations of this kind were made in public at the expense of the prelacy of the Church, they could only encourage Welsh recusants to remain steadfast in the hope that further divisions and dissensions would add to the internal disunity of the Protestant establishment.

That they should feel that time was, perhaps, on their side and working for the eventual disintegration of Protestant supremacy, would be reinforced by the evidence that this absence of decorum and reverence within the precincts of churches was having a harmful effect on the behaviour of Protestants outside them. Judging by the conduct of clergy and parishioners alike, the whole fabric of church discipline and law was being regularly and wantonly damaged by clandestine marriages, the surreptitious appropriation of glebe land, the playing of games in time of divine service, the neglect of church buildings, acts of violence in consecrated ground, the actual condoning of bigamy and connivance at the abduction of young girls by clergymen, and other irregularities. On this point there was considerable criticism in the Welsh dioceses, particularly Bangor and St Asaph, that the Church tolerated certain customs which undermined the sanctity of married life and encouraged immorality.

It is the custom in the said dyosses that every mane and woman, when they shalbe maryed, shall yeld unto the curate the Xth parte of all their goods, as well the woman and the man, or else to fyne therefore, and this as often as a man or a woman shall happen to marye. And yf a mane chaunce to bury his wife or the woman her husband aboute mydsomer, and then payeth all his tythes belonginge to harvest as of haye and corne, and then incontynent after harvest happen to marye, both the man and woman shall paye the tenth agayne, notwithstanding their late tything at harvest. And besydes all this they shall

---

[50] PRO Star Chamber 8 James I 28/6.

paye a certyne some for their bodyes the day of their maryage. But who so lyste to lyve in adultary there, his fyne is but ll^s by the yeare to the ordenary, the which causeth matrimonye to be litle sett by and muche refused in these partes.[51]

There were two almost insuperable difficulties facing the Church at this moment in its slow progress within the Principality, of which the recusants were fully cognisant and which, no doubt fostered their sanguine expectation of a truce – even an uneasy one – with the Crown. The more irksome of the two was the poverty which pressed heavily upon it and constrained it to suffer certain restrictive practices, which were incompatible with its evolution as a source of spiritual zeal, enlightenment and clerical precedence in a country that had not yet surrendered itself completely to Protestantism.

The Church was in the unenviable position of raising more dust than money whenever it put its hands in its coffers. From the time that the Bishop of Bangor had begged to be released from the obligation of being present in the Parliament of 1606 and was excused attendance on the grounds of 'the smaleness of your living' which would not 'sufficiently defraye the charge of your travaile and attendence',[52] all ranks of the Welsh clergy had felt the pinch. Those of episcopal or slightly subordinate status could manage, in some degree, by living on the revenues of more than one benefice, but the lower orders were constantly vulnerable to the threat of poverty.

From all the Welsh dioceses came evidence that for some rural clergymen life was very difficult. During fifty years or so Lewis Evans, the rector of Llanegryn, in Merionethshire had served his flock faithfully, and had never received the slightest increase in his salary of £5.6s.8d, despite the effects of inflation on the actual value of his stipend. He had ventured to protest on one occasion about its insufficiency, but had been rebuffed and had, consequently, resigned himself to his apparently pre-ordained penury for the rest of his life.[53] Gabriel Parry, the curate of Henllan, in Denbighshire, also had good reason to complain of his lot, since he was paid a mere forty marks a

---

[51] BM Harleian MSS 368, fol. 178.
[52] PRO State Papers Domestic, James I 1603–10, vol. 16, fol. 177. King James to the Bishop of Bangor, dated 22 November 1605.
[53] PRO E 134 10 Carl I, Easter 25.

year for his services as preacher and spiritual mentor in that parish.[54]

That many of the parochial clergy failed lamentably to earn enough to lead decent and dignified lives, as well as meet the clerical contributions payable to the Crown, such as first fruits, tenths and subsidies, was inevitable. Part of the difficulty lay with the economic conditions in some parishes, where the inhabitants had to contend with poor soil and the mountainous character of the countryside, and were unable to derive a reasonable income from their labours. But it is also true that an appreciable number of parishes were in the hands of lay impropriators, to whom they represented a source of revenue in the form of tithes which they exploited to the utmost, even to the extent of mortgaging church livings when they found it to their advantage.[55] And their attitude towards the needy incumbent, who was usually allotted a very ungenerous portion of the tithe to carry out his pastoral duties, was often arrogant and sometimes vicious if he questioned their conduct, and did much to detract from the dignity of his calling and his self-respect.

In the event, the Crown found it advisable in 1624 to pardon those who were in arrears with their payments, some of which had remained undischarged since the reign of Edward VI.[56] Some Welsh Bishops also took up the cudgels on behalf of their impoverished clergy. In 1611 the Bishop of St David's made it crystal clear to the Exchequer why the parsons in his diocese were incapable of paying any Parliamentary subsidy until they had received the fruits of their livings. 'No man', he wrote, 'in this country will or dare undertake for friendship or reward to levy the Kings dutyes and pay them unto the Exchequer at the dayes prefixed bycause they can not come by them so soon'.[57] And the Bishop of Llandaff added the weight of his experience to the blunt warning of his episcopal confrère, that the bureaucrats of the King's Treasury would do well to stop their arbitrary meddling with the customary times of collection in the Welsh dioceses, if they wished to see their money at all. They would have to wait, he wrote, until the lower orders of the

[54] PRO E 148, no. 3, pt 2.
[55] PRO C 24, no. 326, pt 2. James I *anno* 4, Easter.
[56] PRO Exchequer and Audit Office. AO 3 333/1.
[57] PRO State Papers Domestic Addenda (SP 46), vol. 69, fol. 160. Bishop of St David's to Sir Henry Fanshawe, King's Remembrancer, dated 29 January 1610–11.

clergy had been given their traditional Easter offerings, for without them they could not discharge their liabilities.[58]

The other troublesome problem for the leaders of the Church was the difficulty of finding enough qualified preachers to indoctrinate their flocks with the Protestant faith by the constant use of the catechism and the sermon. Since the parishioners, for the most part, were unable to read, it was all the more imperative that the spoken word, as the medium of religious instruction, should be simple, clear and convincing. Moreover, the fact that many of the people were, at the time, monoglot Welsh speakers, demanded that the clergy should be thoroughly at home in the language. As matters stood, the situation was unsatisfactory, and far from reassuring as to the future recruitment of suitable persons for the priesthood. To the recusants, the poor performance of doctrinal exercises and the paucity of sermons, could only promote still further the steady erosion of the influence of the Reformed Religion on a nation that had not entirely severed itself from its past.

In his *Instructions* to the clergy of Llandaff Bishop Francis Godwin had to confess that there were only fifty preachers available to serve 177 parishes and thirteen chapels in the diocese.[59] And it is possible that some of them reversed the order of their priorities in the manner of the parson of Coychurch, who was adept in extracting tithes from his parishioners, but considered one sermon every six months to be an adequate return for the money.[60] In the light of the Bishop's sobering statistics, the Earl of Worcester was right in his opinion that much preaching and more effective spoken commentaries would be necessary to contain the growth of recusancy.[61]

But four years later, in 1609, there was no visible improvement in the situation and, during a visit to the Bishop, the President of the Council of Wales, Lord Eure, found him in a most disconsolate mood and more or less convinced that the mounting tide of Catholicism was irreversible because of equally irreducible factors. 'The multitude of recusants as he

[58] PRO *Ibid*, fol. 164. Bishop of Llandaff to the same, dated February 1610–11.
[59] Gruffydd, 'Bishop Francis Godwin's Instructions for the Diocese ofLlandaff', 14–22.
[60] HMC *Delisle and Dudley MSS*, vol. III, p. 399. Thomas Jones to Viscount Lisle, dated 31 August 1607.
[61] HMC *Salisbury (Cecil) MSS*, vol. XVII. The Earl of Worcester to the Earl of Salisbury, dated 5 July 1605.

conceaveth', wrote Lord Eure to the Secretary of State, 'groweth only by the scarcity of preaching ministers, and that also occasioned because of impropriations whereof part beinge the Kinges and let out to lease, and the rest being other mens inheritance, there is so small a proportion allowed for discharge of the cure as a minister will not accept thereof as not able to live by it.' The remedy proposed by the Bishop may have seemed either preposterous or desperate to a man of strict orthodox views and discipline like Lord Eure. 'The Bishop', he continued in his letter to Cecil, 'is enforced to permitt lay people to execute that function (i.e. of a minister) in divers places which otherwise would be altogether neglected and left undone.'[62] A more temperate, if tentative and not over-confident, proposal was that efforts should be made to collect the fines imposed on recusants, but which were often concealed or simply not paid. It was estimated that these amounted to £200 yearly, a sufficient sum, if ever the fines were actually accounted for, to establish five or six selected and proficient ministers in the main towns of Monmouthshire.

The position was not radically different in North Wales. A good resident preacher, or so the Bishop of St Asaph averred, was the only efficacious medium for undermining the influence of the recusants, who were multiplying at a disquieting rate in the parish of Henllan, in Denbighshire.[63] It was alleged that after the death of the last vicar there, and his replacement by curates of limited expository skill and even less scriptural knowledge, 'there arrose and encreased a good manye recusants within the saide parish, whereof some were of the better sorte... and some of them are become recusants for discontentments and some other for feare of their parents and frends and, perhaps, some for want of teachinge'. The consensus of local opinion was that 'if there were a learned preacher resident amongest them, the congregacon in the said church would much encrease'.[64]

The problem was identical with that in the diocese of Llandaff – the absence and insufficiency of ministers; and the remedy, at least in one recorded case, was similar to that enforced on

---

[62] PRO State Papers Domestic, James I 1603–10, vol. 48, fol. 121. Lord Eure to the Earl of Salisbury, dated 23 October 1609.

[63] BM Lansdowne MSS 167, vol. 25b. Bishop of St Asaph to Sir Julius Caesar, dated 3 April 1611.

[64] PRO E 134 8 James I, Easter 11.

the Bishop of Llandaff. It may be that David Jones, a former rent collecter in the service of Sir John Salusbury, was not the only layman, and possibly not the only representative of his profession, who filled a gap in the sorely depleted ranks of the Welsh clergy.[65]

What emerges from all this evidence is the fact that the decision, taken at the famous Hampton Court Conference of January 1605, to plant Wales with schools and provide its people with capable and educated ministers, does not seem to have been implemented, and that the likelihood of its being put into effect was quickly receding.[66]

In the circumstances, it is not surprising that self-confidence, tenacity and boldness, even temerity, directed the actions of not a few Welsh recusants in the years that followed the unsuccessful Gunpowder Plot. Occasionally, they made no secret of their belief that they were strong enough to retaliate if the authorities and their supporters decided to harass them. One of those who learned this vexatious truth was Bartholomew Hughes, of Caerwys, in Flintshire. It would appear that he had found it intolerable that convicted recusants in the neighbour-hood were able to escape the penalty of the law by the favour of certain sympathetic squires there, as well as through the advance warning given them by the high constable of the hundred in which they resided, whenever he received orders from his superiors to lay hands on them. By means of this connivance of squires and constable, they had time to hide themselves. Hughes it was said, unwisely invited the authorities to share his indignation and prosecute the offending gentle-men, whereupon his house was attacked, some of his cattle killed and his corn trampled underfoot.[67]

Violence of this sort, however, was sporadic. The majority of the recusants preferred not to exasperate the Government by deliberately disturbing the peace. To them, a better way of demonstrating their solidarity and inflexibility was not to permit any encroachment on what they regarded as funda-mental to the preservation of their religious observances; but in such a manner as not to give their adversaries the opportunity

[65] PRO C 21 S 58/1.
[66] PRO State Papers Domestic, James I 1603–10, vol. 6, fol. 16. King's summoning of Parliament, dated 11 January 1603–4.
[67] PRO Star Chamber 8 James I 179/20.

of denouncing them as enemies to King and State. And this form of resistance, however passive in appearance, could prove more productive than aggressiveness.

A focal point of opposition to Protestant pressure was the famous well of St Winifred's at St Asaph, resorted to by recusants of all ages and from all parts of Wales. In the neighbouring chapel of Ffynnon Fair, they would congregate at the Feast of the Assumption of our Lady to organize what their enemies anathematized as a saturnalia of pagan jollity, where dancing and singing was punctuated by a hearty consumption of cakes and ale. The chapel was in a ruinous state, but Anglican services were still held in it under the supervision of the Bishop of St Asaph, in order to provide a counter-attraction to the constant presence of Catholics, or, at least, to keep the Anglican flag flying in the face of strong propaganda winds from the direction of Rome. It was on the occasion of this festival in 1606 that the recusants were said to have manifested in no unmistakable fashion both their Catholic zeal and their ingrained contempt for the Protestant establishment.

On entering the chapel to read the service, the Anglican curate, who was officiating, noticed:

That a stone was taken upp and turned to the wall of the said chappell (havinge beene thentofore an altar termed the ladies altar and ther lyinge by the altar in the said chappell), whereuppon this deponent (the curate) and other curats his predecessors did accustome to kneele downe to read the litanie. And after he oppened the said prayer booke with intente to reade service, he founde in the same a thinge made to the likenes or similitude of a gallows with a halter thereunto bounde made of rushes.

Upon inquiry, it transpired that some recusants were said to be responsible for this offence, and the curate made it the subject of a severe reprimand to the congregation before continuing with the service. Later in the afternoon, matters got worse. Returning to read the evening prayers, he found 'a companie of people dauncing and singinge of rimes about the altar in the said chappell, having one or more minstrels with them there, and having pots and cups upon the said altar drinkinge and making merrie'. The Bishop of St Asaph, to whom a complaint was immediately sent, thought it over and regretfully decided that nothing more could be done to decontaminate the chapel of the atmosphere of Catholic revelry than to discontinue all further Anglican services, a decision which, no doubt, met with the approval of the recusants.[68]

The Welsh recusants were much alive to the fact that numbers, cohesion and loyalty were indispensable to the survival of their faith, but they also realized that these were by no means indestructible factors immune from change and influence. As in every other age, proselytism by compulsion or conviction was rampant and, like their Protestant rivals, they were aware that the firmest foundation for adherence to a particular religious faith was regular instruction in its essentials and rigorous performance of its ritual. There was this cardinal difference in the situation of the two parties that, whereas all recognized schools and the universities were at the disposal of the Anglicans, the Catholic minority were dependent, for the most part, on the ministrations of their priests, who were forbidden to hold public services and conventicles, and had to celebrate their sacraments and do their religious teaching in private, sometimes at considerable risk to life and liberty.

What this meant was that the Catholic priesthood, deprived of the opportunity of acquiring theological education and training at home (except where they began their schooling as dutiful Protestants and terminated their studies by going over to Rome), had no alternative but to proceed overseas to the Catholic colleges and seminaries in France, Flanders, Italy and Spain. Some of them were without doubt guided by political motives and imbued with an intense dislike of the ecclesiastical and dynastic regime in England, which they were quite prepared to destroy by conspiracy and foreign intervention. But the greater majority were dedicated servants of their creed and preferred to conserve the Catholic faith, and convert others to it, by the more peaceful methods of preaching and ministration. They regarded the time spent in study on the continent as a useful scholastic prelude to the more exacting demands of missionary work in their native country, where the means of livelihood were exiguous, their labours liable to be interrupted or denounced, and themselves arrested or forced to go into hiding.

Compared with the exodus of indigenous Catholics and the converted from England, those who left Wales to cross the Channel in order to improve their learning and qualify for the

---

[68] PRO E 134 8 James I, Easter 11.

priesthood were relatively few, and rarely emerged from the obscurity to which their eventual status and vocation relegated them. The English College at Valladolid in Spain recorded the attendance there of Edward Morgan, of Bettisfield in Flintshire, and Thomas Mostyn, a member of the well-known Catholic family long resident at Talacre in the same shire. Three brothers from St Asaph, Robert, John and Humphrey Hughes also studied there, but like so many of their fraternity they led a somewhat itinerant scholar's life, moving about freely between various Catholic colleges. South Wales was represented at Valladolid by Nicholas Pritchard and William Phillip of Monmouthshire.[69] Two Welshmen, who were received as students at Douai College were William Price and Hugh Thomas.[70]

What united these Welshmen was that they were all destined for the English Mission, the company of seminarists and Jesuits specially trained and diciplined to return home to propagate the faith and infuse greater vigour and constancy into the Catholic communities. What is pertinent in this respect is that most of them took the title of the Mission to mean exactly what it said, and may have assumed that the English Catholics required more attention, stimulation and enlighten-ment than their co-religionists in Wales, for they preferred to expend their missionary enthusiasm to the east of Offa's Dyke.

For some of them, their exertions culminated in a tragic end. John Roberts, a native of Trawsfynydd, in Merionethshire, and a former student at Valladolid, was executed at Tyburn in 1610, but whether as a result of intemperate advocacy of Catholic doctrines or because of the subtle machinations of the Jesuits is uncertain. He was an inveterate opponent of their questionable interference in political matters, and it is possible that they may have decided to deal with him as they were alleged to have dealt with Watson and his fellow conspirators of the Bye Plot. It was at least rumoured that Roberts had approached the Bishop of London about restraining Jesuit activities and, in the words of one observer 'if he doth soe he shold doe well to look to himselfe for they (the Jesuits) meane him noe good'.[71]

Where priests did choose to serve and succour the Catholic

[69] Catholic Record Society, vol. XXX, Register of the English College at Valladolid, pp. 102, 121 and note, 125 and note, 130 and note.

[70] Ibid, vol. X. Douai College Diaries, p. 85.

[71] PRO State Papers Foreign, Spain (SP 94), vol. 10, fol. 8. Edward Morgan of Bettisfield was likewise put to death at Tyburn in 1642, after enduring fourteen years of imprisonment.

faithful in Wales, they were often men of consummate learning and wide experience, who had travelled extensively in Europe and knew something of the austerities of monastic life as well as of the more congenial atmosphere of the lecture hall. The many peregrinations of Griffith Lloyd, of Llangunnell, in Caernarvonshire, who had taught Hebrew in Milan and received the orders of priesthood from the eminent Welsh scholar Dr Owen Lewis, Bishop of Cassano, led him as far as Poland before he returned to Wales in 1609. It was in 1615 that he came into conflict with the authorities, but not so much on account of his diligence as a priest. There was a belief, strongly held in official quarters, that during his sojourn in Poland he had collaborated with a Polish Catholic polemicist, Caspar Cichocki, Canon of Sandomir, to publish a book entitled *Alloquia Osiacensa*, which was so offensive to the King of England because of its derogatory remarks on him and his House, that it had almost caused a rupture of Anglo-Polish relations.[72] Lloyd was interrogated on this point and vehemently denied the charge of collusion with Cichocki, although he freely admitted to having printed one or two philosophical disquisitions in Poland. This could hardly be held against him as a man of erudition, but his interrogators must have blinked in astonishment when he went on to claim that, during the six years he had frequented the academic and ecclesiastical circles of Poland, he had never even heard the name of Cichocki.[73]

Yet another priest who had set his heart on sustaining the old faith in his native land was Roger Gwyn, of Pwllheli, in Caernarvonshire. Having crossed to Ireland in 1594, he made his way to Seville where he attended a seminary, and then left it for a further course of studies at Valladolid. Eventually he found himself on board a French vessel with the intention of landing in Swansea and introducing himself to the leading Catholic families in the neighbourhood. But a vigilant English ship intercepted the Frenchman, seized upon Gwyn, and thus deprived the recusants of south-west Wales of a learned seminarist who might have rendered them great service.[74]

Potential priests and missionaries, eager to benefit from the instruction and guidance of Catholic seats of learning, were not

---

[72] Jasnowski, *England and Poland in the XVI and XVII centuries*, pp. 30–1.
[73] PRO State Papers Domestic, James I 1611–18, vol. 81, fols 100–1, 17 August 1613.
[74] PRO State Papers Domestic, James I 1603–10, under date of 6 June 1603.

the only recusants to leave Wales. The contemplative aspect of religion and its appeal too, particularly for women, and the opportunities denied at home to renounce the world for the seclusion of conventual life, with its insistence on meditation, prayer and the consummation of religious vows, multiplied with the foundation of many English nunneries in the Low Countries at the beginning of the century.

'There came hither some tenne dayes synce', wrote Sir Thomas Edmondes the English Ambassador in Brussels, to the Secretary of State, 'one Mistress Morgan, sister to Sir Matthew Morgan, with twoe other English [?Welsh] mayds with her, and they are in hand to procure themselves to be received into the English nunnery of this towne.'[75] She was Anastasia Morgan, daughter of Sir Edward Morgan of 'Pettie Coye' [?Cae Bach] in Monmouthshire, and was received into the Benedictine monastery in Brussels in August 1605, where she remained until her death in 1646 at the age of sixty-nine.[76] Other voluntary Catholic exiles from the Principality were men who preferred a military to a religious profession, such as Sir John Salusbury, of Denbighshire, and a 'Mr Gwin, sonne to Mr Gwin of Gwithir', both of whom enlisted in the English Regiment serving the Governor of the Spanish Netherlands.[77] And, occasionally, there came Welsh recusants who were adventurers by temperament, with an economy of scruples dictated by adversity or incurable moral disabilities.

It was in the month of July 1607, that Sir Thomas Cornwallis, the English Ambassador in Madrid, had an unexpected confrontation with one of these errant Catholics from Wales, whose plausibility revealed a skill in duplicity that might have commended itself to that very experienced diplomat, if it had been used to promote English rather than personal interests.

This last weeke [he informed the Privy Council] entred into my house one that caleth himselfe Sir Thomas Wyllyams, a Welshman, and another that taketh for name Peeter Creswell of London. The fyrste hath long traversed his ground in Italy and in these kingdoms, ther contenting himselfe at sometymes with the place of a

---

[75] PRO State Papers Foreign, Flanders (SP 77) Bundle 7, fol. 224. Edmondes to the Earl of Salisbury, dated 28 August 1605.

[76] *Catholic Record Society, Miscellaneous*, vol. IX, p. 179.

[77] PRO State Papers Foreign, Flanders (SP 77) Bundle 7, fols 329–31.

lackey, but of late her and ther also publyshing himselfe to be sonne to the Earl of Worcester, and at times to some Earle of another name; and now lastly a knight, and under thes pretenses and of having lost the favor of his father, the ayre of his cuntry and all his possibilities by his publique profession of the Catholique fayth, hath obteyned a pass from the Pope and divers his and of some byshopps of this kingdom, not only to walke al the wayes of yt, but to requyre and receave what in a case of such compassion he can procure for his sustentation.

The putative Sir Thomas might possibly have disarmed Cornwallis of some of his suspicions if he had been alone, but whatever chances he had of ingratiating himself with the Ambassador were destroyed by Creswell. The latter became uncontrollably drunk and infected the Welshman with his insobriety, so that when they entered the embassy one day and Williams 'sayd and sware that he (Creswell) was his own brother, being both drunke, they so behaved themselves as my men thrust them out at the gate'. The sultry summer air of Madrid had a disastrous effect on the illusory notions already generated by strong Spanish wines. Creswell began to shout that he, a Catholic, was being threatened with death by the Protestant staff of the embassy. An ugly mob gathered around, who might have invaded Cornwallis's house if the Ambassador had not immediately alerted the Madrid police. The Welshman, being, perhaps, less immobilised than his companion, tried to get away but was captured, and both he and Creswell were thrown into gaol 'with strong boults of iron about theyr heeles'. They were eventually sentenced to four years' banishment from Madrid, which Cornwallis regarded as a light punishment and assumed, perhaps correctly, that their profession of Catholicism had persuaded the Spanish authorities to show leniency in their case.[78]

Occasionally, the English Government gave a sharp reminder to its recusants that their flouting of authority and their sanguine speculations on the resurgence of their fortunes did not go unnoticed in London. One way of inducing them to cool their feelings and reappraise their situation was to remind

---

[78] PRO State Papers Foreign, Spain (SP 94), vol. 14, fols 77–77b. Cornwallis to the Privy Council, dated 10 July 1607.

them that, in terms of numbers and influence, they were still very much the inferior section of the community, and quite impotent to resist any resolute action by the authorities to control them.

One fear that periodically haunted the King and his ministers, although there was no longer any real ground for apprehension, was that in a political crisis the Catholic minority might take it into their heads to stake all on an armed insurrection or support of a foreign invasion of the kingdom. As far as the Principality was concerned, the days had long gone by when a self-deluding Spaniard could predict without misgiving that the landing of Spanish troops on Welsh soil would be much welcomed by the inhabitants as an opportunity to take revenge on their English neighbours everywhere for centuries of oppression.[79] A hundred years of Tudor rule had done much to eradicate sentiments of this sort in Welsh minds, but the Government was not prepared to ignore the possibility that religious sympathies could transcend national antipathies, where they existed, and create a dangerous coalition between co-religionists of different languages and backgrounds, as was actually happening on the continent at the time.

To disarm recusants was the natural consequence of this lingering fear, and from time to time instructions were sent from the Privy Council to the Justices of the Peace within the Principality that recusants should be deprived of all weapons except those considered necessary for the defence of their homes.[80] There was little sign of opposition to these decrees, which was due, perhaps, to the fact that they were not implemented with that thoroughness thought desirable by the Government or which it, realistically, did not expect.

---

[79] The Spaniards 'perswad the Welshman that when they (the Spaniards) enter, they (the Welsh) shalbe lords as they were before and revenge themselves of all the injuries which they have receyved by the English, of whom they are kept in tyranny and despised and scorned, that it is a wonder that such valorous and noble people of vertu and antiquity can endure it'. Notes by Thomas Wilson in his letters dated May 1602. *See* PRO State Papers Foreign, Venice (SP 99) Bundle 2, p. 117.

[80] Jones-Pierce, *Clenennau Letters and Papers*, p. 181, no. 283, dated 28 February 1612–13. *See also Acts of the Privy Council, 1613–14*, pp. 356–7, where the recusants, whose homes are to be searched for weapons, are described as 'being persons whome his Majesty and the state have reason to hold in jelousye'. *See also* PRO State Papers Domestic, James I 1611–18, vol. 77, fol. 155. The Privy Council to the Sheriffs and Justices of Wales, dated 14 September 1614.

Another method of clipping the wings of too restless or overbold recusants was to enforce the statutory financial penalties against them, and compel them to take the Oath of Allegiance to the Crown. Both measures were regarded as distasteful and vindictive by the Catholics, but they were supremely effective in enhancing the security and supremacy of the King. For just as the former penalized them if they did not attend the Anglican form of worship and, in this manner, make a show of recognition of the King as Head of that Church, so the latter obliged them to declare their obedience to him as Head of the State and to no other ruler.

The penalties which a refractory recusant could incur were harsh enough. Continual absence from divine service and refusal to take Holy Communion in the parish church were punishable by heavy fines. But what threatened him and his family with ruin was the punitive Parliamentary legislation that allowed the King to strip him of two thirds of his property in land or goods and use them as he wished, either to reward courtiers and seekers of royal favour, or as a temporary restorative to his perniciously anaemic Exchequer. They were rarely employed for more constructive or beneficial purposes. Some Welsh recusants were to feel the full weight of this particular measure,[81] and inevitably many of them found it impossible to devise or discover the necessary resources to disregard the threat of destitution. They had to accept the, to them, repugnant alternative of conforming to the law of the land, to the extent of taking the Oath of Allegiance and receiving the sacraments. In 1613, it was recorded that out of 416 recusants who had capitulated to the pressure of the law since the accession of James, twenty-four came from Wales. It was, proportionally, a low number and suggests, like so much other relevant evidence, that Welsh recusants were not harassed in the same vexatious manner as their Catholic neighbours in England. But it is also clear from the official estimate of the value of their land and goods, that they were in no position to act otherwise. The greater majority of them were natives of Flintshire and Monmouthshire, and possibly belonged to the poorer yeoman

---

[81] For instance, Sir Roger Aston got two-thirds of the property of Edward Morgan, a Montgomeryshire recusant. HMC *Salisbury (Cecil) MSS*, vol. XIX, p. 456. 'Note of such recusants as the King has granted liberty to his servants to make profit of, by virtue of that power which the King has to refuse the payment of 21^{li} *per mensem*, and in lieu therof to extend two parts of their land.'

or lower rural classes who were by no means affluent.[82]

It was a different matter when the Crown discovered that sometimes it was not the case that defenceless and humble recusants had violated the law, but rather that the law had run foul of Catholics who were men of substance and position, autocratic and irascible in disposition, and not averse to demanding or soliciting special recognition, and even exemption, as far as its provisions applied to them. It was obviously not in the interests of the Crown to deliberately disturb the feelings of splenetic Welsh gentlemen on any issue, if it could be avoided. And the political sagacity of the King's advisers, reinforced by the shrewdness of his financial experts, was usually able to devise or welcome a compromise acceptable to monarch and recusant.

The powerful family of the Morgans of Llantarnam, as well as the sixty Catholics whom they were alleged to maintain in their house,[83] were no doubt disquieted by the searing monthly fine of £20 inflicted on the household for not attending church services and ignoring the Oath of Allegiance. To be included in the list of paying recusants testified to the unswerving attachment of Edward Morgan, the master of Llantarnam, to the faith of his fathers. Nevertheless, the relentless exaction of that sum for an indeterminate number of years, as well as its effects on the welfare of a notable and ancient family, could not be contemplated by him without considerable anxiety. In May 1612 he decided to thrash the matter out with the authorities, and took the long road to London to lay his case before the Privy Council. He also wrote a letter to the King's Remembrancer, Sir Henry Spiller, in which he first alluded dolefully to his advancing age before turning briskly to discuss the financial problems which appeared to be as oppressive as his physical infirmities. He had had four sons from his first wife, he explained, and they had reached those years of youthful exuberance, when £500 each annually from the paternal estate was only just sufficient to cover their living expenses. He had added substantially to his domestic charges by marrying a second time and fathering a further six children. His debts were now £2000; nevertheless, he informed Spiller, he was prepared to pay the King as much as £1000 if he were discharged from taking the Oath of Allegiance

---

[82] PRO State Papers Domestic, James I 1611–18, vol. 74, fols 56–63, under date of July 1613.

[83] PRO Star Chamber 8 James I 207/30.

as prescribed by the Government, and permitted to swear to another which merely declared his obedience to the Crown of England. He hinted that the King would find such a concession most advantageous. 'Yf his Matie so please, he maye in these cases make unto his Exchequer a good increase of the revenue and, I assure myself, a great increase of that dutifful affection which his poore Catholic subjects owe and beare both to his Highnes and hys hopeffull and happye yssue.'[84]

The King's reaction to the offer was the reverse of his customary lethargy. In less than a month, Morgan was able to express his satisfaction, in a second letter to Spiller, that James had accepted his proposal. It only remained for the discharge from the Oath of Allegiance to be drawn up – he insisted that it should be both comprehensive and constitutional – and the money would be ready.[85]

This was not the only benefit that Morgan extracted from the transaction. The authorities could, if they wished, add to the difficulties of recusants by restricting their movements and confining them within the limits of the parish in which they resided, thus posing serious problems for Catholics of the professional and mercantile class who had to travel to earn their livelihood. After the transfer of his £1000 to London, Morgan found every request of his for leave to go to London on business or to Bath for his health was invariably granted by the Privy Council.[86] Of all Welsh recusants, he certainly had good reason to hope that the mutual understanding between Whitehall and Llantarnam would continue when the time came for James to be succeeded by that 'hopefull and happye yssue', Prince Charles, in whose life and prosperity the whole Morgan family had a strong vested interest.

In North Wales, on the other hand, the more intransigent attitude of a gentleman in this matter of recusancy, led him perilously near to the downfall of his family.

During the previous reign, John Edwards, of Chirkland, in Denbighshire, had succeeded very well in manipulating his Catholic sensitivites so as to persuade the authorities to entrust

[84] BM *Lansdowne MSS* 153, fol. 78. Edward Morgan to Sir Henry Spiller, dated 22 May 1612.
[85] *Ibid*, fol. 85. The same to the same, dated 15 June 1612. For the King's grant of pardon to Morgan, *see* PRO State Papers Domestic, James I 1611–18, vol. 70 under date of 6 July 1612.
[86] *Acts of the Privy Council, 1613–14*, pp. 44 and 484; 1615–16, p. 438.

him with the offices of a Justice of the Peace and Member of Parliament. But the hard line taken by the Government after the Gunpowder Plot generated a corresponding obstinacy in Edwards, and it was not long before the amicable agreement, which had been observed for twenty years or so, was summarily annulled. Whatever was the reason – a tactless remark about that event or a more defiant demonstration of his Catholic sympathies – Edwards became the object of discrimination and vexation. He was publicly charged with recusancy in 1605 and convicted, but appears to have tried to evade the financial inconveniences of the verdict by conveying his lands to a certain Edward Harris, an associate of his, and pretending that he held them as the latter's tenant.[87] But any subterfuges of this kind were eliminated some years later when he was administered a severe blow, which showed him that he could no longer expect any leniency for his obtrusive allegiance to the old faith. In 1613, all his property, goods and debts were forfeited to the Crown, and granted to Sir Hugh Carmichael to be disposed of by him as he wished.[88]

The material outlook for his family was indeed bleak, but the effect on John Edwards was to impel him to greater extremes of resistance. This was an opportunity for some of his adversaries in Denbighshire to hold him up to execration and contempt, and no one was more assiduous in this campaign of vilification than Sir Thomas Middleton of Chirkland, who with obvious pleasure wrote to the Earl of Somerset, enclosing a copy of the Bishop of St Asaph's letter to the Archbishop of Canterbury about Edwards's activities. 'By the Bishop's letter', he commented, 'your Lordship shall fynd that he [Edwards] is a very dangerous ffellowe of as pestilent disposition as eny in all our countrey; and if he gets his pardon, it may be fearyd that he will doe much mischeef'.[89] The pardon mentioned by Middleton referred, in all probability, to the request boldly presented by Edwards to the King that he should receive his royal forgiveness for not taking the Oath of Allegiance. It was an omission on his part which had led to a warrant for his arrest and the despatch of Richard Christopher, a messenger of the King's Chamber, all the way to Chirk and, later, through

[87] HMC *Salisbury (Cecil) MSS*, vol. XVIII, p. 398. John Edwards, recusant.
[88] PRO State Papers Domestic, James I 1611–18, p. 191. Grant dated 8 July 1613.
[89] PRO State Papers Domestic, James I 1611—18, vol. 76, fol. 1D. Sir Thomas Middleton to the Earl of Somerset, dated 6 January 1614.

the streets of London, to put it into effect.[90] The King, so Edwards alleged, had agreed to pardon him, but for reasons which are not quite clear in the light of his subsequent behaviour.

For some time, Edwards remained acquiescent or, at least, passive in his position as a recusant of more than cursory interest to his neighbours and to local officials. The year 1619, however, proved to be a turning point in his career. Anti-recusant harassment increased in Denbighshire, and it is significant that the sheriff, Fulk Middleton, and various Justices of the Peace well disposed towards the Middleton family, were able to persuade Sir Thomas Chamberlain, Chief Justice of Chester, and Sir Henry Townshend, Justice of Assize in Denbighshire, to order the arrest of a number of prominent Catholics, including Edwards. An excuse for his apprehension, if any were needed, would have been the bitter competition for the salvation of souls between him and the Vicar of Chirk, Robert Lloyd. The latter had recorded some success in this incessant skirmishing, and Edwards was said to be busily undermining the vicar's position by bringing suits against him in various legal courts in the name of other people, with the hope of ruining him financially.

The day chosen for Edwards's arrest was Sunday 15 August 'on which day the wakes have bene and still be used to be held at Chirke aforesaid, and beinge a daye and place of generall meeting of papistes to performe a kind of superstitious singinge to the Virgin Mary'. There were about a hundred of them gathered at Edwards's house, when the under-sheriff and a group of constables and other men approached the manor. Edwards, it was alleged, immediately 'cawsed all the doores to be fast shutt and barred against the said undershreiffe, whereby he could not apprehend any of the said popish persons as he had been directed to take'. If the latter and his subordinates had any thoughts of storming the place, a glance or two at the house would have shown the impracticability of such an attempt. For it was 'moted about with a drawinge bridge over the same mote to come to the said house, soe that noe officer can come thether without sufferance to execute any warrant or process there, besides which he [Edwards] hath an other litle drawinge bridge for a private conveyance over the same mote in the backside of his said house, whereby, if any

[90] Devon, *Issues of the Exchequer during the reign of James I*, p. 168.

officer should enter his said house, a suspitious [suspected] person might escape and flye awaye'.[91]

The under-sheriff and his men prudently retired. If John Edwards had reacted with similar discretion, the matter might have ended there. But he chose not to do so. It was only a person impervious to the danger of drawing attention to his past and present role as a recusant thorn in Protestant flesh who could have written, as he did, an abrasive letter to Sir Thomas Chamberlain and Sir Henry Townshend some ten days after the abortive plan to seize him.

He struck a note of arrogance at the very beginning, when he boasted of his recusancy and added that he was still a 'romishe recusante as well before as after my refusall of the oathe commonly called of allegeance'. He contemptuously dismissed the decision to arrest him as an underhand scheme, by which means warrants were issued 'unto divers base fellowes and common daye labourers, beinge such as doe serve and belonge unto the two Sir Thomas Mydletons, my knowne inveterate adversaries', to lay hand on his person. He made it offensively plain to the two judges that he expected them to make provision in future that no such crude interference with his personal liberty would ever happen again; otherwise, and the threat was unmistakable, he would not fail to complain to the King. But he reserved his most insolent observation for the closing sentences of the letter, in which he bluntly informed Chamberlain and Townshend that they:

> Cannott but be very sensible of the many foulde inconveniences which may happen, when as that obscure base persons, belonginge to mens capitall enemies and such as be knowne in all the countrye to be noe ordinarye and sworne officers of his Ma[tie], shall have secrett authoritie geaven them for the breakinge of houses or apprehendinge of others that be reputed and taken amongst theire neighbours to be of better qualitie and calling then themselfes.[92]

A monarch less sensitive than James would have resented derogatory remarks of this sort about his judicial officials, and

[91] PRO Star Chamber 8 James I 25/8.
[92] PRO State Papers Domestic, James I 1619–23, vol. III, fol. 143. John Edwards to Chamberlain and Townshend, dated 25 August 1619.

Edwards was soon made to realize that the royal displeasure could have as long an arm as the royal courts in London. After deliberating on his case, the Privy Council came to the conclusion that he was an obstinate and perverse recusant, and that his impertinence called for an intensive course of correction and re-education in civic obedience and respectfulness to his legal superiors. On 15 October Edwards was committed to the Marshalsea prison in London,[93] where he spent some months before reluctantly admitting that he had acted impetuously, and submitting with appropriate humility a petition to the King, in which he regretted the trouble and resentment he had caused and asked to be released.[94]

The last years of the reign showed that the inherent powers of resistance, characteristic of recusancy within the Principality, had abated very little. There was still evidence of militant elements who were as aggressive as their elders had been twenty or more years earlier. And, once again, it was Monmouthshire that provided examples of the sometimes domineering and irascible temper of the Welsh Catholics, whenever they considered forcefulness to be the best safeguard of their survival, if not of their ascendancy. It was hardly agreeable news to the Government in 1623, that David Morgan, a recusant of Abergavenny, was such an influential person that he could ensure the election of his partisans as burgesses and bailiffs, and also hold his own in any street fighting with the followers of Sir William Morgan of Tredegar, the steward of Abergavenny.[95] It was an unpleasant reminder of the combative spirit of recusancy in that quarter and, what was more ominous, a reaffirmation that certain acts of violence by Catholics in the town two years previously had not proved counter-productive, as the authorities had hoped.

In December 1621, the House of Commons agreed to receive

---

[93] *Acts of the Privy Council, 1619–21*, p. 40.
[94] PRO State Papers Domestic, James I 1619–23, vol. 112, fol. 11. John Edwards's petition to the Privy Council, undated. He was released on 27 January 1619–20. *See Acts of the Privy Council, 1619–21*, p. 112.
[95] PRO Star Chamber 8 James I 207/30. It would appear that one of David Morgan's servants named Rosser was a competent composer of songs in Welsh, so much so that one who listened to him sing professed to be astonished that 'Rosser could make such songes and recite points of scripture, being illiterate.' He would have been an invaluable purveyor of religious propaganda in songs on behalf of Catholicism.

a petition from Eleazer Jackson, a minister of Abergavenny, in which he itemized seven personal complaints amounting to a serious indictment of the local recusants. That they should have tried to impugn his good name by spreading malicious reports about him, denounced his preaching and Protestant doctrines as blasphemous, and intimidated his supporters with threats, were commonplace enough not to raise a single hair on the heads of most MPs. But that his enemies should have tried to murder him was another story, and his recital of the incident was detailed enough to inspire detestation and condemnation of Catholic bullies.

In the words of the petition:

> Upon the 14th day of October last, about 8 of the clock att night, two convicted recusants intruded them selves into my chamber, first seeking a quarrell by way of disputation, viz, concerning purgatorie and the blessed Virgin Marie. Afterward they reprehended mee for handling matters of controversie in the pulpitt and further charged mee with the procuring of a warrant of the peace against one Roger Howell... whereuppon they laid violent hands uppon mee, beating and sore wounding mee in the head with a dagger and a candlestick, besides a dangerous stabb in the forehead, whereof by the judgment of all men I was nott likely to recover. And if the dagger had not fallen out of the hilts, they had murthered mee att that instance. And further forced mee to vowe uppon my salvation never to preach more in that place, but to leave the contrie forthwith, otherwise they threatened to kill mee.[96]

Because of pressure of other business, the House of Commons had no time to discuss the contents of the petition, but the members were indignant enough to order that a copy of it should be sent to the King for his perusal.[97]

The dissolution of Parliament which shortly followed deprived Jackson of any hope of redress, but it did nothing to diminish the fears of the Government that the petition was one of many indications that the situation could endanger public order, if appeasement were substituted for the control of

---

[96] HMC *Salisbury (Cecil) MSS*, vol. XXIV Addenda 1605–68, p. 242. Eleazor Jackson to the House of Commons, dated before 19 December 1621.

[97] Notestein, Relf and Simpson, *Commons Debates 1621*, vol. II, pp. 544–5.

recusants. In Pembrokeshire, Sir James Perrot and the civic dignitaries of Haverfordwest were appalled at their failure to convince the Privy Council that Anne Hayward, who claimed to be a subject of the Spanish Netherlands and insisted on her right by the provisions of a formal treaty to practise the Catholic religion, should be denied her claim and be classified as a recusant. In his despair at the thought that there should be a resident recusant in Haverfordwest, where none had dared to show his face since the Reformation, Sir James solemnly asserted that if the Privy Council allowed her plea, the way would be open for Jesuits and seminarists to swarm into the town.[98] His astringent speeches in the House of Commons on the subject of recusants, in which he often lamented that they were not being persecuted as the law demanded, were well known in Whitehall and, perhaps, not always taken too seriously. But neither could his warnings and denunciations be totally ignored, and the alleged outrage at Abergavenny seemed to confirm that they were not entirely unrealistic.

They were, in fact, given a greater credibility by an alarming report from Monmouthshire that a number of recusants were maintaining a saltpetre expert at Raglan Castle to manufacture gunpowder, and that there was already a substantial amount of it in the castle. A prominent figure in this ambiguous enterprise was said to be John Winter the son of Lady Winter, whose Catholicism was above reproach. The report ended with the warning that if the King did not grant toleration, there would be serious trouble on the Welsh borders.[99] However much truth lay in this report, the end of the reign, like its beginning, suggested that of the many attributes of Welsh recusancy, self-confidence, resourcefulness and timely pugnacity seemed to be the more enduring.

---

[98] *Acts of the Privy Council, 1619–21*, p. 366. *See also* PRO State Papers Domestic, James I 1619–23, vol. 119, fol. 22. Sir James Perrot to Sir Clement Edmondes, undated, but later than 11 January 1620–1. See *Ibid*, fol. 21, Mayor and Justices of Haverfordwest to the Privy Council, dated 11 January 1620.

[99] PRO State Papers Domestic, James I 1623–25, vol. 168, fol. 102. John Tendring to Sir Robert Naunton, dated June 1624.

3

The Gentry and their interests

It did not take the Welsh gentry long to realize that the King and his ministers had little intention of curbing or encroaching on their manipulation of local politics and their conduct of local affairs. The dutiful behaviour of the majority of the squirearchy at the beginning of the reign was considered to be sufficient testimony that the Crown had nothing to fear from this class in the way of disloyalty. They could therefore be left to enjoy their privileged position as long as they performed their obligations as guardians of public law and order, and co-operated with the officers of the Crown whenever they appeared on the scene, as they had done in the previous reign. This was not too much to ask in return for the Government's inclination, partly because of the distance between the Principality and London, to leave the gentry pretty much to themselves, the more so as the treaty of peace with Spain, signed in 1604, had diminished the danger of invasion along the western seaboard of the kingdom. Most of the gentry were quick to appreciate that this would redound to their personal advantage, and by undertaking the duties of a 'voluntary bureaucracy'[1] in the service of the central authority, they would make themselves immune in some measure from undesirable governmental interference.

The power of the gentry was a cardinal factor in the structure and development of Welsh society, particularly in the countryside. Unlike the members of the corresponding class in England, they were under relatively little compulsion to guard their tongues or restrain their actions for fear of offending their superiors in rank, wealth and authority, who were the

---

[1] This is the expression used by Professor Glanmor Williams to describe the status of the gentry in local government as the result of their collaboration with Whitehall. *See* his *Religion, Language and Nationality in Wales*, p. 157.

descendants of the old feudal families or the more recently created titled dignitaries who made their influence felt in the rural areas, in both Houses of Parliament, at the King's Court and around the table of the Privy Council. To gain the favour or patronage of one family or another belonging to the nobility was almost indispensable to a great many of the English gentry. Without some recognition or protection of this kind, it was difficult for them to conceive of any improvement in their fortunes or, for that matter, of the continuing security of their possessions and status. Whether it concerned their success in the local feuds and rivalries that constantly disturbed rural life; or their nomination as MPs if they wished to transfer their activities to the wider political arena at Westminster; or their ability to escape or survive the danger of governmental censure for objectionable misdemeanours; or for other considerations, the intervention of aristocratic patrons could, and often did, determine the issue.[2]

The Welsh gentry, inside their own country, had little need to seek the favours or fear the frowns of dukes and earls. Such noblemen were few and far between in Wales, and where they did exist, they were but a handful who only occasionally resided on their Welsh estates, and whose attention to events in the Principality was most perfunctory compared with their assiduity in promoting their personal ambitions in London. It was, perhaps, natural that their rank, lands and attachment to the Crown should invest them with an almost inalienable right to become Lords Lieutenant of shires and Stewards of royal manors in Wales, as well as members of the Council of Wales in Ludlow. Robert Devereux, Earl of Essex, unlike his father and grandfather, was more concerned about his possessions in Ulster than his estates in Wales; it is doubtful whether he visited the latter more than once in his life. William Herbert, Earl of Pembroke, was too comfortably settled in his magnificent house at Wilton, in Wiltshire, and too preoccupied with his duties as Lord Chamberlain, to appear but rarely at Cardiff Castle. The same could be said of Edward Somerset, Earl of Worcester, Master of the Horse to the King, except that he took a legitimate pride in his home in Raglan Castle and spent a great deal of his time there. He was also a Catholic, but was

---

[2] The relations between the Earl of Shrewsbury and some of the gentry of Staffordshire is a good example of this. *See* HMC *Calendar of Bath Papers*, vol. V, pp. 6–9.

prudent enough not to excite the resentment of the Protestant squires of Monmouthshire by an excessive display of authority over them, nor to exert too overt an influence over the numerous Catholic gentry in the same shire. Whenever these noblemen were called upon to undertake the duties incidental to their offices in Wales, or were appointed to serve the King in some special capacity, they did so scrupulously. His Catholic faith certainly did not hinder the Earl of Worcester from acting as a commissioner to banish all Jesuits from South Wales. Nevertheless, their commitments in Wales were peripheral in their view; it was the ebb and flow of political fortunes and the fury of factional rivalries at Court that really fascinated and involved them.

It would have been an abnegation of their natural instincts if the Welsh gentry had not exploited this situation. With only a distant monarch, and the strictures, but not always enforceable penalties, of the Council of Wales, to restrain them, they were in a commanding position to regulate the affairs of the community in conformity with their interests and the requirements of their status as the dominant social class.

That this power could be arbitrarily used was generally recognized, and at times it must have appeared to some of its victims that there was no authority on earth that could overrule it. When one of the servants of Sir John Wynn of Gwydir delivered a message to a local yeoman that he should surrender his tenement to Sir John or face the possibility of being charged with the theft of a heifer, the yeoman was said to have protested his innocence.

Whereupon the servant said, look upon these stones (being a walle or hedge of stones, my Master (meaninge Sir John Wynne) ys able to make theese stones to be greene cheese if he list. And being demaunded what he (the servant) did conceve or meane by uttringe these said words, he (the yeoman) saieth that he verylie beleveth in his conscience that his meaninge was that the said Sir John Wynne was able and could prove any thinge against him, though the same was never so untrue.[3]

Landed gentry confederating, as they often did, to procure some advantage to themselves, or families linked by marriage

[3] PRO E 134 8 James I Mich. 3.

co-operating to gain their own ends, could only heighten this feeling of impotence in the Welsh countryside. Led by John Bodwell, a number of Caernarvonshire squires allegedly supported a claimant to a certain property at Abererch, on the condition that he would allow them to erect a mill on it and enjoy the profits. In return they guaranteed his immunity from legal proceedings 'the said Bodwell being a gentleman of great power and might in the said county and having a great command over diverse of the freehoulders of the said county, would assist, ayde and mayntaine him for obteyning and keeping of the same messuage...and would be able by his acquaintance and credit with Juriemen and his power in the said Countie, to overthrow any suit'. The death of the claimant did not deter the gentlemen concerned. They were accused of forging papers to the effect that the deceased had conveyed the property to them, bribing a complaisant jury to declare that the documents were valid, building the mill and turning a nearby stream from its course to serve it. This, seemingly, provoked a local protest which Bodwell crushed with the threat that 'if water could not be gotten to turne the same millne, yt should turne with bloud'.[4]

In the same shire, when Sir John Wynn was on one occasion the defendant in a case involving titles to holdings at Penmaen Llysfaen, the squire of Gwydir was said to have arranged an unpleasant surprise for the bold band of free-holders who had dared to challenge him. They found that the four commissioners nominated to investigate the case and instruct the jury – Robert Thurbridge, Thomas Vaughan, David Hillard and Fowke Vaughan – were not only Sir John's good friends but that:

> The wiefe of the said Mr Turbridge is aunt unto the defendents wiefe, viz her fathers sister; the said Mr (Thomas) Vaughan brother in lawe to the said defendent, viz havinge formerly married the said defendents sister; the said Mr Hillard and the defendent deare and lovinge ffrends in sight; and the said Mr Ffowlke Vaughan cozen german removed, viz the said defendents cozen within the third degree.

It was generally concluded, without much effort of thought,

---

[4] PRO Star Chamber 8 James I 14/3.

that 'theis gentlemen aforementioned weare appointed to execute the busynes aforsaid by the nomination of the said defendent'. And the treatment meted out to the dispirited freeholders could not have astonished them or any one else in the circumstances; for when they tried to produce evidence to validate their titles, they 'were taken by the shoulders and thrust out of doores from the commissioners and jury', or so they complained.[5]

Such absence of scruples on the part of the gentry was hardly conducive to good relations in the countryside, but it did not necessarily mean that there was an uncompromising antagonism between them and their less fortunate neighbours. There were occasions when both parties could approach each other in complete confidence. It still remained the custom in some districts, for instance, to refer disputes between heirs over property to local squires, who, it was commonly accepted, were sufficiently conversant with the lineage and history of the contending claimants, to be in a position to make a fair and impartial award or division.[6]

Moreover, where gentry and tenants alike felt that their interests were being threatened by extraneous pressures or intervention, they sometimes closed their ranks to resist them. In Radnorshire, a dispute between John Bradshaw and William Vaughan, gentleman steward of the manors of Elfael, Aberedw amongst others, over the right to hold manorial courts appears to have ended in a public challenge to established authority by the latter. He allegedly reinforced his claim by assembling two hundred armed men from the neighbourhood at Painscastle. And being handed a warrant from no less an eminent person than the Lord Treasurer of England forbidding him to hold a court, he read it and then announced most emphatically: 'I will not deliver up my office (as steward) nor forbeare to keepe

---

[5] PRO E 134 11 James I Easter 17. It would seem that the dispute had originated some years previously when Sir John Wynn actually arbitrated on behalf of the same freeholders and obtained a concession for them whereby they paid a reasonable fine for the retention of their lands. Later, he secured a lease of the same lands and threatened to evict his former protégés unless they paid him a fine, considerably greater than the one he had awarded them as mediator. The Bishop of St Asaph, who tried to emulate Sir John as arbitrator, was soon advised, in view of the latter's violent temper, to plead ignorance of the niceties of the case and withdraw from the scene. PRO State Papers Domestic, James I 1603–10, vol. 58 fols 11 and 62 under date of 16 November 1610.

[6] PRO E 134 11 James I, Easter 17.

courte for any Lordes letter in England.' If true, it was a bold statement, even for an outraged Welsh gentleman, which may have persuaded him to qualify it with the discreet and prescribed formula of all loyal subjects 'excepte my soveraigne Lorde and King command me soe to doe'. What alarmed many people was not his inflammatory language, but the fact that so many local inhabitants should have assembled with weapons to support him. One of them remarked that he had never witnessed or experienced such a concourse 'within the marches of Wales'. It certainly suggested that the fierce independent spirit, and a residual lawlessness, of the old Welsh border districts had not yet totally expired.[7]

The domination of the gentry over their tenants and servants was almost absolute, not unlike the system of retainers that had been suppressed, at least partially, by the Tudor monarchs in the preceding century.[8] Without the unqualified obedience of those who were immediately dependent on them, it would have been difficult for the squires to create the image that approximated to their appraisal of their own power. And that was of a caste which, although subject to the authority of the Crown, was in a position to impose its will on other classes of the community, and had the physical means to do so. When Sir William Maurice of Clenennau ordered his servants to seize a tenement, which he claimed as his property, they allegedly evicted the occupants with unnecessary violence. To the charge of brutality they replied that 'the said Sir William Maurice did bidd and command them so to do, and that the said Sir William Maurice was sufficient to answere it, able to beare it out, and to make good whatsoever they had done, committed or attempted'.[9] And in Carmarthenshire, a husbandman of Llanpumsaint was, apparently, overheard to declare that he was bound to fulfil the will of the gentleman who was his master, even if he should order him to commit murder.[10]

Such blind attachment was, inevitably, open to be exploited

---

[7] PRO E 134 2 James I Trinity 1.

[8] The system had not entirely disappeared in Wales. One of the charges brought against Sir John Vaughan of Golden Grove, in Carmarthenshire, in 1611, was that he maintained a number of people – thirty-three of them are named, all freeholders who wore his livery contrary to the statutes prohibiting retainers. PRO Star Chamber 8 James I 302/31.

[9] PRO Star Chamber 8 James I 133/15.

[10] *Ibid* 118/9.

and abused, and in the case of the more unprincipled and aggressive of the gentry it could, and did, introduce an element of instability and tension in the daily life of the community. Nothing was more calculated to make the common people more sensitive to this, and more aware of their impotence, than the ability of the squires to override the law, seemingly with impunity. For instance, the *comortha*, or so-called voluntary contributions, had been declared illegal from the days of Henry VIII, but it persisted up and down the Principality despite the efforts of the Council of Wales to suppress it by means of heavy fines.

John William Lloyd, of Llanbadarn Fawr, in Cardiganshire, a gentleman of considerable wealth, power and authority, was said to have inflicted for three successive years a *comortha* on various inhabitants in the commote of Perfedd, and exacted from them as many as thirty-one sheep averaging six shillings apiece. His victims were defenceless people who 'durst not deny upon his demands so to give him the said giftes, for that he threatened them, if they did stand out and refuse so to doe, to trouble them and undoe them in those poore estates which they then enjoyed'.[11] But not all the gentry guilty of this offence behaved as despotically and callously as did James Games, of Aberbran, in Breconshire, who was said to have toured the fairs and markets of Breconshire with a troop of armed servants, and extorted money on all sides. With his tongue in his cheek, for he could hardly have been serious about it, Games handed out IOUs to those whom he had robbed, with a promise to redeem them at the end of seven years.[12] It was, possibly, the same uninhibited feeling of power that prompted Thomas Prys of Plas Iolyn, in Denbighshire, to establish an unauthorized fair at Spyty, and impose a toll on all animals and commodities sold there.[13]

There was little the Council of Wales or any other court

---

[11] *Ibid* 242/24.

[12] *Ibid* 241/31 and 307/27.

[13] *Ibid* 215/25. The *comortha* was not restricted to illegal exactions in money and kind. Walter Powell in his diary refers to the 'great comorth to impale and inlarge Lantilio Park' in July 1617. On this occasion, the tenants of the Earl of Worcester were summoned to give a number of days' work in fencing and extending the park. See Bradney, *The Diary of Walter Powell*, p. 8. And on another occasion, the *comortha* was used to raise funds towards covering the costs of a commission issued by the Chancery to investigate a complaint. PRO E 134 1 James I Trinity 6.

could do to restrain these high-handed practices. When it was notified of cases of *comortha* involving gentlemen or local officials, such as bailiffs, the Council subjected them to financial penalties, but this scarcely helped to reduce the incidence of this particular offence. What is interesting in this connection is that the *comortha* was often resorted to by the lower rural classes, on the occasion of a wedding, to solicit gifts in money and kind in order to assist the newly married pair to set up a home. As a violation of the law, it could not be ignored, but it could be exonerated. Very often the Council of Wales, aware of the poverty in the countryside, imposed the lightest of fines and then, conveniently or deliberately, may have forgotten to collect them.[14]

The *comortha* was an infuriating burden, but compliance could ward off the danger of physical violence or some other unpleasantness. What was more alarming was the possibility of disturbances and excesses resulting from personal animosities and feuds amongst the gentry. With their explosive temperament, Welsh squires did not have to look very far for motives which could set them at loggerheads with one another. It was not always an altercation over disputed lands, although that occurred often enough to keep lawyers busy in Wales and London, and could erupt into an open conflict with its inevitable casualty list. But family pride or hyper-sensitivity, where family honour was involved, could sometimes galvanize the most sluggish gentleman into volcanic action.

There was, for example, the troublesome matter of family burial places. In general, the gentry had little respect for ecclesiastical property – the disposal of monastic property, a century previously, had taught them that. But to secure and monopolize, even appropriate, a piece of hallowed ground, preferably within a church, to inter their dead, was calculated to enhance their social eminence as well as to keep alive some flicker of reverence for religious observances. But what added an element of contention and potential violence was the fact that, according to an old and recognized custom in Wales, anyone entitled to a pew or kneeling place within a parish church could sell or dispose of it as he wished, just like any other piece of property.[15] Real estate in a parish could

[14] BM Harleian MSS 4220, fols 35 and 40.
[15] PRO C2 James I D 14/56.

therefore carry with it a seat in the church and a burial place under that seat or near it.

Any conflicting claims to a property were liable to be fought out, not in a court of law, but in the chancel or nave of the parish church. The readiness of the squires and their followers to brawl and commit outrages inside churches was symptomatic of the gradual decline of the old sense of respect for places of worship, for which the decay of the ancient belief in the efficacy of church and churchyard as places of sanctuary and protection against violence was, no doubt, partly responsible.[16]

There was a bitter quarrel between the related families of the Vaughans of Bodrichwyn and Eyton in Denbighshire on this issue,[17] and the parishioners of Llanuwchllyn in Merionethshire were appalled by the hatred shown by the Vaughans of Glanllyntegid towards the Prices, a branch of the same family, during a similar dispute. The Vaughans claimed a particular burial place in the parish church, which was marked by a stone in the shape of a man, as that where their ancestors have been laid for generations. Their opponent, Edward Price, would have none of this, and when his father died, he decided to inter him in the disputed grave. He seems to have decided too that the occasion called not only for an exhibition of family sorrow, but for an imposing demonstration of force that would add tears of humiliation to those of grief in the eyes of the Vaughans. With the support of a few local gentlemen – the Lloyds of Rhiwaedog, the Morgans of Talyllyn and others – Price was reported to have invaded the church at Llanuwchllyn during divine service, irreverently ejected the coffins of the departed Vaughans from their resting place, threatened to bury alive anyone who dared challenge him, and claimed an undisputed and irreversible decision as to who should be buried there in future.[18]

When the gentry felt that something more persuasive than polite request or indignant expostulation was required to safeguard their interests, armed servants or friends were useful accessories. In some cases these were too few to provide the requisite pressure, but there was always available a reserve of ruffians who were ready to commit any outrage for money.

---

[16] PRO Star Chamber 8 James I 202/1.

[17] *Ibid* 287/31.

[18] *Ibid* 25/18. For a closer inquiry into the subject *see* Morgan 'Disputes concerning seats in church before the Consistory Court of St David's', 65–89.

They were the brigands and outlaws who infested the mountainous regions of Wales. In some localities, their inhumanity had become proverbial. It was said that their way of dealing with unco-operative people in Radnorshire was to put them to 'extreeme tortures of bodie and many inhuman usages, as by causing them naked to sitt on hott brandeirons to their extreeme torments and dainger of life'.[19] Such was the fear caused by their activites in Montgomeryshire that, in the Lordship of Arwystli, officials refused to keep watch and ward as required by law, leaving the countryside to be terrorized at will by gangs of cut-throats.[20]

With such lawless elements at the disposal of malevolent squires, enemies and rivals could be assaulted and sometimes fatally wounded or maimed; refractory occupiers of contested lands evicted; and whole rural communities reduced to submission. Because of the vicious feuds of certain gentlemen in Flintshire, ordinary people were known to refuse to work on the estate of one squire engaged in an acrimonious dispute with his neighbours. In these circumstances he had no hesitation in replacing them with labourers from Staffordshire and Cheshire.[21]

Land and the revenue derived from it was, as it had always been, the principal source of the gentry's power, and the extension of ownership by the acquisition of property remained their chief concern. This was not only in accordance with their traditional way of life. It was also forced upon them by economic considerations, not least by the steady rise in the cost of living and the inflationary processes which had been at work within the kingdom, as in other European countries, since the previous century, and had afflicted all classes. To meet the burden of taxation and loans to the Crown which fell heaviest on them; to provide for their children in the form of

---

[19] PRO Star Chamber 8 James I 91/3. There is a hint of employing people out of work for lawless purposes in *Ibid* 23/2.

[20] *Ibid* 304/25. A tenement held by bond tenure could impose the most menial or degrading obligations on the person who occupied it. But the service exacted at one time from the occupier of a holding in the Lordship of Cedewain, in Montgomeryshire, was out of the ordinary, for it was no less than to carry a ladder to the gallows for the execution of felons. This is suggestive of the brutalizing conditions of life in that Lordship which still existed in the seventeenth century. PRO E 134 9 Carl.1, Mich. 65.

[21] PRO Star Chamber 8 James I 134/4.

estates, legacies and dowries; and, in general, to maintain their privileged status in society, became more difficult with the passage of time. The cardinal problem for many of the squire-archy was to procure a sufficiency of ready money for their occasions,[22] and while these were numerous, cash was short as it commonly was outside the prosperous trading and commercial circles in towns and seaports. However, it was far from being an irremediable problem, for the Welsh gentry were not lacking in opportunism and resourcefulness.

Naturally enough they would look, in the first place, to improvements effected in the exploitation of their property, for an easing of their financial difficulties, beginning with the rents of their tenants. There were, however, certain obstacles in the way of enhancing their value and productiveness. Normally, they were payable at fixed times during the year, and landlords were expected to abide by traditional customs and usages as much as the tenants. Neither was it always advisable to anticipate rents in order to discharge liabilities – a constant temptation when creditors became insistent and unmanageable, since rents could be affected by unforeseen circumstances. In North Wales, for instance, the agricultural slump of 1622, not only brought about a fall in prices, but saw rents tumbling. Many tenants were so impoverished that they left their farms as soon as their leases expired, and were reduced to begging. One of their number, who had been worth £300 a year when he took a five year lease in 1618, was so poor a few years later that he was imprisoned for non-payment of rent. As a result of this crisis Sir Richard Bulkeley, faced with a drop of £60 in his rental, showed much shrewdness in directing an Anglesey drover to buy the cattle of those of his tenants who were in arrears with their rents, at reasonable prices, to enable them to pay their debts.[23] At Gwydir too, Sir John Wynn was most concerned to find that his tenants had paid him £400 less in rents than they had done in 1622.[24] Such sums might not have been large enough to discourage land-lords in general from continuing to enjoy a comfortable life.

---

[22] In South-West Wales this constant need for cash forced some squires to mortgage parcels of their land, and there was a significant increase in the number of mortgages between 1600 and 1625. *See* Lloyd, *The Gentry of South-West Wales*, pp. 46–8. Dr Lloyd adds that some of these mortgages may have been resorted to for the accumulation and consolidation of estates.

[23] PRO C 21 O 9/11.

[24] *Calendar of Wynn Papers*, p. 173, no. 1073.

But to be reminded that the law of diminishing returns could operate in their case was not too reassuring for some of them.

Not all rents, of course, showed this disconcerting downward trend. Even in Anglesey, where they could be erratic at times, a tenement which had been formerly leased for seventy years at eleven shillings and 'presents and services', was acquired by a tenant in 1612 who was willing to pay £10 in rent together with four geese, four capons and four days' services to his landlord. The latter, with a keen eye to a possible future surge in the value of land, stipulated that the lease should be for six years only.[25] In Caernarvonshire too, a holding which produced £8.9s.0d in 1579 had increased in value to £20 annually by 1614.[26]

It would seem that shorter leases, with more onerous financial terms, wherever they could be introduced offered one avenue to higher cash returns, but the scale on which they could be infiltrated into the agrarian economy was limited. Other more ancient and tenacious kinds of tenure barred the way – those enjoyed by freeholders; by tenants in possession of long leases, such as the conventual leases granted by monasteries before their dissolution, and which were often valid for ninety-nine years; and, above all, by the customary tenants who maintained that the manorial practices governing the continuity of leases, the inheritance or division of land, and the payments in money and services, were inviolable, and that they themselves were untouchable, at least as far as their rights of ownership were concerned.

Some of the gentry employed every means, including intimidation, to contravene or undermine those leases and customs they regarded as incompatible with their notions of profitable returns from their estates. Immediately after purchasing the properties of Llanddewi Velfrey and Lampeter Velfrey in Pembrokeshire, George Barlow, the squire of Slebech, announced that he considered their inhabitants to be his 'vassals', and intended to replace their freehold tenure with that of copyhold, which would be more advantageous to him. His tenants revolted and went to the length of voluntarily organizing a fund to defray the expense of research into

[25] PRO E 134 18 James I, Hilary II.
[26] PRO C 24 398, pt II, no. 54. By the first year of James's reign, the rents of the Crown lands at Dinorwig, in Caernarvonshire, had been at least doubled, compared with those paid to Queen Elizabeth. PRO E 134 3 James I, Mich. 8.

documents in the Tower of London, to enable them to confirm their freehold tenure and defend it by legal means.[27] Barlow, in fact, waged a long legal battle with his tenants in the Lordship of Narberth as to whether they were under an obligation to pay him rent, and perform certain services for the lands they held of him. It was a costly affair as his son was to find out some years later, when he was forced to mortgage large portions of the family estate to meet the bills.[28]

Rather than venture into disputes and litigation that might prove inconclusive or protracted some of the gentry preferred to try other alternatives that promised more immediate and durable gains. For example, enclosures were regarded as a source of wealth, if they could be successfully appropriated without undue dislocation of the communal economy. Slow and steady acquisition of pieces of waste and common land had been illicitly practised for generations, and no amount of prohibitions, threats and penalties had been able to control it. Almost all classes in the countryside were guilty of it in one form or other, and the individual or collective benefits accruing from it tended to outweigh recriminations and criticism, except when the parties involved showed excessive greed or a lack of consideration for other people's interests. In this respect, the lack of scruples amongst avaricious gentlemen was most noticeable, and at times it could lead to bitter opposition and violence.

Edward Nevill, Lord Bergavenny, who resided in Kent and owned extensive estates there, but who had some land in Monmouthshire, was one nobleman who discovered that enclosing property for personal profit could ignite more than resentful feelings. Claiming that he intended to enclose an extent of land traditionally held to be common pasture, called Drinos in the lordship of Abergavenny, for the benefit of the inhabitants, he justified the project by saying that 'the said countrey is for the moste parte mountaynes and very poore and populus and little corne or any other grayne sowed there at all'. The inhabitants objected that they had always pastured their cattle on Drinos common and travelled over it 'with their horses to goe to the mountaynes adjoininge to the cole to make lyme'. What is more, they had a healthy suspicion of what was

---

[27] PRO E 134 12 James I, Easter 15.
[28] For details of this dispute *see* Lloyd, *The Gentry of South-West Wales*, p. 24, n. 3 and p. 69, nn. 5, 6 and 7.

in his Lordship's mind, which was amply confirmed when the Justices of the Peace of Monmouthshire were asked to bring about a compromise on the matter. For no sooner had Lord Bergavenny been persuaded by the Justices to relinquish his plan for Drinos in return for the right to enclose other parcels of land, than he turned them over to a Bristol merchant for an annual rent. It was not surprising that when the merchant proceeded to enclose them with a wall, the inhabitants retaliated by dismantling it.[29] Neither did his Lordship have better success with his scheme for enclosing a woodland called Coed Morgan, in Llanddewi Rhydderch parish, with fences and a gate to increase the value of the timber, possibly with a view to selling it. On this occasion, as many as eighty people from the parish took part in a massive raid, destroying the fencing, burning the gate and rescuing their cattle which had been impounded by Lord Bergavenny's officials.[30]

Local opposition to a landlord's intemperate appetite for enclosures could not be better exemplified than by the sixty year struggle between the tenants of the manor of Trefgrug in Monmouthshire and the Williams family, into whose hands it had come towards the middle of the sixteenth century. The manor had some 800 freehold tenants, who had always exercised common of pasture in the waste known as Coed mab Paun or Paynswood and Sychffynhonnau. In 1564, Roger Williams instituted proceedings in the Court of the Marches at Ludlow to force them to forgo their rights of common, but the Court dismissed his case. Twenty years later he renewed his attempt, this time by packing the leet court of the manor with a jury of freeholders whom he considered to be amenable to pressure, but even this obsequious group declared in favour of the ancient rights of common. In 1623, his grandson, Sir Charles Williams of Llangybi, proposed to succeed where the grandfather had failed. Taking advantage, as it was implied, of, 'being great by allies and a knight, and one of the justices of the peace of the same county', he and his servants were said to have entered on the waste and dug burrows for rabbits on certain portions of it, which they enclosed with fencing. The intention might have been to convert the place into warrens for hunting. Moreover, by means of other fences, Sir Charles was alleged to have tried to prevent the cattle of his freeholders

[29] PRO Star Chamber 8 James I 49/19.
[30] *Ibid* 120/9.

from drinking at a spring near or on the waste, and to have hired men armed with guns to keep his tenants at arm's length. Their reaction was to invade the waste at night and destroy both burrows and fences.[31]

Some more moderate and perhaps enlightened squires chose not to agitate their tenants by riding rough-shod over their tenurial rights, and actively encouraged them to enclose pieces of land, in particular of the local waste, in order to bring them into cultivation or improve them as pasturage. When this had been achieved, their rents were revised and increased on a more realistic evaluation of the newly extended tenements, and were termed 'improved' as opposed to the old or 'customary rents'. On the manor of Wentsland and Bryngwyn in Monmouthshire, the former estates of Llantarnam Abbey and now in the possession of the Morgan family of Llantarnam, rents had climbed from £6.13s.4d to £11 by 1616, following upon the annexation and resourceful exploitation of the waste.[32] It was a policy that was also successfully pursued by some landowners in the mountainous districts of Montgomeryshire, but, in this case, the tenants were obliged to compound for the waste which they had converted into their private property.[33]

Opportunistic and discriminating land management of this kind no doubt allowed some of the gentry to derive profits from their estates, but others found it more difficult to cope with financial worries. They were not slow in grappling with the problem by other methods, in order to keep the flag of solvency flying above their ancestral homes.

Judiciously arranged marriages offered one way out of their troubles, especially when cash was urgently needed to liquidate debts or mortgages. Hugh Nanney or Nannau of Nanney, in Merionethshire, not only gave his daughter to John Vaughan of Caergai, but also 'bestowed a large maraige porcion to the said John Vaughan in preferment of his daughter to the said maraige, as threescore head of beasts, threescore sheepe and a great sume of money to redeeme sum parte of the said John Vaughans lands being then in morgage',

---

[31] *Ibid* 291/16.
[32] PRO E 134 13 James I, Mich. 16.
[33] PRO C 21 P 17/6 and E 134 6 James I, Mich. 42. The rents issuing from the Lordship of Ewloe had been considerably enhanced by an identical policy of fining and increasing the rents of those tenants who had encroached on the waste. PRO E 134 21 James I, Hilary 2.

the sum being the substantial one of £500.[34] John Price of Rhiwlas, in the same county, hoped to recoup his money losses and restock his fields at the same time by marrying his son to the daughter of John Owen, a neighbouring squire. The latter agreed to lend the young man £30 in cash, as well as six oxen, eighteen head of cattle, two mares and a horse, to begin a new lease of farming life. Unfortunately for Price, his son died before attaining a marriageable age.[35]

Being in debt was no uncommon experience, particularly amongst the more improvident or imprudent gentry, and it could lead on some occasions to consequences which they would be anxious to avoid.[36] John Williams, of Llangollen, certainly made no bones about confessing why he had married the widow of one of the Nanney family, who had prospered as a mercer in London. Her late husband, as he bluntly avowed, was reputed to be, 'a man of good estate when he died, and that it was sufficient to pay his (William's) debts with a good surplus, for otherwise, he saieth, he would not have married the said Nanneys widow'.[37]

To incur liabilities, of course, was not always a gentleman's fault, but the law cared little about that. Sir John Phillips of Clog y Frân, in Carmarthenshire, must have cursed the hour when he permitted himself to become a surety for a party to an agreement. The party defaulted, leaving Sir John to face the stiff financial penalties resulting from this defection, and which his means did not allow him to pay. What followed made his life rather miserable. 'By non performance thereof, the said Sir John Phillip was dampnified in that there cam extents against him, his body, lands and goods, whereby he was fayne to keepe home for diverse yeares. And when he had occasion to ryde for London, he could not walke the streets about his none (owne) affayres, but keepe to Milford Lane for the most part.'[38]

It was a situation that was eagerly exploited by ambitious yeomen and enterprising small farmers, who wished to improve their own and their children's social standing. It was said that, where squires married off their daughters with liberal dowries of £300 or more, the local yeomen emulated them with marriage

[34] PRO C 21 V 6/1.
[35] PRO C 24 401, pt 1, no. 92.
[36] The rate of interest for loans could be as much as two shillings in the pound. PRO Star Chamber 8 James I 210/20.
[37] PRO C 24 463, no. 84.
[38] PRO E 134 20 James I, Easter 1.

portions of £100 or more.[39] But a much more desirable achievement was to find or force admittance into the ranks of the
gentry by a marriage of financial convenience – at least, for the
acquiescent or desperate squire, since class distinctions were
often waived in return for pecuniary advantage. To effect the
'better advauncement' of his daughter, John Fowkes of Mostyn,
in Flintshire, married her off to the son of John Griffiths, the
squire of Gwaunysgor, and not only provided her with a fairly
sizeable dowry, but also agreed to furnish the children of the
marriage with food, apparel and accommodation for four years.[40]

There were, one may assume, certain proprieties to be
observed in any union between gentlemen and commoners. A
minimum of acceptable social behaviour, even of education,
was thought desirable in a young man who aspired, or whose
father undertook to aspire on his behalf, to a higher rank than
that decreed by the circumstances of birth. John ap John, a
yeoman of Carmarthenshire, had somehow or other accumulated
property worth £200 a year which, with paternal ambition and
cautious optimism, he was prepared to employ to push his son
up the ladder of worldly success. He, first of all, sent him to
the Grammar School in Carmarthen, to acquire, at least, a
smattering of higher education. The intention was sound, but,
unfortunately, son David was inquisitive or impressionable
enough to be distracted from his studies by the non-academic
recreations of that town. He developed a taste for strong drink
and the corrosive tobacco of that age, so much so, that the
landlady of the tavern which he patronised tried to take
advantage of his periodic bouts of drunkenness to persuade
him to marry her daughter. He might have succumbed if his
father had not appeared on the scene and removed him to the,
perhaps, more elevating influences of the Grammar School at
Hereford. What is more, he successfully arranged a marriage
between his son and Lettice, daughter of Sir Walter Rice, a
Carmarthenshire squire. Young David's contacts with learning,
however intermittent, probably helped to cover up his
aberrations in Carmarthen; as did his father's money which,
wisely distributed amongst the ecclesiastical officials of the
county, enabled the wedding ceremony to be celebrated
without bans or other dilatory preliminaries.[41]

[39] PRO C 21 W 74/4.
[40] PRO C 2 James I G 13/52.
[41] PRO Star Chamber 8 James I 188/21.

A few Welsh gentry saw no reason why the, to them, advantageous political union of the Principality with England should not be matched by profitable matrimonial union with English heiresses. Their readiness to promote Anglo-Welsh harmony in this manner was not always reciprocated on the other side of the border, where it was considered by many that Wales was out of England and its eligible young squires best left alone.[42] This attitude of aloofness not unexpectedly invited some equally uncomplimentary comment, and it came from Sir John Wynn, of Gwydir, who observed that it was easier to find good women in Wales, where their sex was simple, unsophisticated and innocent of vice, than in England. It was true that much virtue was taught in that country; nevertheless, Sir John was persuaded that English women were more inclined to questionable behaviour because of the liberty allowed them by English fashions.[43] This did not prevent the squire of Gwydir from marrying an English woman, nor finding English wives for two of his sons.[44]; and other Welsh families followed suit, including the Vaughans of Golden Grove, in Carmarthenshire, the Bulkeleys of Anglesey, the Morgans of Llantarnam and the Perrots of Haroldston. No doubt, most of these marriages were successful since, despite differing cultural and social backgrounds the families concerned, both Welsh and English, shared identical ideas as to the acquisition of wealth and influence.

But there was the occasional misadventure or miscalculation when the process was reversed, and an Englishman tried his luck in winning a Welsh bride. Richard Ireland, of Shropshire, was allegedly inveigled into marrying the daughter of John Lewis Owen, a Merionethshire gentleman, with the promise of a dowry of £1,000. Instead of enjoying this money in peace, he found himself signing a bond for the payment of debts accumulated by his wife's family, and had to sell some of his own estates to discharge them, or so it was claimed. But his disillusion with the match, from which he had anticipated financial as well as connubial rewards, was not complete until the day when he complained of having been assaulted by his father-in-law and his confederates.[45]

---

[42] *Calendar of Wynn Papers*, p. 58, under date of January 1604/5.
[43] *Ibid*, p. 108, under date of 7 March 1614–15.
[44] Sir John Wynn, senior, married Sydney, daughter of Sir William Gerrad. His son, Sir John, junior, married Margaret, daughter of Sir Thomas Cave, and another son, Sir Richard, married the daughter of Sir Francis Darcy.
[45] PRO Star Chamber 8 James I 184/27.

A similar piece of chicanery was said to have occurred in West Wales where Sir Arthur Chichester, Lord Deputy of Ireland, showed too much keenness in advancing the fortunes of his wife's niece, Jane Phillips, daughter of John Phillips of Picton, in Pembrokeshire. He arranged a marriage between her and Sir James Hamilton, to which Phillips had no objection but regretted that he had no money at the time to pay the dowry of £400 agreed upon. Chichester willingly paid it on his behalf, and in an access of liberality, added £200 of his own money. Years passed without the slightest move on Phillips's part to refund the £400 or even to provide security for its eventual payment. And to add to Chichester's discomfiture, there was no written evidence available concerning the transaction.[46]

Necessitous gentlemen, sometimes, found it very difficult to resist the temptation of misusing their position as the local administrative officers of the Crown. As sheriffs, feodaries and Justices of the Peace, they were expected to perform their duties without any remuneration from the Government, and to be satisfied with whatever prestige and perquisites were attached to these offices. But certain abuses had crept in which, though offensive in the eyes of the law, were so common as to be accepted as inseparable from a social system in which patronage was a well-established practice.

Perhaps the most evident of these, and the most lucrative for those squires who were in a position to exploit it, was the opportunity to sell or otherwise dispose of local goverment posts and sinecures which were under their control in the shires. There were few places in Wales where a brisk market in private deals for jobs and situations did not flourish, and the sums involved were quite respectable. Edward Kemys, High Sheriff of Glamorgan, was alleged to have openly flouted the law by selling the bailiwicks of Senghennydd, Neath, Llangyfelach and Cardiff, the first three for £12 each and the last for £8. A good bargain over the Clerkship of the County Court netted a

---

[46] In West Wales the landed gentry normally married within their own circle, rarely outside it, with the result that they were related to one another in near or remote degree. This kind of consanguinous matching could lead to matrimonial tangles, not the least extricable being that of the relationship by marriage between the Stedman and Vaughan families, which Francis Jones in his study on the subject describes as 'more of a conundrum than a pedigree.' See *Ceredigion, Journal of the Cardiganshire Antiquarian Society*, vol. IV (1960–3), 15–16.

further £36 for him, the Keepership of the gaol in Cardiff fetched £14, and Kemys saw no reason why he should not get something for the Cryership of the shire. He did, to the tune of forty shillings.[47] In Pembrokeshire, Alban Stepneth, the sheriff, sold seven bailiwicks – Cemaes, Narberth, Cilgerran, Dewisland, Daugleddau, Rhos and Castlemartin for the total sum of £66.[48] Other instances of this illicit trade in public offices occur in North and South Wales.[49]

The amount of money that could be realized from their sale was not, necessarily, the sole criterion of their usefulness. The sheriff of Carmarthenshire, David Lloyd Jones of Trimsaran, struck a most judicious balance between financial benefits and family ties in his disposal of offices. He sold the under-sheriffwick to a nephew for £30; the bailiwick of Elvet to his natural brother for £12; that of Derllys to another nephew for £10, and the post of itinerant bailiff of the county to his brother-in-law for £6. From these and the sale of other posts he reaped £116, as well as the tremendous advantage of having some of his nearest relatives strongly entrenched up and down the shire – a valuable asset should he, at any time, be involved in a dispute with opponents of his own social class.[50]

Control over subordinates by the sheriff was essential to the ordinary working of local administration, as it was to the exercise of his personal power and influence. This was more or less ensured, when the distribution or sale of posts synchronised with family interests and ambitions. Where it did not, there was another method of bringing refractory subordinates to heel. This was simply to force them to sign bonds, when entering into office, not only to carry out their duties, but to exonerate the sheriff from any responsibility for faults of theirs, and to idemnify him for all financial penalties arising from their remissness or ignorance.[51] How this commitment could be operated to the advantage of the sheriff was obvious to any

---

[47] PRO Star Chamber 8 James I 197/29. Fiddling with jobs and money, which did not belong to him, seems to have exercised a fascination on Kemys. It was he who, when his bailiffs had gathered fines and amercements in the hundred courts to the amount of £100 and handed the sum to him, accounted for only £36 to the King's collectors and pocketed the rest for himself. PRO Star Chamber 8 James I 192/28.

[48] *Ibid* 290/5.

[49] *Ibid* 118/9 and 187/25.

[50] *Ibid* 215/20.

[51] PRO C 2 James I H 37/20; J 2/33 and C 21 I 18/1.

bailiff or official who toyed with the idea of opposition.

The purchasers of local government posts – they included gentlemen as well as yeomen, had every intention of recouping the money they had paid out, and a little more, from the perquisites attached to them. They were inclined to do so with little regard for the feelings of the community, and it was their exactions that led to one of the rare revolts of the oppressed lower orders in the Welsh countryside during the early years of the century.

The office of Raglorship in the hundreds of Caio, Manordeilo, Cethiniog and Mallaen, in Carmarthenshire, had been leased to two gentlemen, Thomas Alisbury, an Englishman, and Henry Vaughan, of Derwydd, whose treatment of the inhabitants had obviously not been exemplary. According to a report, the first indication of resentment towards them was the interruption of divine service in some of the neighbouring churches by groups of people, who declared openly that the parishioners would support any resolute action against the exactions of the two lessees. This was followed by an un-equivocal and bold challenge to the two gentlemen. The leaders of the aggrieved inhabitants proceeded to rate and tax the community according to the customary assessment, and not at the inflated standard imposed by Alisbury and Vaughan. They then appeared at the Court leets of Caio and Mallaen to demonstrate their opposition to the lessees, and amongst other exhortations to one another it was said that they 'used a Welsh fraze Trech gwlad nag arglwith which ys in English, a whole countrye ys to hard for a Lord'. They also, so wrote Vaughan later in his complaint to the Star Chamber:

> Threatned to do with your said subject what there (their) auncestors had done in foretimes with one David ap Rice, sometimes fermore of the said duties or customes, who so daring to demaund the said customes or duties of the said riotors auncestors, they compelled and forced him with his horse to take his way over a river and ride for safeguard of life...and soe would they use your subject if they had any spark of their auncestors blood in them.[52]

The Welsh gentry were essentially a class rooted in rural life and pursuits, but some of them were shrewd enough to see

---

[52] PRO Star Chamber 8 James I 41/13.

that there were advantages in engaging in trade wherever that was feasible. The difficulty was that, depite the increasing sea power of England and the consequent greater security of the ships that flew her flag, facilities for mercantile enterprises were rather restricted in Wales. There were few ports with adequate accommodation for large vessels, and the amount of shipping available for trade, coastal or international, was limited; although it would need much more than the prescribed grain of salt to swallow the sensational statement made by the MP for Radnor, Charles Price, in the House of Commons that 'there is in Wales but 4 sail of ships'.[53]

The principal trade routes were those leading from West and North Wales to Ireland, and from South Wales to the English shires on the other side of the Severn and the Bristol Channel. Most of the cargoes carried along them were of coal and agricultural products, and something more lucrative than these indigenous commodities was needed to stimulate trade. To some degree, this had been achieved by the development of the wine trade with France and Spain. Claret and the wines of Gascony were conveyed from Bordeaux to Beaumaris,[54] and sherry and sack from Cadiz to Cardiff,[55] with Milford Haven and Tenby playing a profitable role in distributing the wines throughout West Wales.[56] This particular branch of trade, in fact, had assumed such proportions by the end of the reign of James I, that it was estimated that as many as seventy-seven licensed wine-sellers were operating within the Principality, most of them in South Wales and Pembrokeshire.[57]

But commercial initiative in Wales as a whole was sometimes hindered by government policy, which often controlled it in the interests of national security, or chose to subordinate it to

---

[53] Notestein, Relf and Simpson, *Common Debates 1621*, vol. II, p. 389.

[54] PRO E 134 16 James I, Hilary 13.

[55] *Ibid* 9 James I, Mich. 18.

[56] *Ibid* 7 James I, Easter 21.

[57] PRO E 163 17/22. Attempts were made by the authorities to restrict the number of alehouses on the grounds that they were conducive to riotous or lax behaviour. But their suppression was not always popular with those who gained profit from them. Sir Francis Mansel, Justice of the Peace of Carmarthenshire, kept a number of alehouses in the vicinity of Kidwelly for the sale of his own tithe corn which was converted into malt 'whereof he hath great store yearely to the value of eight or nyne hundred pounds'. The closure of some of them by his fellow JPs in 1607 infuriated Mansel beyond words. PRO Star Chamber 8 James I 288/4.

the claims of trade monopolies in England. A case in point was the export of the cloth woven in North Wales. For many years, Welsh cottons and friezes had been exclusively bought by the drapers of Shrewsbury at Oswestry market and, after the process of dyeing and dressing, they had been sent to Blackwell Hall in London, to be sold to merchants, who disposed of them at home and on the continent. In 1611, the Company of merchants who traded this cloth to France sent their own agents to Machynlleth to buy up as much cloth as they could and ship it directly to France from Aberdyfi without troubling to dress it. There followed indignant protests from Shrewsbury, the Privy Council ruled that there were too many ancillary businesses and workpeople dependent on the industry for it to be meddled with, and the Company of merchants were warned to keep out of Machynlleth and Aberdyfi. Welsh cloth continued to be sent to London, and the weavers of North Wales were tied more than ever to the market at Oswestry and the prices that were fixed there.[58] The laws against exporting Welsh butter did some damage also to dairy farming in Glamorgan, although they could be by-passed by paying heavy fines for the privilege of taking butter out of the Principality in limited amounts.[59]

Government interference was, likewise, responsible for the decline of another viable export trade in South Wales. As far back as 1604, ships bringing iron ordnance from Glamorgan were constant visitors to Spain; so much so, that an English observer in that country wrote to Sir Robert Cecil that 'all the ports of Spayne are full of English artigliary (artillery), and more and more dayly brought thither out of Wales'.[60] By 1614, the trade in ordnance had been switched to the Netherlands, and was concentrated to a great extent in the hands of a Dutchman, Peter Semeyne, who transported great numbers of guns, forged in his furnaces in Glamorgan, from Cardiff to the ports of Holland. But in their apprehension of Dutch rivalry on the sea and in the Indies, and with the weakening of their influence on the foreign and military policies of the Dutch

---

[58] *Acts of the Privy Council, 1613–14*, pp. 9–10, 34–40 and 51–3.

[59] PRO E 148, no. 3 pt 2. State Papers Domestic, James I 1611–18, vol. 94, fol. 180. The state of the case concerning the transportation of Welsh butter out of Glamorgan and Monmouthshire.

[60] PRO State Papers Foreign, Spain (SP 94), vol. 10, fol. 147. Endorsed: 'November 1604. Mr Wilson. Note of certain points most subject to discours of Ambassadors abroade'.

leaders at the Hague, the English Government ordered the total suspension of the trade. For two years or so, Semeyne managed to ignore or side-step the official prohibition but, eventually, the Privy Council issued the strictest possible instructions for his arrest, his furnaces were closed and 'his fyer quit put out soe as there may bee noe meanes leaft for his servaunts or anie others to worke ther anie more'.[61]

Interference of this sort was bound to be exasperating and frustrating, but looking around them, Welsh squires who wished to supplement their incomes from commercial transactions believed that there was sufficient evidence to raise their hopes of profitable investments. However precarious the international situation might sometimes appear, with its constant and not entirely unfounded rumours of military and naval preparations, Welshmen still travelled from Denbigh to Bergenop-Zoom and from Cowbridge to Utrecht, 'about certen their affaires'.[62] And Welsh merchants of Caernarvon despatched their ships to Flushing with a load of lead and exchanged it for a cargo of soap, flax, hemp and other goods;[63] and to La Rochelle to bring back an assortment of luxury commodities, including French furniture, tobacco, vinegar, aquavite and wines.[64] One bold Welshman adventured as far as the East Indies, where he remained for eight years, but, unfortunately, his activities there are not recorded.[65] No less notable a member of the aristocracy than Lord Herbert of Chepstow, son of the Earl of Worcester, tried his hand at mercantile speculation. He built a ship at his own expense in Chepstow, and invited local merchants to freight her with their wares. The ship made, at least, one voyage to Spain, and Herbert acquired enough profit from the freight charges to pay the crew and to compensate himself for his venture.[66]

---

[61] *Acts of the Privy Council, 1613–14*, pp. 427 and 446; and *1616–17*, p. 47. Semeyne's efforts to avoid government investigations into his business affairs did not go unnoticed by the Customs officials at Cardiff but, not surprisingly in an age of easy financial virtue, they turned a blind eye to his clandestine consignments of guns, munition and shot to foreign parts, in return for unrecorded but probably satisfactory gratuities. PRO Star Chamber 8 James I 142/18.

[62] PRO E 157, no. 13.

[63] PRO C 2 James I G 6/51.

[64] PRO C 24 550, pt 11, no. 110.

[65] *Calendar of Wynn Papers*, p. 168, no. 1046a.

[66] PRO HCA 13, no. 42 under date of 16 July 1614.

Where their estates were adjacent to the coast or within reasonable access to ports and havens, the aspiring merchant-squires of Wales did not lack enterprise. In Pembrokeshire, a number of them co-operated in the export of wheat, rye and malt from Milford to Dublin, subscribing to an agreement that each should receive a return proportionate to his share or shares in the venture.[67] Sir John Carew, of Carew Castle in the same county, found it to his advantage to sell cereals to a merchant from Somerset, although, on one occasion, his consignment of barley, apparently, left much to be desired. After it had been carried to Minehead 'the water wherein the said barley was washed would look, when the same was put from the corne, as if it had come from durt'. It was, in fact, too coarse in quality to be offered even to the destitute people in Minehead. On the other hand, Sir John found his overhead expenses appreciably reduced by the fact that the Somerset merchant could navigate his ship almost up to the gates of Carew Castle.[68]

Richard Bulkeley of Beaumaris had a more ambitious scheme to increase his fortune with the help of a pinnace of thirty tons and a crew of five Anglesey mariners. In view of the ever-increasing demand for tobacco, he decided to buy certain goods in Chester and sail with them to the West Indies. He was persuaded, however, to revise his plan and take part in a voyage to Virginia with other ships, but was forced to abandon the project in circumstances which seem to suggest that, like mariners and merchants in all ages, he could spin a good yarn. If his story is to be believed, his ship had been boarded and seized by the crew of the very person, Sir Ralph Bingley, who had induced him to join the expedition to Virginia, and from whose clutches he had escaped with much difficulty to Cardiff.[69] Virginia, certainly, had a fascination for some Welsh gentlemen, like Matthew Griffith, of Llandaff, who readily agreed to a proposal by a friend of his, Sir John Zouch, of Codnor Castle, in Derbyshire, that they should both venture to that colony; but for some reason or other, he failed to make his way across the Atlantic.[70]

A few of the mercantile-minded Welsh squires may have made a little profit from their risky undertakings, but they

[67] PRO C 2 James I P 12/44.
[68] PRO Star Chamber 8 James I 104/4 and C 24 421, pt 11, no. 5.
[69] PRO HCA 1 vol. 48, fols 335b–37.
[70] PRO C 24 398, pt 11, no. 73.

were the fortunate few. Even a reputable Merchant Adventurer like Sir William St John, of Highlight, in Glamorgan, who was Governor of the Company of London merchants trading with Guinea and other parts of Africa, suffered considerable losses because of the incompetence of captains and crews, and the constant wrangling amongst them as to the best methods of dealing with the natives.[71]

There were, of course, other hazards to be run. Shipwrecks on the inadequately charted coasts of Wales were only too common, and those mariners who survived them were hardly treated better than pieces of wreckage by the local population. A bark laden with beer and cloth worth £800, and bound for Cork, was driven off its course by foul weather and forced to seek shelter at Aberystwyth. It was, apparently, invaded by the inhabitants of that town, abetted by the country people around. They rifled the vessel of everything that was detachable or transportable, and stripped the crew and passengers of their clothes. Moreover, it was stated that 'where they were not able to carry away the said beere, they did steeve (stave) the barrells to lett the beere run out that they might carry away the casks'.[72] Nothing was safe, sometimes not even the ship itself. When the *Anne* of Neath, of eighteen tons burthen, went aground not far from the Mumbles near Swansea, the local people took to their hatchets and axes, chopped her into pieces and carried them back home in their carts as firewood and building material.[73]

On the high seas piracy was rampant, and the notorious English freebooters Bishop, who set up his headquarters on Lundy Island, and Sackeld played havoc with merchant shipping between Land's End and St David's Head. If a report to the Privy Council on 27 March 1610, is to be believed, Sackeld was daring and brutal enough on one occasion to raid Milford Haven, where he killed a number of the inhabitants and burned some houses and a church.[74] Other pirates chose to hug the Welsh coast with an intimacy that suggested a degree of improper collusion between them and the residents. Certainly Tenby and Milford had a bad name for providing

---

[71] PRO C 2 James I G 18/13.
[72] PRO HCA 1b, no. 38, fol. 203.
[73] *Ibid*, vol. 39, under date of 10 March 1607–8.
[74] HMC *Salisbury (Cecil) MSS*, vol. XXI, p. 209. Enclosure of examinations, dated 27 March 1610.

ways and means of disposing of goods seized by pirates, and there was an ugly rumour that George Owen of Henllys, deputy Vice-Admiral of Pembrokeshire, was involved in surreptitious transactions with members of visiting Dutch warships, which were eager to rid themselves of articles which their crews could not claim as being their rightful property except by the most specious of arguments.[75] Such was the attitude of receivers of pirated cargoes in this corner of the Principality that, when a more conscientious or law-abiding member of the community was commissioned by the Admiralty to investigate and, if possible, stop this irregular trade, he was heartily abused by his neighbours who were alleged to have accused him of having 'begged a commission of the Lord Admirall to undoe his countrie'.[76]

At least one Welsh gentleman found the dangerous but exhilarating life on board a pirate's ship very much to his taste. From the moment that Owen Blayney of Penegoes, of the eminent Montgomeryshire family of that name, set foot on the *Jane* of Dartmouth, he temporarily renounced any allegiance he had or owed to the sovereignty of law, and his statutory obedience to the King of England who detested pirates, applauded their harassment and destruction, and needed a great deal of persuasion to reprieve any who qualified for the gallows. The first action of the *Jane*'s captain, Christopher Holland, showed only too clearly that the company recognized no restrictive practices in their trade. Although provided with letters of reprisals, which stated most categorically that they were to confine their attacks to Spanish shipping, peace with Spain having not yet been signed, their first victim was a vessel manned by Hollanders, England's allies in the war with Spain, which they captured and used her cargo of deal boards to convert her into a man of war.

What followed showed how flexible and unpredictable were the relations between the nations inhabiting the Mediterranean seaboard. Despite the religious animosities of Christians and Moslems, these had been tempered for some time by the realization that political and commercial advantages could be gained by a common front directed against Spain, the one temporal power that represented a threat to many countries in Europe, both Catholic and Protestant. Venice had come to

[75] PRO HCA 1 vol. 48, fols 123 and 193; vol. 46, fols 340–1.
[76] *Ibid*, vol. 47, fol. 244.

terms with Constantinople, France had followed suit, even the Netherlands and England had resident ambassadors in that city. This did not mean, of course, that the trade routes in the Mediterranean were made safe. Merchant ships continued to be attacked and despoiled by the Sultan's subjects, and their crews captured and sold in the slave markets of North Africa. But representations could be made, not always effectually, on their behalf by accredited diplomats, and the Sultan requested to moderate the excesses of his subjects, which he occasionally did. However, the people who really benefited from this situation belonged to the international fraternity of pirates, who sought, and often obtained, the connivance of the Moslem authorities on the North African coast, since their common enemy was Spain. It was this situation that allowed the *Jane* to sail to Tunis without hindrance, with Owen Blayney acting as Lieutenant of the company.

Their next move was imprudent and almost cost them their liberty, if not their lives. Off the island of Madona in the eastern Mediterranean, they took a Venetian vessel with a rich cargo of silk, pepper, cotton and other wares, and were misguided enough to offer them for sale to the Turkish governor of the island. It was only when Christopher Holland, their captain, was arrested on land and the *Jane* itself threatened by a Turkish warship, that Blayney and the rest of the crew remembered that all Venetian ships enjoyed the protection of the Sultan. Blayney had enough sense to cut the *Jane*'s cable, managed to escape through a hail of shot to the open sea, and thus avoided the fate of the captain who was condemned by the Turks to be hanged.[77]

Souza and Tripoli were other ports where Blayney and his company felt very much at home, and it was to their credit that they not only treated their prisoners with consideration, but, on one occasion it was claimed, ransomed fifteen of their countrymen who were slaves in Tunis. Eventually, the company divided into two groups; those who wished to return to England, and those who had become too inured to the customs and manners of North African Moslem society to contemplate a painful readjustment to ordinary English habits. A bout of nostalgia proved too strong for the squire from Montgomery-shire, and it was while he was sailing past Sicily, on his way

[77] PRO Calendar of State Papers, Venetian (SP 99) vol. X, 1603–7, p. 31, no. 51 and p. 39, no. 65.

home, that he was involved in the second serious blunder of his sea-roving career. And it was Venice, again, that was partly responsible for it. Boarding a French vessel, Blayney and his fellow pirates momentarily forgot about its cargo of muscadel, aniseed and currants in speculative observation of a number of trunks which, so the French captain informed them, were the property of the Venetian ambassador to England, who was not aboard, however, since he had chosen to travel overland to London. To seasoned pirates the idea was preposterous and, no doubt, greeted with something more boisterous than nods and winks. The trunks were taken aboard the pirate ship and opened. They contained 'thre Cannapies, two of red and white silke lyned throughe with yellowe taffitie fringed with white and redd, and one greene one of silke unlyned; twoe gownes, one of blacke ritche taffitie lined through with Coniefurre, and the other of fine damaske lined with foxes furre; one Crucifix of Ivorye sett in a frame of Ibonie, and certaine wax Candles, and two other gownes more'. It was pronounced to be fine haul, and the articles were divided according to custom.

Unfortunately for Blayney and his companions, the French captain had not lied. Upon their arrival in England, they were summoned to appear before the Court of the Admiralty to account for their activities. However much they may have convinced the authorities that they had been dictated to by circumstances beyond their control in the Mediterranean, their affront to the ambassasador of a friendly state like Venice could not be overlooked.[78] It might have gone hard for Blayney if the King, for one reason or another, had not granted him a pardon in November 1604.[79]

The element of risk inseparable from overseas trading may have persuaded not a few Welsh squires that their native land might, after all, offer better security and easier profits, if its mineral resources were properly exploited. They were obviously impressed by the dramatic expansion of industry in England, with its intensive and often government-sponsored investigation into the mineral wealth of the kingdom. They were also probably aware, to some extent, of technical improvements in the extraction of ores and the utilization of available sources of energy to that end; as well as of the multifarious projects for

[78] PRO HCA 1 vol. 46, fols 119–23.
[79] Phillimore, *Index to the Signet Office Docquet Books*, p. 65.

the manufacture of all kinds of consumer goods as viable by-products of this general industrial development. Judging by the evidence on all sides, the way was open for personal initiative in the matter of beginning new industries or promoting existing ones, either on one's own property or in localities where conditions appeared to be favourable; or, again, by throwing in one's lot with other speculators and sharing their success or failure.

Some Welsh gentlemen entered into the spirit of industrial enterprise with enthusiasm and confidence and, where the initial outlay was reasonable and overhead charges not too burdensome, they could expect some return from their investment. A good example of co-operation between North and West Wales was provided by the all-Welsh company launched by Lewis ap Richard, of Merionethshire, and Richard Gwillim and Francis Merrick, of Pembrokeshire. Appreciating the general demand for salt in Merionethshire, they erected a salt house and salt works there for the production of 'fine whyte sawlte'. It proved a profitable venture and was regarded as being most beneficial to a county 'which stoode in grete wante of sawlte of that nature'. There was, apparently, no lack of customers, who were allowed to buy the salt at an enormous price and in any quantity they desired. It was, perhaps, inevitable that the lucrative dealings of the company with the inhabitants should have excited the envy of competitors, one of whom was accused of going so far as to throw 'some venemous, poysonous and pestilent matter and stuffe' into one of the pans in which the crude salt was being boiled, thereby destroying an amount calculated to being equal to twenty barrels of salt worth at least £40.[80]

Farther north, in Flintshire, the millstones produced by the numerous quarries within the county were considered to be a very reliable source of revenue to those who either owned or operated them, particularly as there was a steady demand for them, not only from mills in the immediate neighbourhood, but also from Denbighshire and Merionethshire. Here, too, competition was extremely keen, and the acute rivalry between two gentlemen owners, Lewis Yonge, of Bryn Holkyn, and George Hope, of Broughton, led to some unpleasant incidents. Yonge was alleged to have attempted to entice the most expert worker in Hope's quarry at Caergwrle to enter his service and,

[80] PRO C 2 James I P 24/56.

when all his blandishments failed, to have made every possible effort to run him out of the country. Finally, a number of millstones at Caergwrle were mysteriously destroyed and suspicion, not unnaturally, perhaps, fell upon Yonge rather than upon the hobgoblins and apparitions which were popularly believed to haunt Hope's quarry. The latter retaliated at the first opportunity. Hearing that Yonge had dismissed one of his servants, he was said to have induced the man to confess that Yonge had pressured him into demolishing the millstone. This Hope did, according to one report 'very prophanely in making religion the shadow of his mallice'; for he caused 'the minister of the parish church of Hope in the said countie, in the face of the congregation, publiquely to make a solempe prayer that the breaker of the said millstones might be revealed; which being doen and performed accordingly, thereupon forthwith the said George Hope caused the said Llywelyn (Yonge's late and perjured servant) to confess unto others the comytting of the same ffact by the procurement of...Yonge, as if the same discovery had come by Divine Revelation'.[81]

These enterprises were simple and straightforward exploitation of primary materials, which were readily accessible and required relatively little processing to convert them into useful products for the whole community. Matters were, of course, more complicated in the case of major industrial operations such as coal and lead mining, the smelting of iron ore, glass-making and like activities, all of which demanded higher technical knowledge and experience, advanced organizational skill and, above all, adequate capital. Generally speaking, these were beyond the capacity of most Welsh squires, who were aware of their limitations in this respect. They had no illusions as to what this deficiency might mean; that without the co-operation of people, who had both technical expertise and money, they could remain spectators of, and not participators in, the free-for-all competition in the industrial field. They did not have to look far afield, however, for partners and associates with those qualifications. There were plenty of Englishmen, especially businessmen, eager to try their luck in industrial speculation, not to mention foreigners with an eagle eye for profitable investments. But, as in every sphere of feverish money-making and intense commercial rivalry, there were unavoidable hazards here also.

[81] PRO Star Chamber 8 James I 311/28 and 166/19.

The Mathew family of Radyr, in Glamorgan, were much alive to the possibilities of the rapidly expanding iron industry, which was proliferating in the south-east of the Principality. Edmund Mathew erected an iron forge on a property leased by him from More Waters at Monmouth, which cost him £300 and spent an equal sum in stocking it with coal, iron ore and implements to convert the ore into iron bars and pieces. He then struck a bargain with Robert Chauntrel of London, that the latter should act as agent and general supervisor at the forge, while he himself assumed all responsibility for maintenance and stockpiling. According to other testimony, it was Chauntrel who had been the moving spirit in this enterprise, and who had leased certain works known as Walk Mills with a view to re-building and re-equipping them as a 'doble forge and hammer for the makinge and forging of iron'.[82] Be that as it may, the forge seems to have paid handsomely until such time as dissensions alienated the partners from one another. These grew apparently out of an insidious and successful attempt by Waters, the lessor of Walk Mills, to subborn Chauntrel into violating a condition of the lease by deliberately omitting to pay the rent within fifteen days as agreed. Mathew heard of the conspiracy and managed to pay the money in time, but he could scarcely have anticipated the consequences of such a declaration of honest intent on his part. The forge was invaded by a gang of ruffians, led by Waters in person, who manhandled the workers and took possession of a great quantity of iron and coal. To his credit, an Englishman, Bartholomew Maskal, who was the clerk of the works, put up some opposition to the intruders 'whereupon he, the said More Waters, did threaten to pull the bearde from the said Maskals face and to break his knaves pate, telling him that he had paied for the breaking of many better mens heads than his'.[83]

A divergence of views on the proper use of company funds was one factor, amongst others, that seemingly brought about the failure of the ironworks at Nannau, in Merionethshire. Here, in the previous reign, Hugh Nannau and Gruffydd his son had leased the site to John Smith of Newcastle under Lyme, and sold him the wood at nearby Penrhos to provide the necessary fuel. In his turn, Smith persuaded William Dale, a London mercer, to invest the considerable sum of £15,000 in the

[82] PRO C 2 James I C 22/69.
[83] PRO Star Chamber 8 James I 218/16.

enterprise. It soon became evident, however, that if anyone was deriving profits from it, it was the Nannau family and Smith, but certainly not the London businessman, who was constantly at loggerheads with Smith. There were broad hints that the latter had no difficulty in disposing of the iron, but was quietly misappropriating the proceeds 'for that by the report of the workemen there and others which were then neighbours, he [Smith] at the beginninge of these works was held to be a very poore man in his estate, but within a short time after, he was gotten unto his satten or taffety dublett and his velvet hose, and was thought to be a man of good estate'.[84]

This, however, did not prevent further collaboration between the Nannau family and Smith. The latter proceeded to modernize the existing works by converting them into a blast furnace with forges, and obtained enough capital to do so from the ever optimistic London mercer and a third partner, William Grosvenor, of Shropshire. It is thought that the reorganized company hoped to retrieve its fortunes by producing iron to feed Grosvenor's own forge at Chester, which was turning out armaments for use in Ireland. Again this scheme came to nothing, but on this occasion it is possible that natural causes were primarily responsible for the abandonment of the Nannau ironworks, early in the reign of James I; the river in the vicinity of the forge overflowed its banks, poured into those parts of the works which were underground and, before counter-measures could be taken, choked them with stones and gravel.[85]

Close association between Welsh gentry and English investors, some of high rank, was signalled from other parts of the Principality, where industrial initiative and activity intensified with the passage of years. In Pembrokeshire, the Crown had granted the royal mines to Sir James Perrot, but when the time came to request a renewal of the grant, he thought it prudent to accept as his partners such prominent members of the English aristocracy as the Marquess of Hamilton, who was Lord Steward of the King's Household, Lord Chichester and the Countess of Bedford.[86] The Privy

---

[84] PRO C 24 448, pt 1, no. 19.
[85] PRO C 2 James I D 6/24. *See also* Parry 'A Sixteenth Century Merioneth Ironworks', 209–11.
[86] PRO State Papers Domestic James I 1623–5, vol. 167, fol. 9 under date of 2 June 1624.

Council, in fact, took a close interest in Pembrokeshire mines, and when they were informed that tests on lead deposits in Crown property near the coast yielded satisfactory results in silver and lead, they encouraged the Crown tenant, John Canon, to set up leadworks, promising him a patent for further development if he did so. In the meantime, the sheriff of Somerset was directed to send ten or twelve experienced leadworkers from the Mendips to assist Canon in the initial stages of the enterprise.[87]

The lead deposits of Cardiganshire, notably rich and productive in the early years of the seventeenth century, were eagerly sought after. The most conspicuous Welshman in this branch of mineral exploitation was, of course, Sir Hugh Middleton, the opulent silversmith and public benefactor of London. In conjunction with Sir Bevis Thelwall, of the reputable Denbighshire family of Bathafarn, he came to an arrangement with Thomas Russell, a mining expert, to employ his most recent inventions for the extraction of silver and the improved efficiency of the mines, and to recruit workmen of experience and skill.[88] This collaboration proved highly successful and beneficial to both parties, so much so that the King was sufficiently impressed by it as to warn aggressive prospectors not to encroach on Sir Hugh's territory. In one case, James even rejected an offer by an English entrepreneur of £10,000, if he were allowed to supersede Middleton.[89]

This was in direct contrast with the exclusive English company formed by Thomas Best, of Bristol, who leased the lead mines formerly exploited by Sir Richard Lewkenor at Llanafan and Llanfihangel-y-Creuddyn, and hired professional miners from Somerset and Gloucestershire to supervise the smelting of the lead ore. A special furnace was installed to accelerate the conversion of the ore, and teams of horses specially brought to carry the lead to storehouses in Aberystwyth. Once again, a commercially viable business was undermined by a conspiracy, for the imported English miners were said to have combined with some of the local workmen to steal the stored lead.[90]

---

[87] *Ibid*, vol. 152, fol. 12. Undated but endorsed: about Mynes of silver in Wales.
[88] *Ibid*, vol. 169, fol. 3 under date of 2 July 1624.
[89] *Ibid*, vol. 152, fol. 25. Endorsed: His Ma[ts] warrant concerning the Mynes in Wales, dated 8 September 1623.
[90] PRO Star Chamber 8 James I 49/13 and 75/10.

Sir John Wynn of Gwydir was likewise anxious to improve his financial prospects by uncovering a portion of the mineral wealth, which he confidently assumed had been allotted by Providence to the north-west corner of Wales. He started by diligently searching for lead and copper on his estate in the Conway valley,[91] and much to his gratification he found enough lead to justify its exploitation. Not only was the ore free from dross, but it was apparently good in other qualities which persuaded Sir John, in the first flush of anticipation, to announce that two tons of it would produce one ton of lead. Furthermore, his elation led him to convince himself that he would have little if any difficulty in selling lead at home and abroad, particularly in Holland and Spain. On the advice of one Thomas Jones, of Halkin, in Flintshire, he set up a furnace to smelt the ore. This was in 1621, and it required less than twelve months to dispel Sir John's hopes of an assured income from his mine. Unfortunately for him, his venture coincided with a fall in the price of lead, which became one of the cheapest commodities on the market, and this was forcibly brought home to him when he dispatched a consignment of his lead to Middelburg in Zealand, and got a very low price for it from the Dutch merchants of that town. At one time Sir John may have thought of closing the mine, which was far from supplementing his income as he had expected, and was actually swallowing a good proportion of the rents which he received from his tenants. His only consolation in this period of declining fortune was the advice conscientiously doled out to him by his son Maurice, who was a commercial agent in Hamburg, that he should exploit the silver content of the lead ore, or make an effort to find a market in Lisbon and Leghorn, where lead was needed and appreciated, or forget about lead altogether and concentrate on copper mining. There was a slight advance in the price of lead by 1624, which gave some impetus to lead smelting. But Sir John may have paused to consider, when examining the meagre results of his efforts, whether Lewis Bayly, the Bishop of Bangor, had unintentionally summed up the purpose, as well as the productive capacity, of the Gwydir lead mine, when he wrote to him that the Almighty had conferred on the squire of Gwydir the privilege of discovering lead deposits unknown to his ancestors, and that he should offer at least a portion of the lead towards the

[91] Dodd, *The Industrial Revolution in North Wales*, pp. 18–19.

work of repairing Bangor Cathedral. There was enough money in the church funds, the Bishop added, to pay Sir John for three or four tons.[92]

Novel industries had few adherents or practitioners in Wales, where it was assumed that wealth could only be drawn from the expeditious working of the available mineral resources of the country and, when it was feasible, from the manufacture and sale of those consumer goods that could be derived from them without too much effort and expense. An eminent example of this was the wireworks at Tintern, in Monmouthshire, which were so successful and profitable that, according to one report, they not only employed the exceptional number of 600 workmen, but produced wire in sufficient quantities to provide a livelihood for 20,000 people, who used the wire to make various articles for the home market.[93]

But Sir Robert Mansel of Margam, in Glamorgan, refused to be guided by such a cautious attitude towards the hazards of industrial speculation. As one of the younger members of a numerous family, he was alive to the inescapable fact that, if he was to make his way in the world, it would have to be through his own exertions. His experience as a soldier in the Low Countries and as an investor in the East India and the Virginia trading Companies, had strengthened his predisposition to take risks where others chose to take shelter. In 1615, he obtained the monopoly of glassmaking and, at first, was satisfied to confine his activities to London. There he specialized in the manufacture of looking-glasses and employed no more promising a young Welshman than James Howell, later, the author of the *Familiar Letters*, as his agent. Howell was entrusted with the task of travelling on the continent to find the best materials and the most skilled workers in the craft of producing crystal glass; and this gave him the opportunity to acquire foreign languages and a taste for other national cultures.[94]

There followed a period of experimentation, during which Mansel did not conceal his exasperation with the problems that plagued the industrialists of that age. He even went to the length of addressing his complaints to the House of Commons, where he represented Glamorgan, but in such an outburst of

---

[92] *Calendar of Wynn Papers*, pp. 143, 145, 147, 153, 155, 164, 170, 202, 232.
[93] PRO Requests 2 390/486.
[94] See his letters to his father, dated 1 March 1618, and to Dr Francis Mansel, Principal of Jesus College, Oxford, dated 20 March 1618, in his *Familiar Letters*.

bad temper that some of his fellow members protested and told him to hold his tongue. Others, however, were impressed by his bellicose style of oratory and countered with the encouraging cry of 'Let him speak... he speakes like an open hearted Welshman and like a soldier.'[95]

Gradually, Mansel came to the conclusion that one requisite fuel for making glass was coal of the right kind, wherever it was cheap and available. He also thought that he would be able to find this kind of coal in Pembrokeshire and, in addition, would discover in Milford Haven a convenient port for the transportation of the glass to other parts of the kingdom. He was to be disappointed on both counts. There was no lack of coal in the shire, some of the most productive mines being in the parish of Roche, at Nolton[96] and in other localities. Unfortunately, as Mansel was to find to his vexation 'this coale and all the coale in Pembrokeshire is a base stone much inferior to the common cole of England, for it cannot worke any mettal or serveth to any use but for the common fuel of these parts'. Moreover 'the coleworkes in those partes are generally subject to the fall of waters which suddenlie drowneth them and the vaynes of cole doe sone ende after they are founde with greate labor and chardge, whereby ther is greate discouragement to undertake them'. There would be little inclination later on to condemn the anthracite coal of Pembrokeshire, but for Mansel's purpose it contained little gas or smoke, and this failed to provide the necessary hot flame for glassmaking. He chose not to look for the coal he needed, in other parts of the Principality, and left to prosecute his glassmaking in the north of England.[97]

In their periods of relaxation from the pursuit of wealth and property, and the assertion of their authority, peacefully or otherwise, the Welsh gentry could be appreciative of scholarship and the arts as their contemporaries in other countries. Many country houses up and down the Principality reflected the wide cultural background and artistic tastes of the families who lived in them. Lady Anne Morgan, the wife of John Morgan of Pencoed, in Monmouthshire, went to considerable

---

[95] Goodman, *The Court of King James the First*, pp. 56–7.
[96] PRO C 2 James I H 27/35. *See also* HMC *Salisbury (Cecil) MSS*, vol. XVI, p. 120, petition 2414.
[97] The fullest account of Mansel's glassmaking project in Pembrokeshire is given in Godfrey, *The Development of English Glassmaking*, pp. 80–4.

trouble and expense to beautify her home and provide tangible evidence of the catholicity of her cultural interests. She had 'many good books, a paire of virginalles,[98] one Irish harpe, one mappe and diverse pictures, that is, the pictures of Sir William Morgan, late of Pencoed, Sir Walter Montagu and his Lady. Sir John Morgan and the Lady Anne, Sir Edward Randolph and his Lady, and the picture of Mistress Grace Morgan, the pictures of king Henry the Eight and of Queen Elizabeth and others'.[99] The latter, of course, were not original portraits but reproductions made in London and sold throughout the kingdom, for it had become fashionable in the reign of the late Queen to exhibit her portrait as a symbol of loyalty to the Crown.[100] In the case of the Morgan family, the sentiment of fidelity in allegiance would be reinforced by a feeling of national pride in the Welsh affinities of the Tudor dynasty. In Carmarthenshire, John Prothero of Hawksbrook could boast of valuable household furniture, but it was scientific learning that held a special fascination for him. It is to be regretted that a more detailed inventory of his library was not compiled, for he had 'a truncke full of papers of severall sorts, some of them being manuscripts in the mathematicall arts, and the same stood him in a great deale of chardge and paines takinge, some parte whereof had been brought him from beyond seas, and the same the said Mr Prothero did very highlie estimatt'.[101]

Of the gentry in North Wales, it was Sir John Wynn of Gwydir, who showed, to all appearances at least, the most active interest in scholarship and literary matters. The books which he and his son Owain acquired for the library at Gwydir suggest that they would have endorsed the opinions of Sir Edward Herbert, later Lord Herbert of Cherbury, that a good knowledge of governments, manners, religions, the relations between sovereign states and their respective military strength, was indispensable to a gentleman's education.[102] Sir John's collection included Camden's *Brittania*, Sir Walter Ralegh's *Chronicles* and Purchase's *Pilgrimages*. He kept in touch with international and political affairs of the day by reading the

---

[98] That their daughters should learn to play the virginals was thought highly desirable by some of the gentry. For examples see Jones-Pierce, *Clenennau Letters and Papers*, p. 67 and *Calendar of Wynn Papers*, p. 151, no. 967.

[99] PRO C 21 M 1/1.

[100] Strong, *Portraits of Queen Elizabeth*, p. 22.

[101] PRO C 21 L 10/11.

[102] Lee, *The Autobiography of Edward, Lord Herbert*, p. 27.

Mercurius Gallobelgicus and the *Belgicke Pismire*.[103] He also found time to help the cartographer John Speed with his maps of the shires of North Wales, and with his description of Caernarvonshire.[104] His son, also Sir John Wynn, inherited some of his father's exactitude in topographical knowledge. While on a continental tour in 1614, he contracted a fever in Italy and died in Lucca at the age of thirty-one. On his deathbed he made his will and entrusted it to Robert Allen, an English draper in that town, who later recalled that Sir John was so meticulous about the accuracy of his last testament that 'he dyrected this deponent (Allen) how to expresse in true orthographie the names of certain Welsh towns or parishes in the said will mentioned, which otherwise this deponent of himself would not have done but as he, the said Sir John, taught this deponent then to spell the said names'.[105] There may have been pronounced bibliophilic tendencies in the Nannau family also. When Robert, one of Hugh Nannau's sons and a mercer in London, died, he left a library consisting of a Bible worth twelve shillings, as well as many printed books dealing with divinity, physic and surgery, which were not normally the reading material of a Welsh business man in the city of London.[106]

Sir John Wynn the elder was as much at home in Welsh poetry as in English prose, for he was able to discuss the merits of the traditional strict metre forms with his friend Sir William Jones, a Justice of the Common Pleas.[107] In this he showed his attachment to his native culture in its various manifestations, which he shared with many other squires. Their affection for the language was genuine and uninhibited, which was natural since a number of them spoke no other.[108] Sir Edward Herbert's parents thought it imperative that he should learn Welsh well 'to enable me', so he wrote in his autobiography, 'to treat with those of my friends and tenants who understood

---

[103] *The Belgicke Pismire* was a popular tract written and distributed to prejudice its readers against the proposed marriage between Prince Charles and the Infanta of Spain. The author was Thomas Scott, preacher to the English garrison at Utrecht, who published virulent anti-Catholic pamphlets until his assassination by an English soldier in 1626.

[104] *Calendar of Wynn Papers*, p. 160, no. 1014.

[105] PRO C 24 430, pt 1 no. 119.

[106] *Ibid* 463, no. 84.

[107] *Calendar of Wynn Papers*, p. 158, no. 1005.

[108] PRO C 24 562. This refers to a gentleman residing near Dolgellau, in Merionethshire, who knew only Welsh and had to be interrogated through an interpreter.

no other tongue'.[109] This spontaneous and deep-rooted loyalty towards the language explains why so many landed families adhered to the traditional way of patronage, to preserve the national heritage of bardic compositions which had been the quintessence of Welsh culture for centuries.

The cardinal feature of this relationship between patron and bard was that the latter was maintained and given a privileged status in the household of the patron. In return, he addressed adulatory poems to him and celebrated in verse domestic events of significance and interest. The Nannau family could trace their association with household bards as far back as the fourteenth century, and these links were still strong when Hugh Nannau died in 1623 and his bard, Richard Phylip wrote a moving elegy on that occasion. And it is from his compositions and those of other bards, who enjoyed the open-handed hospitality of Nannau, that one learns that Hugh Nannau was imbued so much with the enthusiasm for building characteristic of his period, that he went to great pains and expense to improve and beautify the mansion at Nannau with unusual architectural features, that won the admiration of all who passed that way.[110] In Caernarvonshire, the Glynns of Glynllifon saw no reason for renouncing their cultural upbringing in their unremitting pursuit of money and prestige. On the contrary, Thomas Glynne and his son Sir William Glynne prided themselves on their ability to compose poetry in the strict Welsh metres, and while they lived (Sir William died in 1620), Glynllifon continued to dispense hospitality to the bards who depended so much for their livelihood and welfare on the patronage of the gentry.[111]

Despite the respect shown for age-long cultural practices, the latter were being slowly eroded by changes in attitudes and beliefs. This was inevitable, partly because of the growing appreciation of the benefits of education which, although conditioned by an increasingly English-orientated commercial and political environment, was generally found acceptable as a

---

[109] Lee, *The Autobiography of Edward, Lord Herbert*, p. 20.

[110] Jones, 'The Family of Nannau', 5–13. For the patronage extended by the landed families of Cardiganshire to bards, *see* Roberts, 'Noddi Beirdd yng Ngheredigion', 14–39.

[111] Roberts 'The Glynnes and Wynns of Glynllifon',25–40. For the relations between the Price family of Gogerddan in Cardiganshire and the bards, *see* Robert's 'Noddi Beirdd yng Ngheredigion', 14–39.

means of gaining entry into new fields of individual effort and achievement. There is little doubt that a belief in education for practical ends was spreading throughout Wales at this time. It was reflected in the opinion of a contemporary German traveller and topographer, that the inhabitants were ambitious that their children should enjoy schooling, and that they showed a strong predilection for the study of law as one sure way of attaining success and status.[112]

The few existing Grammar Schools in the Principality offered the younger generation a chance to familiarize themselves with the humanities and, consequently, to find their way, either through the English universities of Oxford or Cambridge or the legal societies in London, to remunerative employment in Church and State, particularly in England. Many Welsh squires, however, were not satisfied with them, not necessarily because they thought their system of instruction defective. They simply preferred schools with an entirely English atmosphere and, occasionally, at an appreciable distance from Wales. John Thomas of Goytre, in Caernarvonshire, sent his niece and heiress to be educated in a school at Ludlow.[113] And Meurig Llywelyn of Pendeulan, in Glamorgan, was so keen on seeing his sons well equipped for successful careers, that he took them to school in Oxford and lived with them there, while the rest of the family stayed at home.[114] A similar notion of the superiority of education and upbringing in England appears to have captivated the father of John Lloyd, who sent him to Yorkshire 'for his better breeding' and was most gratified to observe, when the boy returned home, that he was, 'gentleman-like cladd'.[115] Sir John Wynn also seems to have recognized that there were advantages in sending two of his sons to Westminster and Eton, although the problem as to which university to send them caused much suspense at Gwydir, until Sir John was induced to order the better scholar of the two to pack his bags for Cambridge.[116]

It is likely that many of the young men educated across the border, who came back to Wales, were too influenced by English manners and the constant use of the English language

---

[112] Zeiler, *Itinerarii Galliae et Magnae Britaniae*, pp. 50–6.
[113] PRO C 24 549, pt 11, no. 49. Another source alleges that she was educated in Shrewsbury and Ludlow.
[114] PRO Star Chamber 8 James I 197/3.
[115] PRO C 21 L 5/1. This particular John Lloyd was a native of Denbighshire.
[116] *Calendar of Wynn Papers*, p. 76, no. 464.

to be reintegrated into the society which had formed their earlier character and dictated their ideas. They were inclined to disregard or, at least, not promote with the enthusiasm of their fathers, that cultural heritage and patronage which had distinguished the Welsh gentry for so many centuries. Nevertheless, some considerable time was to elapse before the landed class yielded that privilege and time-honoured responsibility to other social classes and to various institutions and movements within the Principality.

Local politics were, in essence, a running conflict between landed families for dominance, but there were occasions when they were overshadowed by events which intruded abruptly into the constant manoeuvring and scheming of the contending parties, and forced them to think and act on a much wider scale. Such an occasion was the summoning of a Parliament, and the arrival of a writ from London to the sheriffs of the Welsh shires, directing them to arrange that the freeholders of the counties should meet together at a specified time to choose a knight 'girt with a sworde', that is, a properly qualified gentleman, to represent the shire in the House of Commons. It was a signal to forget trivial advantages, reinforce and expand alignments, influence the non-committed, and browbeat the dissident; and, where it was thought necessary or feasible, to ignore the law of the land, if that could help to overthrow the opposing candidate.

By the time the first Stuart King took the reins of English politics into his hands and convened his first Parliament in 1603, the gentry of Wales had had seventy years or so to acclimatize themselves to the atmosphere and the procedures of the House of Commons. On the whole, they had not made their presence felt, nor won recognition as rhetorical or persuasive speakers on the outstanding issues of the day. This may have been due to the fact that they had not been particularly concerned with them; and also that they had not been elected to become intimately involved in Parliamentary disputes which might bring them into confrontation with the Government.

Ascendancy over rivals within the shire, and the assertion of local prestige, was one factor governing the ambition to become a Member of Parliament and, probably, the predominant one, but there were others. Attendance in the House of Commons brought undoubted benefits, not the least being the possibility of forming friendships and alliances with the English gentry, and finding an entry into the cosmopolitan life of seventeenth century London. It was recognized that this helped to broaden the understanding of the Welsh MPs of the outside world and its intricate problems. What was equally important to them was the chance of establishing contacts with the Court and with the imperious, self-confident courtiers and men of affairs, who had it in their power to dispense favours in employment and money. The latter, in their turn, valued complaisance and the tactical advantage of having devoted supporters in the House of Commons, upon whose fidelity they could count if required. In this way William Herbert, Earl of Pembroke, was assured of the vote of the Herbert family who dominated Montgomeryshire in the persons of Sir William Herbert, knight of the shire, and George Herbert, who sat for the borough of Montgomery. They were both cousins of the Earl and looked to him for advancement.[117]

It was a situation which did not commend itself to all Welsh squires. When Sir Roger Mostyn understood that his son, Sir Thomas Mostyn, wished to contest Flintshire for the Parliament of 1624, he pronounced that, if Sir Thomas were elected, it would not benefit him or anyone else and might, indeed, cause him to ignore his own and more immediate interests at home. Sir Roger believed, like some others, that the House of Commons had little say in national affairs, as compared with the gentry who had a great deal to say in local affairs,[118] a point of view that held its ground up to the events which precipitated the Civil War. However, few aspirants to, or holders of, the status of a Member of Parliament subscribed to this opinion. Sir Robert Mansel, who sat for Glamorgan, feared that the aversion of the House of Commons to monopolies might jeopardise his control of glassmaking, but concluded that he had a better chance of protecting his interests personally on the floor of the House. His eloquence on the subject impressed his fellow members, but he also skilfully enlisted the sympathy of the King by advocating military expenditure, to enable

---

[117] Ruigh, *The Parliament of 1625*, p. 130.
[118] *Ibid*, pp. 91–2. A contrary opinion was expressed by John Gruffydd the younger of Llŷn, in Caernarvonshire, who wrote to Sir William Maurice of Clenennau in 1620: 'You knowe best the experience that is obtained in beinge of a parliament, and that every true lover of his countrie should endevoure to do service therein.' Jones-Pierce, *Clenennau Letters and Papers*, p. 113, no. 398.

James to assist his son-in-law, the Elector Palatine Frederick, whom the forces of the House of Austria had evicted from the throne of Bohemia and his ancestral lands in Germany. Similarly, Sir Hugh Middleton, MP for Denbighshire, exploited his position in the Commons, not only to secure the monopoly of the lead mines in Cardiganshire, but also to seek Parliamentary confirmation of the privileges granted to his New River Company in London. He anticipated little hindrance in this matter, since the King himself was a partner in the Company, and the House of Commons would have no reason to oppose the Crown on this particular issue.

An eye to the main chance in gratifying personal as well as family ambitions, and advancing one's fortunes in a world open to opportunistic talents, was generally accepted as a legitimate and satisfactory reason for wishing to enter the House of Commons. But Parliamentary candidature could and did camouflage less commendable motives. What happened in Radnorshire during the elections for the Parliament of 1621 illustrated how a recourse to illegality could subvert a sense of responsibility, when dubious motives were allowed to dictate the actions of local leaders and officials.

According to the complaint of William Vaughan of Llowes, one of the two candidates (and the loser) who contested the election, the sheriff of Radnorshire, Thomas Rea, the under-sheriff, Thomas Phillips and their confederates, including a Doctor of Divinity, Dr Richard Vaughan, agreed amongst themselves that James Price of Mynachty should emerge the victor at all costs and without reference to the genuine wishes of the electors. In the judgment of his opponent, Price had the minimal degree of virtue and aptitude to recommend him for the distinction. Besides, he was at odds with the law 'being a man very muche indebted unto many creditors in divers greate somes of money, and one that of longe tyme hath and still doeth for the same debtes contempteously stande outlawed both before and after judgement at the suites of many severall persons in divers of your Ma^{ts} Cortes of Recorde at Westminster'. Moreover Price, having no lands or goods, 'hath and doeth live and lurke obscurely in secrett and priviledged places in and about your Ma^{ts} Cittie of London'. However, the cardinal objection to him as a candidate was that, 'being very indigent and needy [he] woulde desire a longe Parliament therby to be protected from being arrested for his said debtes'.

Despite these tangible disqualifications, Price's friends and relations (Dr Vaughan being his son-in-law and the under-sheriff his brother-in-law) were said to have devised a scheme to ensure his election; first, by concealing the writ directing that a knight should be chosen for Radnorshire until three days before the actual election in the town of Presteigne; and, secondly, by releasing Dr Vaughan in the countryside on a campaign of intimidation, during which the formidable divine put the fear, not so much of God on this occasion as of the Church, into the hearts of many freeholders by threatening to summon them periodically before the ecclesiastical courts on ill-defined charges and keeping them there at their own expense. To confront him was no joke. When one or two bold spirits in the parish church of Nantmel ventured to question the suitability of Price as an MP, no irate prophet in the Old Testament could have presented a more terrifying picture. 'The said doctor', so said one report, 'being much enraged with fury did then and there come from his seate out of the Chauncell into the bodye of the said churche, spreading forth his armes and handes [and] saye and exclayme with a low voyce in very passionat and threatening manner these and the lyke woordes, vzt, ys ther any man heare that doeth say any thinge against James Price of Monaughty. Lett me see any one that dares oppen his mouth againste him or to give his voyce against him in that cause'. Nobody opened his mouth, but it was alleged that, at least, one hundred of the freeholders there decided privately not to put in an appearance at Presteigne on polling day.

Not content with this strategem, the confederates then threw aside any pretence of respect for the electoral law, by deciding to augment the ranks of genuine freeholders with people who had no valid claim to vote at all;[119] and the irrepressible Dr Vaughan saw to it that these included clergymen without the divine or any other right to take part in the election. By means of these subterfuges, Price was declared to head the poll.[120] The unsuccessful candidate, William Vaughan, not

[119] The fraudulent creation of freeholders without any pretence to that status and the electoral privilege it carried, was quite common at the time. For another example, see Gwynne Jones, 'County Politics and Electioneering 1558–1625', 42–6, which describes the electoral contest between Sir Richard Wynn and John Gruffydd, and how both parties competed in investing other sorts of people, especially their own servants, with the rank of forty shilling freeholders.

[120] PRO Star Chamber 8 James I 288/9.

unreasonably refused to accept the figures after the hands had been counted, and complained to the Star Chamber after Parliament had assembled. It was an error on his part. For when the Star Chamber prudently decided that the case was one for the House of Commons to examine and judge, the news created an uproar on the benches at St Stephens and vehement protests that Vaughan had behaved offensively towards the House 'in flyinge to the Star Chamber with a cause dureinge the parliament which belongs to our jurisdiction'.[121] It was an opportunity for the House to reprimand Vaughan, who was summoned to London to answer for his transgression, and to advertise their independence of the Star Chamber, embodying the Crown's prerogative power, which the Commons were never slow in emphasising at all possible times. But, probably to the relief both of the triumphant Price and the aggrieved Vaughan, the dissolution of Parliament in February 1622 halted all further proceedings.

During the short life of this fourth of James I's Parliaments, one Welsh squire had attracted the attention of the House of Commons for his ready disposition to speak on all kinds of matters. Not even the disclosure that Sir John Trevor, MP for Denbighshire, and Theophilus Field, the Bishop of Llandaff, were not entirely strangers to corrupt practices,[122] occupied so much space in the Journals of the House and other reports on its proceedings, as did the views of Sir James Perrot, the loquacious Member for the borough of Haverfordwest.[123] Sir James had been a member of previous Parliaments, and both the House of Commons and the Court of St James knew of his undeviating attachment to the cause of the Protestant religion and the confounding of its enemies. But it was in this Parliament that his eloquence and outward demonstration of piety impressed his fellow members and, incidentally, led him to commit an indiscretion which even they could not exonerate completely on the grounds of his impenitent Protestant fervour.

When it was decided by the House that the persistent gap in the King's revenue should be partially filled with money issuing from the sequestrated lands of recusants, Sir James was

[121] Notestein, Relf and Simpson, *Commons Debates 1621*, pp. 172–3.
[122] Both were named in the House as being at one time implicated in the notorious system of bribery, which was the principal accusation levied against the alleged corruption of the Lord Chancellor, Francis Bacon.
[123] Lloyd summarizes and comments on Perrot's speeches and activities in his *The Gentry of South-West Wales* pp. 104–7.

nominated member of the committee set up to enforce that resolution. In his enthusiasm, he injudiciously granted a warrant to certain persons to examine the records of the Exchequer for information on recusant property. This drew an angry expostulation from Sir Henry Spiller, an official of the Exchequer, that Perrot had acted without consulting the committee, and had hardly shown exemplary discretion in the choice of people to look through financial records, since one of them 'had been free of almost all the prisons of the town', possibly, a charitable way of saying that he had been something more than a casual visitor to them. The Chancellor of the Exchequer, Sir Fulke Greville, finally ruled that Sir James had undoubtedly exceeded the conditions of his commission by ignoring the committee of which he was, after all, only an ordinary member like the others. Neither did Greville refrain from adding an admonition, which may have annoyed the Member for Haverfordwest by its supercilious tone, that his censurable failure to observe the procedures and the specific authority of a House of Commons committee should be salutary warning to all other members not to be guilty of a similar misdemeanour.[124]

Whether, as a result of their preoccupation with material gains and personal credit, the landed gentry of Wales became men of considerable substance, thus belying the popular belief that they remained a relatively poor class, is an open question. There is documentary evidence that an appreciable number of them acquired wealth, which placed them on an equal financial footing with their compeers in other parts of the kingdom. Hugh Gwyn of Llanrwst, in Caernarvonshire, had money, plate and household goods to the value of £6,000 in addition to the £700 a year paid to him by his tenants.* He was certainly in the comfortable position of being able to offer a liberal dowry of £1,200 with the hand of his daughter Jane in marriage, and it was the gallant but aberrant Thomas, the son of Thomas Prys of Plas Iolyn, who secured both prizes.[125] Sir William Herbert of Swansea died in 1609, leaving behind

---

[124] *Proceedings and Debates of the House of Commons in 1620 and 1621*, vol. 1, p. 144.
* Professor A. H. Dodd estimated (1952) that £4500 in the early seventeenth century was roughly equivalent to £5,000 in our money. See his *Studies in Stuart Wales*, p. 2.
[125] PRO Star Chamber 8 James I 235/11.

property worth £10,000, besides ready money, plate and jewels estimated at £7,000. Much of this inheritance was bequeathed to Sir John Herbert, the junior Secretary of State, and it enabled him to assign a respectable legacy to his wife upon his demise in 1617.[126] Rice Rhydderch of Laugharne in Carmarthenshire must have been exceptionally wealthy for a man of his rank. Becoming acquainted with an English gentleman, Sir John Kennedy of Tunbridge, in Kent, he proposed to sell him his estate in Wales and, in exchange, purchase some portion of Kennedy's lands. The fact that Rhydderch could contemplate paying as much as £11,000 in this transaction singled him out as a person enjoying enormous credit or possessed of an unusual amount of cash and securities in addition to land.[127] Even Thomas Williams, a squire residing in Ystradffin, a remote district in Carmarthenshire, could boast of having property that brought him £200 a year; also jewels which, with furniture and other household accessories, could have realized as much as £2,000.[128] And Sir Henry Jones of Abermarlais, in the same county, had sufficient income to pay an annuity of more than £300 to his mother during her widowhood, and after her marriage to Sir William Maurice of Clenennau.[129]

The estate of John Salisbury of Bachymbyd, in Denbighshire, came to about £2,000, but this gentleman could also survey with pride other tangible tokens of his opulence. He owned eight geldings, two horses and two mares, three nags, three breeding mares and three colts, side by side with large numbers of cattle and sheep. Inside his house he could handle a good store of plate and silver, including a white silver salt cellar, three white silver candlesticks, a dozen silver spoons and a gilt bowl. And it would afford him great pleasure at times, no doubt, to wear his rapier and dagger gilded with gold or silver complete with girdle and hangers of pearl, and silver buckles and hooks.[130] Thomas ap Morris of Aber, in the same county, with £3,000 in jewels, gold, silver and household stuff, was accounted a most wealthy knight and accorded every respect until he succumbed to senility, and gave his sons by his first marriage an opportunity to exploit and rob him,

---

[126] PRO C 2 James I H 7/29.
[127] PRO C 24 443, pt 1, no. 44.
[128] PRO Star Chamber 8 James I 241/11.
[129] PRO C 21 M 44/12.
[130] PRO C 24 377, pt 11, no. 101.

and chase his second wife back to Anglesey.[131] And Sir Richard Price of Gogerddan, in Cardiganshire, was reckoned to have a personal estate of £6,000 and an annual rental of £700.[132] Such examples could be multiplied and, in their light, it is highly questionable whether one contemporary opinion, which held that it was rare to meet with a Welsh squire possessing land to the value of £40, corresponded to the actual financial position of the gentry in Wales.[133]

It would not be irrelevant, in this context, to refer to an event in the House of Commons in 1621. Towards the end of the session, after the House had acceded to the King's wishes in the matter of a subsidy, James expressed his thanks to those members who had expedited the passage of the bill and, particularly, to 'those Gentlemen what serve for the country of Wales, who were soe desirous that this free guift might be to his Majestys most advantage, as they willingly relinquished all pretences to precedents of former favour or dispensacions for the time of payment, and most readily and dutifully joyned with the rest of the Kingdome in the speedie leavie therof'.[134] These 'dispensacions' were an ancient custom which stipulated that no new subsidy could be collected in the Principality until previous subsidies or mises had been fully accounted for. The subsidies granted in 1610 were still in the process of being collected, and the Welsh members of the House would have been within their rights if they had demanded a strict observance of this immunity. They chose not to do so and voted to suspend it when the House proceeded to discuss the King's request for money.

This may have been a sudden detonation of patriotic fervour: Catholic and Spanish armies were victorious on the continent, and the future of Protestantism looked bleak; the King was visibly shaken by the flight of his daughter and her husband, the Elector Palatine, from their beautiful capital of Heidelberg. Whatever the reason, it is difficult to believe that these Welsh

---

[131] PRO Star Chamber 8 James I 307/4.

[132] PRO C 21 E 7/12.

[133] This was the rather superficial observation made by Major General James Berry who was put in charge of Wales by Cromwell in 1655–6. *See* Dodd, *Studies in Stuart Wales*, pp. 2 and 14.

[134] HMC Buccleuch and Queensberry MSS (Montagu House), vol. 111, p. 224. His Majestys message about the subsidy, under date of December 1621. *See also* Notestein, Relf and Simpson, *Commons Debates 1621*, vol. IV, p. 145 and vol. VII, p. 578.

gentry would have agreed to waive such a financial concession and commit themselves, and the freeholders they represented, to an additional fiscal burden if they had not had the means to discharge this voluntary obligation.

4

The King's needs and Welsh resources

As the ruler of an impoverished and isolated kingdom like Scotland, James I had lived nearer to the poverty line than most of the European monarchs of his day. It was a situation that offended his sense of personal dignity and his conception of a ruler as being the fount, not only of authority and justice, but of reward for meritorious service to the Crown. He despised parsimony in a King as being totally at variance with his exalted idea of royal patronage. He had also learnt, in common with some of his contemporaries, that it could be dangerous. There was nothing so likely to breed active opposition and discontent among the nobility and administrative hierarchy of a state, upon whom a monarch relied for the maintenance of his prerogative powers, than a failure to win their good will and loyalty by a judicious distribution of gifts, offices and favours. James had shown some dexterity in procuring the benevolence, even the friendship, of some of the landed magnates of Scotland with his limited resources. It had been a drain on the latter, so heavy a drain that he had had no objection to placing himself in a position analogous to that of the recipients of his bounty. For he too had been the pensioner of the Queen of England.[1]

No sooner was he crowned in London than he reacted most vigorously against many years of enforced financial abstinence. His journey from the Scottish border to the capital had opened his eyes to the affluence of his English subjects, while his inheritance of the territorial estates and Customs revenues of the Crown presented him with the opportunity of indulging his long frustrated taste for extravagance. He took it with both

---

[1] By the terms of the Anglo-Scottish treaty signed at Berwick in July 1586, James was to receive a pension of £4,000 from Elizabeth. *See* Wilson, *King James VI and I*, p. 72. Elizabeth also assisted him to meet expenses incurred by his marriage to Anne of Denmark. For his relations with Scottish nobles *see ibid* p. 115.

hands. There followed uncontrolled spending on clothes and jewels; the number of household and court officials multiplied at an almost vertiginous rate, as did the King's bills for paying and feeding them; entertainments and masques were organized and staged with a bland indifference to costs. One of these had a distinctly Welsh flavour, although it was not to the taste of some Welshmen at the Court. In January 1618, Prince Charles, who had succeeded his dead brother Henry as Prince of Wales, gave a masque at Whitehall on Twelfth Night. It was a dismal failure although the Earl of Buckingham, the King's favourite, had danced in it; and it had also led to a diplomatic uproar, because of the heated protest of the French Ambassador that he had received a colder welcome to the entertainment than his Spanish and Venetian colleagues. To mollify the disconsolate Prince and the irritated diplomat, it was decided to give a repeat performance a month later, and to embellish the masque with 'som few additions of goats and Welsh speeches sufficient to make an Englishman laugh and a Welshman cholerique'. This time, the masque was a resounding success. 'It was much better liked then Twelvth Night by reason of the new conceites and ante-masks and pleasant merry speeches made to the King by such as counterfeyted Welshmen and wisht the Kinges comyne into Wales.' James probably enjoyed the performance but ignored the invitation.[2]

The Treasury was so ransacked to gratify the avarice of favourites and others who presumed on the King's liberality that, within a short time, James had lavished money gifts to the value of £68,000 or so, and awarded a further £30,000 in pensions.[3] There were, indeed, occasions when his prodigality appeared to be nothing short of an addiction. When in 1604, a Spanish embassy arrived in London to treat for peace, not only did he bestow chains of gold on them but, as one observer wrote: 'He hath given away more plate than Queen Elizabeth did in her whole reigne.'[4] No Treasury could have survived such systematic pillage. By 1608, James had accumulated debts

---

[2] PRO State Papers Domestic, James I 1611–18, vol. 96, fol. 46b. Nathaniel Brent to Sir Dudley Carleton, dated 21 February 1617–18. *Ibid* fol. 51, Gerrad Herbert to the same, dated 22 February 1617–18; and *Ibid* Nathaniel Brent to the same, dated 7 March 1617–18.

[3] Prestwich, *Cranfield*, p. 14.

[4] PRO State Papers Domestic, James I 1603–10, vol. 8A, fol. 58b. Dudley Carleton to John Chamberlain, dated 27 August 1604.

of about £600,000,[5] and was faced with the unpalatable fact that his coffers were after all, as one of his courtiers fancifully described, a cistern that could be more easily drained than filled.

Long before this belated exposure of the King's irresponsibility in matters of finance, his subjects in England and Wales had been called upon to extricate him from his difficulties, which had been anticipated by the Archbishop of York in a letter to Sir Robert Cecil.

His Majesty in Scotland lived like a noble and worthy king of small revenues in comparison because he wisely foresaw that *expensae* should not exceed *recepta*, which I fear His Highnes does not in England, but not minding his yearly *recepta* and *Recipienda* (although great yet not infinite) yields almost to every mans petition. If this should continue, this kingdom will not serve but that His Majesty, contrary to his princely nature, must be compelled to be burdensome and grievous to his most loyal and obedient servants.[6]

The first indication that James was feeling the pinch of his extravagance came in July 1604, when Privy Seal letters were addressed to a selected number of the more comfortably off among the landed and urban communities, asking them for a voluntary loan. This was no innovation, for the late Queen had made similar requests when she had been hard pressed to meet her liabilities. However, it must have surprised many that the King should have needed ready money within a year or two of his accession. The general feeling of good will and optimism which attended the beginning of the reign had not yet evaporated, and the response gratified James. The loan realized almost £112,000, to which the Principality contributed £3,485 in sums ranging from £525 in Glamorgan to £105 in Anglesey. This was quite a substantial amount of cash to transfer from private pockets to the royal purse, particularly as only 119 individuals in Wales were involved. It may also be illustrative of the distribution of wealth within the twelve shires and Monmouthshire, that whereas four persons in

[5] Prestwich, *Cranfield*, p. 16.
[6] HMC *Salisbury (Cecil) MSS*, vol. XVI, pp. 220–1. Matthew Hutton, Archbishop of York to Lord Cecil, dated 10 August 1604.

Radnorshire disbursed £100 between them, eighteen in Flintshire were invited to contribute £485.[7]

The work of collecting the loan, however, did not proceed without a hitch. In Denbighshire, £210 were paid by eight people, but it would appear that the Privy Council had originally issued their letters to twenty. Some persons had ignored them while others had gone to the extent of mortgaging their property to pay. It was also debatable whether Sir John Salisbury of Llewenni, who had been appointed collector, had accounted to the Treasury for all the money received by him. His explanation that, when in London he had been told not to hand over the sums subscribed by those who could ill afford them, was accepted with considerable reservation, the more so as he had somehow omitted to give receipts to the lenders, or so it was said.[8]

The loan of 1604 did little to ease the financial embarrassment of the Crown, and it became increasingly difficult to effect a compromise between what James felt he owed to his friends and servants and what he unquestionably owed to his creditors. The King may have regretted his rather unseasonable magnanimity in turning down the offer of the House of Commons, in their first session of the reign, to grant him a subsidy. When the time came to repay the loan of 1604 and other debts, he was glad enough to accept two subsidies in 1606, and even tried to persuade the House to increase them to three. The assessment and collection of subsidies, however, was a complicated and protracted business, and was usually spread over a number of years. Since austerity seemed to be the last solution that the King's ministers, with the exception of Cecil, would think of urging on the self-willed monarch, other means had to be devised to keep insolvency at arm's length.

Wales could scarcely hope to escape the scrutiny of hard-pressed Exchequer officials casting around for expedients to raise money. It was only a matter of time before they realized that there was one special tax, which its inhabitants could be legitimately called upon to pay. This was the Mise, traditionally payable by the Principality upon the demise or change of monarch, and which had been levied since the reign of

[7] PRO State Papers Domestic, James I 1603–10, fols 120–79. Books of loans lent to his Majestie. The Welsh counties are dealt with on fols 164–179.
[8] PRO Star Chamber 8 James I 198/5.

Henry VII. The belated discovery of the tax may have been due to the fact that it had not been imposed since the accession of Elizabeth, and the intervening forty-five years led to some uncertainty as to the correct procedure for assessing the Mise. The commissioners and others appointed to supervize its collection were given a free hand in the matter; but one method employed was to consult ancient assessment rolls and invite the oldest inhabitants in the shires to draw upon their recollection of previous assessments.

The reception given to the Mise was mixed, and the commissioners soon found themselves treading a thorny path in some localities. At Holt, in Denbighshire, they were definitely snubbed. The inhabitants of that borough made it quite plain to them that by their charter they were free from any obligation to pay the tax, and that any challenge to their immunity would recoil on the heads of those foolish enough to attempt it.[9] At the other end of Wales, in Monmouthshire, it was almost dangerous to demand the Mise in open daylight in some places. Rather than risk personal injury by levying it on the lands and goods of the tenants in the Lordship of Rhymni, whose violence was a byword in the county, the under-sheriff, Thomas Powell, resorted to the safer tactics of distraining upon their cattle at night.[10]

In Radnorshire, the Mise was unequivocally denounced by Brian Crowther, a Justice of the Peace, who was also a prominent counsellor in the Court of the Marches at Ludlow. He did so while he was sitting on the bench at the Quarter Sessions held in Presteigne. 'Intendinge in a vayne and popular manner', as one of his critics alleged, 'to gaine to himself the good wills of the said countrey and to bring only hatred and slander to the proceedings of the said Commissioners, to the manifest disturbance and interruption of your Ma[ts] service, and with no small daunger of some more perillous consequence, he did animate and encourage the countrey not to yield to the payment of tallage or mizes, deliveringe openly in his words and speeches, due or payable unto your Highness.'

Crowther argued that the King should have claimed a Mise immediately after his accession, and that by not doing so, he had forfeited it. Moreover, Radnorshire had not received a free pardon, as was customary at the beginning of a new reign, and

[9] PRO E 178 5088 3 James I and 4 James I.
[10] PRO E 134 7 James I Mich. 13.

had continued to pay arrears of amercements, fines and rents when these should have been cancelled by the pardon.

The closing passages of Crowther's protest were most outspoken, for he was reported to have declared, 'very scornfully and seditiously that if your Matie would looke to have customes performed to you, you should likewise performe for your part what belonged. By which speeches and perswasions of the said Crowther, the country did then and doth now generally refuse to pay any Mizes at all'.[11]

The sum realized by the Mise fell far short of the sanguine expectations of the Treasury. It had been estimated that if the Principality responded, as custom and loyalty demanded it should, then North Wales would contribute about £3,500 and South Wales a little over £2,000. To make payments easier, it had been conceded that the money could be paid over in six instalments between Midsummer 1606 and Michaelmas 1608, but this made little difference. When the date of the final instalment arrived, it was found that only about half of the total sum of £5,653, anticipated by the Treasury had been received in London.[12]

If this was a source of disappointment and irritation to the Lord Treasurer, the Earl of Dorset, he might have called to mind one very pertinent fact. The Mise had been imposed on the people of Wales when a number of them had not finished paying their share of the Parliamentary subsidies granted to the late Queen as far back as 1601.[13] One of the collectors of that grant in Cardiganshire, Edward Vaughan, declared in a petition that the poverty of the shire made it impossible for him to collect the £111 odd due as first payment.[14] To find sufficient cash to discharge so many fiscal liabilities concurrently was a heavy burden on what was a thinly populated and poor country.

That evasion and deception should have been practised was not at all surprising. In Carmarthenshire, John Lloyd of Llanllawddog parish was rated for £8 in land and assessed at

[11] PRO Star Chamber 8 James I 202/23.
[12] PRO State Papers Domestic, James I 1603–10, vol. 57, fol. 100. Wallis, A Certificate of the Mizes, 27 September 1610.
[13] The Queen had been granted four subsidies and eight fifteenths, which were expected to realize some £300,000 in the money of those days.
[14] PRO State Papers Domestic Supplementary (SP 46) vol. 68, fol. 21. Petition of Edward Vaughan to the Earl of Dunbar, Chancellor of the Court of Exchequer, dated 11 April 1606.

21s 4d, but he contrived to avoid payment by arranging somehow that the money should be levied on other inhabitants of his parish. When charged with irregularity, he declared that it was customary for some of the parishioners who escaped taxation, to contribute towards the payments of those who did not 'in such sorte as had bene formerly a use amongst them to do by consent amongst themselves'. As Lloyd and his brother were said to have a bad name for extorting the illegal *comortha* or 'voluntary' gift of sheep from the more submissive of their neighbours, such an explanation must have sounded somewhat fanciful.[15]

Other temptations were not lacking, as had happened in the case of David Gwyn, of Breconshire, who had been entrusted with conveying a portion of the 1601 subsidy, collected in that county, to London; and who, it was alleged, had taken the first available ship to the continent with the money. If true, it was an uncharitable deed as well, for by the law of the land, the unfortunate collector, who had consigned the cash to Gwyn, was expected to make good the loss out of his own pocket.[16] The business of sending money to London from the outlying regions of the kingdom was always a hazardous one, but even as regards the despatch of cash destined for the Treasury, the Government would seem to have allowed the local authorities to decide how best to ensure its safe arrival.

The auditors of the Treasury had barely had time to reckon up the disappointing results of the Mise, when the King confronted the country with another demand on its money and patience. It happened that in 1609, his eldest son, Prince Henry, was fifteen years of age and eligible for knighthood. Both feudal custom and common law allowed that on this occasion, as on that of the marriage of the King's eldest daughter, Crown tenants holding their land by military or knight service and by socage were under an obligation to contribute towards defraying the expenses of the ceremony and the celebrations that followed. It was more than a hundred years since Henry VII had demanded the Aid for his eldest son, Prince Arthur, and if the ordinary citizens of the realm had long forgotten its

---

[15] PRO Star Chamber 8 James I 116/11. But according to an entry in BM Stowe MSS, no. 397, fol. 17, the charge against him was dismissed for want of proof.

[16] PRO State Papers Domestic Supplementary (SP 46), vol. 67, fols 73 and 74.

existence, the fiscal officers of the Crown had certainly not. There was a wealth of precedents to authenticate the claim, from the Plantagenets to the Tudors, and the commissioners nominated to enforce it were carefully briefed on the legality of the Aid. But James had reigned long enough by this time to realize that even his law-abiding subjects could become restive and un-cooperative under the pressure of constant exactions. The commissioners were therefore instructed that they should try to persuade the tenants concerned to agree to a free and easy valuation of their lands for assessment, and only empanel a jury to determine the amount when sweet reasonableness proved no match for obstinacy.[17]

There seems to have been some doubt at first whether commissions should be issued to collect the Aid in Wales, possibly because of a reluctance to impose what could appear to the Welsh to be another unwelcome Mise so soon after the vexations of the previous one. Or, possibly, because of the much greater difficulty in identifying the two tenures of military service and socage in the Principality, where there were better opportunities of concealing them or changing their nature.[18] Eventually, it was decided to send the commissions out. Otherwise, it was argued, suspicions would be aroused that there existed hidden motives for not doing so, and it would become correspondingly harder to find persons who would be ready to act as commissioners.

Unlike the Mise of 1606, the Prince's Aid only affected a minority of people in the Principality – Crown tenants, the Bishops and the corporate bodies of certain boroughs. Nevertheless, resistance to it was sometimes strong. There was little disposition in Welsh counties, in contrast to some English shires, to regard it as an occasion to show affection for the young Prince.

In Radnorshire, the borough of New Radnor presented an awkward problem to the commissioners, since it had been

---

[17] PRO State Papers Domestic, James I 1603–10, vol. 43, fols 177–8. Instructions given to his Ma[ts] Commissioners for the levyeinge of Ayde to make the most heigh and noble Prince Henry his Ma[ts] eldest sonne, knight. February 1609.

[18] The body of commissioners in each shire was to explain to those assessed for the Aid that it was grounded on ancient authority and the common law of England. In this particular case too the investigations they were called upon to carry out would not prove too difficult, since it had been decided that everyone holding by knight's fee would have to pay twenty shillings, and that the same sum should be charged for every £20 of land held in socage.

granted in fee farm to the bailiff and burgesses by the late Queen, in return for an annual rent of £37 18s. 'And therefore', one report stated, 'the said Baylief and Burgencies (*sic*) are very unwillinge to cesse or rate any mize there, alleadgeinge that they are informed that they ought not to pay any Mize' – in this case, the Prince's Aid. But the commissioners were not without hope that instinctive loyalty to the Crown would ultimately triumph over municipal pretensions, however legitimate. It was claimed that:

> Thomas Myles, now Baylief there, hath done his best endevor to perswade the inhabitants to be contented to pay this Mize. But the multitude of the inhabitants will not assent thereunto. Nevertheles, some of the best sorte of the gentlemen in that libertye desyre to be resolved from your Lordshyppe. And yf your Lordshyppe shall thincke by law that they ought to pay Mizes, notwith-standinge their said fee fearme, that then the said Corporacon would with all humblenes submytte themsylves thereunto.[19]

In Caernarvonshire, the commissioners did their best to dispel the notion that the Aid was a burden to be shuffled off by any subterfuge that could be invented. A hundred pounds, fairly apportioned between the hundreds of the county, they thought, would not be too much to ask for.[20] Moreover, they were ready to allow that all socage tenants should pay only one sum for all the lands they held within the shire, irrespective of the extent and value of their separate holdings.[21] These concessions fell on as barren a soil as any that could be found

---

[19] PRO E 101 Bundle 526, no. 17. Undated but endorsed: 'A letter from certen of the Commissioners there assigned for the taxing of the Mizes due unto the late Princes highnes sent unto the right hon. Sir Julius Caesar.' The local dignitaries and burgesses were summoned to appear with proofs of their exemption from mises. PRO State Papers Domestic Supplementary (SP 46), vol. 70, fol. 72. Sir Henry Williams, Robert Mill and Edward Carne to the Bailiff, Aldermen and Burgesses of New Radnor, dated 25 October 1613.

[20] *Calendar of Wynn Papers*, p. 81, no. 500. Sir William Thomas to Sir John Wynn, dated 31 May 1609 and p. 98, no. 620, the same to the same, dated 31 May 1613.

[21] Jones-Pierce, *Clenennau Letters and Papers*, p. 72. The Privy Council to the High Sheriff and Commissioners in Carnarvonshire, dated 24 March 1608–9. *See also* State Papers Domestic, James I 1603–10, vol. 44, fol. 96, dated 19 March 1608–9.

in the mountains of Snowdonia. After two years, little money had been collected, and a letter addressed to the commissioners from London was, not surprisingly perhaps, more of a supplication than an admonition. They were asked to redouble their efforts to bring in the money, and were solemnly promised that if they succeeded, their endeavours would be brought to the attention of Prince Henry who, it could safely be said, would never forget their service in the matter.[22]

It was not only the laity who felt disinclined or unable to put their hands in their pockets. The Bishops of Bangor and St Asaph, too, were of that number who refused to consider the Aid as a matter of priority, and remained impervious to the entreaties of the harassed commissioners. The Bishops of St David's and Llandaff, however, were willing to pay, but their example was lost on their flocks.

In the shires of South Wales, active hostility and passive resistance would seem to have combined to make the work of the commissioners both arduous and unproductive. The situation was described by Sir Edward Carne, the general collector of the Aid, in a letter which held out little hope that much money would be forthcoming from one end of the six counties to the other.

> Ffirst I will begin to acquaint your Honor [he wrote to Sir Julius Caesar, the Chancellor of the Exchequer] of one proceeding in Glamorgan, which is the county wherein I dwell. The Commissioners, standing upon the direct points of his Ma[ts] instructions, would not agree to rate or compound with any but His Highnes immediate tenaunts, in which county his Ma[tie] hath but one little mannor which is parcell of the Duchie of Lancaster, and all the residue of the county is held by my Lord of Pembroke except two or three mannors which the Erle of Worcester hath. Soe that the whole some that is rated in the said county is but three score and seaventeene pounds, whereof six knights have rated themselves in five pounds a peece, and the cleargie in fourteene pounds. Where if they (the Commissioners) had held a course to rate all the Earle of Pembrokes freeholders and knights fees held of him, it would have amounted to the som of two or three hundred

[22] Jones-Pierce, *Clenennau Letters and Papers*, p. 75, no. 258, dated 31 July 1611.

pounds at the least.[23] Brecon being the next county adjoyning wherein the King hath very many lardg and goodly mannors is rated to a lesse some then one hundred markes. Pembrokeshire to some hundred pounds. The Commissioners for Carmarthen have not spared any freeholders within the County, soe that there is rated some eight score pounds, which is a reasonable some in soe barren a country. The Commissioners for Radnor and Cardigan have not as yett rated any some on their counties, for that they expect new commissions, as by my Lord Treasurers and your Honors letters this last summer hath been promised them and the other shires; the expectation of which commissions hath been a meane of very slow proceedinge of the service in all these counties; for, as yet, I have not received one peny but some ffourtye pounds or thereabouts out of Breconshire, which hath been paid me within these six dayes, neythyr had I the rowles untill the beginning of this month whereby I might collect them.[24]

In the circumstances, the officials of the Exchequer had no alternative but to brace themselves against further procrastination on the part of those in Wales who could not escape their liability to the tax. And as the years passed without much visible improvement in the situation, other changes supervened to make it unlikely that the mood of the Welsh would change materially, at least to the benefit of the Exchequer.

---

[23] This criticism raised the ghost of an old dispute between the King's tenants of the Lordship of Glamorgan and the Earl of Pembroke, to whose father the Lordship had been granted in the reign of Edward VI and confirmed by Elizabeth. The first Earl had claimed that by virtue of that grant and as lord of Cardiff Castle, he had a prescriptive right to all aids and mises. The tenants, at least those of them who were bold enough to challenge the Earl on legal grounds, argued that despite the grant, the seignory or ultimate lordship still remained with the Crown, and that all aids and mises were inalienable pecuniary rights of the monarch, to whom they should be paid and not to the Earl. Carne's attitude suggests that he believed the tenants to be in the right. The 2nd Earl of Pembroke's influence at the Court and the King's avowed friendship for him may have dissuaded the commissioners from stirring up possible trouble for themselves by levying the Prince's Aid on these tenants. See *Cardiff Borough Records*, vol. III, pp. 72–8.

[24] PRO State Papers Domestic, James I 1603–10, vol. 49, fol. 29. Edward Carne to Sir Julius Caesar, dated 8 November 1609.

Prince Henry himself died in 1612, and the King ordered that the proceeds of the Aid should be paid to his youngest son, the fifteen-year-old Prince Charles, destined within a few years to take the place of his dead brother as Prince of Wales. Since the proceeds were practically non-existent, it seemed possible that the Prince would grow to manhood without seeing a penny of the money, as far as the Principality was concerned. Sir Edward Carne still remained in charge of the Aid in South Wales, but the passage of years must have almost extinguished his hope of discharging a thankless task with some degree of success. Pembrokeshire, he recorded dolefully, had not contributed a penny. Of the two subordinate collectors in Cardiganshire, one had dutifully handed over his portion; but the other, and a deputy-sheriff at that, was keeping a tight grip on the money that he had managed to extract. And as for Carmarthenshire, he added 'some collectors pay and some pay not, by reason of the multitude of them, for in every parish there is apointed a collector, but I hope we shall do reasonably well for that shire. But in Radnorshire I cannott receive one penny'.[25]

Sir Edward had written more optimistically of Carmarthenshire than of any other county, but he had underestimated the intransigence of some of its inhabitants. In 1621, there were still twenty persons there who, by skilful manipulation of evidences, had fought off every attempt to force them to pay the Aid.[26]

On 22 September 1613, Sir John Digby, the English Ambassador to Spain, sat down to write a confidential letter to the King of England. With the connivance of a highly placed official in the Spanish Department of Foreign Affairs, he had been able to peruse the latest despatch from the Spanish Ambassador in London and, what is more, to summarize its contents. He now proceeded to transcribe and translate his notes without bothering to moderate the bluntness of some of that ambassador's observations.

For matter of treasure and money [the latter had written] there was never any King of England so poore as this at

---

[25] PRO State Papers Domestic Supplementary (SP 46), vol. 70, fol. 93. Edward Carne to William Hill, Auditor of Wales, dated 12 May 1614.
[26] *Ibid*, fol. 199. Edward Carne to Sir James Fullerton, dated 10 February 1620–1.

the present. For besydes that very muche of his rents is impayred, he oweth five millions (? crowns), muche whereof he hathe borowed upon Privy Seales of all his subjects that have been able to lende him. As likewise of diverse merchants strangers living in London. He hathe allsoe solde many offices and titles of Honour of Knightes, Baronetts by which he hathe raysed a greate summe of money. But hath spent all without doing anything of consideration.

His extravagance had generated much criticism and hostility in the country at large and so 'the King hath now resolved to sell his parks and forests together with their herds of deer'. 'Fyrste, yt is sayd that the deare shall be solde which will be above a hundred thousand; then the wood and afterward the fee simple of the ground. All which will amount to above three millions.' It was not only James's money problems that had forced him to take this step. The Spanish Ambassador also wrote that 'he (the King) groweth fatt, so that hee is not able to followe his violent hunting without some paine, although his greatest pleasure'.[27] The fact that he had just managed to survive two hunting accidents may also have convinced him that it was time to moderate his passion for that sport.

In any case, when Parliamentary subsidies and financial expedients like forced loans failed to provide for the needs of government and royal debts, there remained the alternative of exploiting the resources of Crown property and, when absolutely necessary, of selling portions of it. Some of the King's Tudor predecessors had done so, but, although at the time of his accession, the Crown's patrimony had been reduced in extent, it was still considerable enough to produce a third of the King's revenue. Faced with the necessity of taking drastic action to salvage some remnants of the Crown's dignity and credit, James and his ministers proceeded to place a number of royal estates on the market. As long as Cecil, who became Lord Treasurer in 1608, retained that office, the disposal of Crown lands in this manner became so regular a method of raising money for the famished Exchequer, that it realized as much as £400,000 before his death four years later.[28]

---

[27] PRO State Papers Foreign, Spain (SP 94), vol. 20, pt 1, fols 81–6. Sir John Digby to James I, dated 22 September 1613.
[28] Prestwich, *Cranfield*, p. 30.

It was not without its danger and, in some cases, it was to prove prejudicial to the revenue of the Crown. This happened in the Duchy of Lancaster, where so much property was sold that not enough remained to pay the salaries of the Duchy officials.[29]

To extract a good economic return from Crown lands, where these were not sold, it was necessary to examine the actual state of their management in order to see where improvements could be introduced, abuses eradicated, restrictive and customary practices modified, and the price of land itself, as well as rents, made to reflect the rise in the value of property, which had been a feature of the economic life of the kingdom since the middle of the sixteenth century. This called for the employment of astute and experienced surveyors and land commissioners, who could be relied upon to work in the interests of the Crown, without unduly antagonizing Crown tenants and offending the landed gentry, to whom the intrusion of Government officials of any kind was generally suspect.

Those who were sent to Wales soon found themselves in troubled waters. On the face of it, their task was not a particularly exacting one. The country was small, and since the rents and revenues within the twelve shires and Monmouthshire produced only about £4,600 out of the £66,870 annually received by the Exchequer from all the Crown estates in England and Wales,[30] they might have reasonably expected that their labours would not prove too complicated and protracted. Any such opinion quickly disappeared when they got down to their main task, which was to investigate whether the extent of the King's property had been diminished and the King's revenues correspondingly curtailed, and to identify the party or parties responsible for this deliberate filching of Crown estate.

The general practice of the land commissioners was to empanel a jury of freeholders to locate, and establish the King's title to, pieces of land which were known to have been part and parcel of Crown property, but had been surreptitiously appropriated by people who had no valid claim to them. The jury were not only put on oath to declare their

---

[29] PRO State Papers Domestic, James I 1611–18, vol. 96, fol. 20. Edward Harwood to Sir Dudley Carleton, dated 7 February 1617–18.

[30] PRO State Papers Domestic, James I 1603–10, vol. 46. 'A booke of all his Maties mansions houses, castles, parkes, fforests etc.' May 1609.

knowledge, but were sometimes required to beat the bounds of the King's property, to see whether there had been any encroachments on it and to identify the persons guilty of them. It soon became evident from this inspection that the Crown had suffered appreciably in two respects; in its rightful claim to escheat lands and in its heritage of forest, waste and common land.

Escheat lands – those which reverted to the Crown for such reasons as the lack of heirs or offences against the King – were not always easy to discover. This was particularly the case where they consisted of a few acres, and had been skilfully concealed amongst neighbouring and inadequately marked properties. On the manor of Penmaen, in Caernarvonshire, no less than one hundred parcels of Crown land were scattered amongst the land held by the freeholders, and the work of locating them was further complicated by the fact that they were 'severed with baulkes or furrowes from the said freeholders lands, and the said baulkes and markes may be altered att the ploughmans pleasure if his conscience may serve him'.[31] It was a situation that certainly made it easier for an unco-operative or hostile jury to obstruct the enquiries of land commissioners. At Tregarnedd, in Anglesey, after witnesses had been interrogated and boundaries surveyed 'the jurie did then fynde by verdict that the Kings Majestie had right to the eight parte of the towne of Tregarneth...but they could not distinguishe or sever the said escheat lands from the lands of the freeholders within the said towne'.[32]

It was a simpler matter to investigate the illicit appropriation of waste and common land, which formed an extensive part of Crown property within the Principality. Here, the evidence was too visible to be hidden or denied. Besides, too many interests were involved for the guilty parties to hope to avoid denunciation and detection. Any diminution in the extent of the waste or common could affect and prejudice the customary rights of pasture which were indispensable to the manorial economy, and jeopardise the livelihood or depress the status of many who were dependent on it.

The information disclosed in some of the inquiries may have startled the commissioners, for it revealed what appeared to be a wide-spread conviction, not confined to one class, that the Crown could be robbed of its property almost with impunity.

[31] PRO E 134 10 James I Hilary 17.
[32] *Ibid* 5 James I Mich. 9.

Within the liberties of the town of Montgomery, which was Crown land, houses had been erected on the waste and about one hundred acres of it enclosed or concealed. The most prominent guilty party here was Lord Herbert of Cherbury who, despite his profound knowledge of law and reverence for the King, was discovered – after James's death – to have added more than sixty acres of that monarch's patrimony, without his connivance, to his property Lymor Park.[33] The situation was worse in the neighbouring Lordships of Ceri and Cedewain. There the inroad into the waste had been extensive and indiscriminate. *Lluestai* or cottages had been built in all directions and the land around them enclosed. The entire population of the township of Dwyriw was said to have taken part in what seemed to have amounted to an organized invasion of the waste in the neighbourhood, and converted 300 acres or so into private property.[34]

Wales had been rich in forests from time immemorial, but by the early years of the seventeenth century, it looked as if its natural resources in timber would soon be irremediably exhausted by ruthless exploitation and negligence.

It was, perhaps, on the royal estates that the appalling destruction of trees was at its worst. Gilbert Thacker, who had been appointed to survey and sell the King's woods in four of the South Wales shires, found that the value of those in Cardiganshire and Radnorshire was so small that the profits from their sale would not even defray his expenses.[35] His ominous report was matched by that of his fellow surveyor in North Wales, Gilbert Fludd, who lamented that the value of the royal woods in the counties of Caernarvon, Flint and Merioneth, amounted to no more than about £212, £10 and £87 respectively. He informed Cecil, then Lord Treasurer, that he found:

The quantitie thereof in discretion to be but sufficient for tennancie, they beinge in state poor and in nomber many in theis countreys, they having also graunted by theire leases sufficient timber for reparations and ffireboote; but where any mighte be spared it will yield no proffit at

---

[33] PRO C 21 H 46/14.
[34] PRO E 178 5125.
[35] HMC *Salisbury (Cecil) MSS*, vol. XXI, p. 68. Gilbert Thacker to the Earl of Salisbury and Sir Julius Caesar, dated 13 June 1609.

all, for the unaccessabilitie thereunto in the craggie mountaynes. Only I have in Carnarvonshire made sale of 40s worth, which uppon the retorne of my survey of woods I shall accompte for unto your Lordship as parte of the £40 I should have received for imprest of moneys growing of sales of woods to have been made in theis partes; for default whereof I am constreyned to take up money for the performance of my service in survey of his highnes landes within the counties aforesaid.[36]

Much of the evidence produced at the inquiries into these depredations pointed to the local gentry as active amongst the despoilers. The Nanneys of Merionethshire certainly had a bad name in this respect, so much so that the allegation that they were responsible for cutting down some 60,000 trees in the Crown forest of Snowdon does not seem to have strained the credulity of the commissioners.[37] On their home ground in Llanfachreth, it could be proved, apparently with greater certainty, that they had felled 10,000 out of 30,000 oak trees, valued at ten shillings each, and sold them for conversion into charcoal. Lacking confidence in the impartiality of a jury composed of their countrymen, the Nanneys had their case tried before a jury in Middlesex, who found the evidence of witnesses brought all the way from Merionethshire too convincing to be rejected.[38]

In West Wales, the officials chosen by the Crown to administer and guard its property were occasionally tempted to exploit their privileged position to make a little money at the King's expense. The woodward of Cilgerran Forest was said to have organized the spoliation of the trees in his care in a generous manner. Ignoring a royal proclamation prohibiting their felling, he invited the burgesses of Cardigan to purchase as much timber as they wished, for the renovation or construction of their houses in that borough, and sometimes actually allowed them to select the choicest trees in the forest. The fact that many of these trees were marked JR, indicating that they were specially reserved for the King's own use, made not the slightest difference.[39] The same disrespect towards Crown

---

[36] *Ibid*, p. 103. Robert Fludd to Lord Salisbury, dated 28 July 1609.
[37] PRO E 178 5111.
[38] PRO Star Chamber 8 James I 223/17.
[39] PRO E 178 5863.

property was shown in Narberth Forest, in Pembrokeshire, where the steward of the manor was said to have turned a blind eye to the King's regulations concerning the protection and conservation of the trees. Here, the prospects of private deals and undeclared profits were enhanced by the needs of the coal mines and the rural economy in the southern part of the county, which required a constant supply of timber for industrial and agricultural uses. The work of destruction continued without interruption until long after James's death, when it was discovered that out of the original 8,000 trees marked with the King's initials, only 800 were standing in 1632.[40]

One salient and indisputable fact that emerged from the investigations carried out by surveyors and commissioners alike, was that the landed gentry had taken advantage of the negligence of the Crown and the connivance or supineness of its local officials, to integrate portions of the Crown's property with their own. But this fact was not established without considerable opposition from the parties who stood to lose by the disclosure. It was not confined to such passive resistance as a refusal to give evidence or an attempt to conceal knowledge, or even a blunt rejection of the findings of the commissioners and their juries. There were other forms of non-collaboration with which to persuade the latter that, if they pushed their noses too far into gentlemen's business, they were liable to get pinched.

The Nanneys, for example, staged an impressive demonstration of their contempt for commissioners and their like in the first year of James's reign, when the Lord Treasurer, the Earl of Dorset, ordered an inquiry into their alleged devastation of Penrhos Wood at Llanfachreth. No sooner had the representatives of the Government appeared on the scene to conduct the inquiry, than Hugh Nanney and his son Gruffydd were said to have summoned their kinsmen, friends and retainers, and forcibly abducted one of the commissioners as he was attending divine service in Dolgellau church. This being done, Hugh Nanney reassumed his office of Justice of the Peace, which he had temporarily relinquished to organize the kidnapping, committed the defenceless official to prison and kept him there until the commission had, in some form or other, completed its inquiry.[41]

[40] PRO E 134 7 Carl. 1, Easter 13 and 7 Carl. 1, Mich. 11.
[41] PRO Star Chamber 8 James I 225/15.

What occurred in the Lordship of Kidwelly, in Carmarthenshire, the following year was more serious than an act of discourtesy towards a Crown official, to say the least. There, the commissioners chosen to survey the Lordship came face to face with Sir Francis Mansel, who was in possession of most of the King's demesne lands and very determined to hold on to them. The squire of Muddlescombe, the commissioners complained:

> Did not only refuse to shewe unto us any deeds or other evidences whatsoever for any lands that he held within the said honore, but in contempte of the said commission and authoritie did also sende worde in the nature of a proclamation to be made in the parishe church of Llanellie situate within the said honore upon a Sundaie in the tyme of devine service, that noe persone or persons whatsoever should shewe any deeds, writings or evidencies unto us or paie anythinge to the deputie surveyor for the entrye, survaie and examynacon of any of them.

Sir Francis Mansel also promised quite openly

> That he would undertake to discharge them if it did cost him a hundred pounds, and that wee (the commissioners) had no authoritie at all to requyre or command any suche thinge of any persons within the said honore, and that we came thither to connycatche and extorte upon the cuntrie and dyvers other words to the like effect.

They were, however, no idle words, for by bringing his influence to bear on the tenants at Pembrey, Llandyfaelog and other localities to deny what they had deposed on oath, and by other means, Mansel made it almost impossible for the commissioners to carry out their survey properly and thoroughly.[42]

Whether the practical results of these enquiries always justified the expenses incurred is, perhaps debatable. The Government may have been very relieved to understand that, in the Lordship of Kidwelly, escheats 'have not beene so plentifully among them (the tenants) as in former tymes of discencon, they being now more civysied (sic? civilised) then in those days'. But this improvement in respect for the law meant

---

[42] PRO DL 44, no. 665.

a corresponding decline in the Crown's revenues from fines. There was little doubt, however, that the survey, despite Mansel's disruptive manoeuvres, halted a concerted effort by gentry and tenants slowly to divest the Crown of its lands and revenues at Kidwelly. But the salvaging of the surviving remnants of royal property was partially undone by the distressing cupidity of Gerard Bromley, the chief surveyor. Aware of the value of materials, and how and where they could be extracted from Crown buildings within the Lordship, he was reported to have joined in partnership with a local gentleman to strip the castle of Kidwelly of its timber and lead – there was, apparently, enough of the latter to provide two boat loads – and sell or otherwise dispose of them for his own profit.[43]

The restitution of filched Crown property to its rightful owner, the King, however desirable it may have been, presented one particular problem in Wales, to which the Government could not remain indifferent. There were vast tracts of royal waste in various parts of the Principality which only served as a refuge or sanctuary for the lawless element in society, the thieves, brigands and outlaws who distinguished themselves by their particular brand of terrorism. The conversion of pieces of waste into private property, the erection of cottages on them, the attempts at tillage and the rough and ready exploitation of minerals under their surface, however illegal they might be, were, in essence, the first steps towards a more civilised way of life and the rule of law in localities which had rarely, if ever, experienced them before. In Breconshire, the waste in the Lordship of Dinas called Grwyn Fychan had gradually passed into the hands of a large number of people, who had diligently set about cultivating it. When challenged to prove their title to the waste, they wasted no time in legal technicalities, but stated baldly that it was to the Crown's benefit that the population in that desolate part of Wales should multiply and have a vested interest in the preservation of law and order. Their argument ran that 'it was a strength to his Ma[ts] king-dome that the said cottagers did so encrease, for the more the subjects be, the greater is his Ma[ts] face and strength'.[44] No more persuasive argument could be put to the King, who could never quite convince himself of the loyalty of his subjects,

[43] *Ibid*, no. 983.
[44] PRO E 134 8 James I Hilary 26.

especially along the Welsh border and some English shires adjacent to it, where recusants seemed to abound.

It was powerfully reinforced by a petition from Thomas Canon, the King's surveyor of South Wales, who went so far as to advocate some kind of programme of colonisation of the waste on Crown lands:

> There are severall large tracts of wastlands not unfruitfull according to the quality of land in those partes, which having bine withheld for many ages from all hope of habitacon or manuring by a succession of thieves and outlawes as their hauntes and receptacles of their praies, are now like to be reduced to good use by the late honorable care of the Lord President and Council of Wales and of your Ma^ts Justices of the Great Sessions. [Canon pointed out that most of this land belonged to the Crown, and once liberated from the robbers and thugs who roamed over it]...may be planted with divers families of your Ma^ts good subjects to the raysing of divers churches (needfull for the multitude of the ignorant people there), and to the advauncing of the revenue, service and wealth of those contryes, whereby also your good subjects inhabiting those partes, and epecially the poor Borderers, shall stande the better secured of their goods that have hitherto bine subject to the spoyle of those malefactors.[45]

Canon proposed that where the waste was Crown property, groups of houses should be built, not more than ten in number, and occupied by tithing men, that is, by a community that would be collectively responsible for the lawful behaviour of its individual members. Leet courts should be held twice a year in which the tithing men would give an account of their activities, renew their oath of allegiance to the Crown, and provide information about misdemeanours and the whereabouts of brigands in their neighbourhood. From such small but organized centres of law-abiding and dutiful subjects, Canon believed that it would be possible to push forward the frontiers of justice and good administration, and eventually

[45] PRO State Papers Domestic, James I 1619–23, vol. 109, fols 192b–93. Petition of Thomas Canon, Surveyor of Crown Lands in South Wales to James I, dated 18 June 1619.

pacify or extirpate the dwindling remnants of those who disliked a well-ordered society. It was a plan that recommended itself to the King, and may have reminded him of a similar scheme initiated by himself to curb the lawlessness of the Highlanders by settling colonies of more amenable Scotsmen from the Lowlands amongst them. It had failed, and James had had recourse instead to treachery, punitive expeditions, even physical extermination before achieving some sort of success.[46] But Canon's moderate project, although endorsed by the King and the Lord President of the Council of Wales, the Earl of Northampton, was never implemented.

Such impositions as the King had hitherto inflicted on his subjects had been occasioned by his personal extravagance and his inability to govern the country within his income. Even in the later years of his reign, it would appear that he was as incapable as ever of discriminating between the needs of a stable and credible government and the avaricious demands of a whole legion of parasites who infected the Court. The situation was best illustrated by the fact that whereas in 1618 the King's ambassadors in various European capitals had to content themselves with £12,000 divided between them, and his secret agents with £14,000; and whereas the navy, the first line of the kingdom's defences, received only £29,000 towards its maintenance, James's pensioners and others were able to extract more than £76,000 from the Treasury.[47] It was a state of financial misrule and a source of embarrassment to all concerned, and Parliament did little to alleviate the situation with the few subsidies that it doled out to the Crown. But the chronic want of cash in the Treasury had had one result that met with the fairly general approval of the country. It had been one factor, and not the least decisive, in restraining James from pursuing an aggressive foreign policy which might have involved the people in military commitments with a consequent further strain on their good will and purses.

The King personally had little objection to having his hands tied in this manner. His congenital timorousness, combined with a belief that he had been singled out by Divine will to preserve the peace of Europe, led him to think that by exploiting the formidable reputation of England, so imposingly

[46] See Introduction, n. 2.
[47] PRO T 48/87, fol. 1.

built up by Queen Elizabeth, he could dictate to continental powers and command respect, if not always compliance, from them. England's adversaries and allies alike, however, were fully aware that James was the only European sovereign of importance who could be safely ignored, his advice rejected, his threats discounted, and his efforts at mediation publicly acclaimed but privately ridiculed. He simply did not have the money or any other means even to create the impression of a monarch capable of fulfilling the minimal military obligations undertaken by him. And when, for the first and last time in his reign, James was called upon to engage in an enterprise of this nature, the financial implications for his subjects were as unwelcome as any they had previously experienced.

It was in 1618 that the Elector Palatine, Frederick V, who had married the King's daughter Elizabeth,[48] imprudently allowed himself to accept the Crown of Bohemia, thereby seriously challenging the political ambitions and military might of both the Hapsburg dynasty and the King of Spain. Within a short time, he had been defeated at the Battle of the White Mountain, which put an end to the independence of Bohemia, had lost his crown, had suffered the humiliation of seeing his own patrimony of the Palatinate invaded and occupied, and himself and his family forced into exile.

At first, James hesitated to take up his son-in-law's cause. He disapproved of the Bohemian venture, and when it ended in disaster, he did little more than make diplomatic represen- tations on Frederick's behalf in Madrid and Vienna, which proved quite ineffectual. Neither did he allow any one else to show more enthusiasm for the Elector Palatine. When Bishop Bayly of Bangor stood up at St Paul's Cross in London and prayed for the success and welfare of the King of Bohemia, he was reprimanded by the Privy Council for exhibiting unseasonable zeal.[49] On the other hand, any attempt to disparage his son-in- law's character or actions could arouse a feeling of vindictiveness in the King, as Edward Lloyd of Llwyn-y-Maen learnt to his cost.

A lawyer by profession and member of a prominent Catholic family near Oswestry, Lloyd found himself in Fleet prison in

---

[48] The comote of Eifionnydd, in Caernarvonshire, is recorded as having been assessed for an aid to Elizabeth, the King's daughter, on the occasion of her marriage. Jones-Pierce, *Clenennau Letters and Papers*, Addenda, p. 154.

[49] PRO State Papers Domestic, James I 1619–23, vol. 112, fol. 10. Sir Francis Nethersole to Sir Dudley Carleton, dated 8 January 1620–1.

London when the fall of Prague was announced in the capital, in December 1620. The misdemeanour, which had led to his detention, became insignificant in comparison with his behaviour when the news reached his ears. He not only made it perfectly plain to all that he welcomed Elector Frederick's downfall, but, as it was alleged, he 'did term the Prince and Princess Palatine, the King's daughter, by the ignominious and despiteful terms of Goodman Palsgrave and Goodwife Palsgrave, calling him "that poor lad" and scoffingly, with great jollity, related a Stage-Play of the Princess running away with two children, the one under one arm and the other under the other arm, and the third in her belly, with the Palsgrave following with the cradle'. What was more reckless and, potentially, more dangerous for Lloyd was his alleged declaration to another prisoner in the Fleet that 'now we may freely speak it, I or any nobleman have as good a right to be king of Wales as he, meaning the Palsgrave, to be King of Bohemia'.[50]

Lloyd's defamatory remarks were serious enough for the House of Lords to sit in judgment on him, and his failure to put up a reasonable defence merely strengthened the opinion of its members that there was nothing to exonerate. What is, perhaps, surprising is that the penalty imposed for such an offence was not carried out in all its brutality. That he was a gentleman may, possibly, have saved Lloyd from being flogged and having his ears nailed to the pillory. In other respects, the sentence was severe and humiliating enough. He was to be placed on the back of a horse with his face to its tail and holding the tail in his hand, with papers on head and breast describing his offence; to stand in the pillory in Cheapside for two hours; to be branded with the letter K signifying knave in his forehead; to pay a fine of £5,000 and to be imprisoned for life in Newgate gaol.[51] To be also deprived of his right as a gentleman to bear arms, and to have any testimony of his henceforth discredited, may have been the least of his immediate worries when his sentence was read out to him.

It was only when his protests and pleadings fell on deaf ears in the Courts of Europe, that James reluctantly turned to the alternative and more hazardous way of liberating the Palatine, by raising and equipping an expeditionary force for that purpose. And in due course imperious requests for contributions

[50] *The Parliamentary History of England*, vol. V, 1603–21, pp. 443–7.
[51] *Calendar of Wynn Papers*, p. 150, no. 954, under date of 16 May 1621.

came flowing into Wales.[52] Once again, too, they synchronised with a – to the Government – regrettable state of indifference and impecuniosity within the Principality. With the exception of the Earls of Worcester and Pembroke, few members of the landed aristocracy were sufficiently impressed by the disasters in Bohemia to show their sympathy in a practical manner. But neither were the Welsh clergy, or, at least, the episcopal hierarchy, unduly afflicted or depressd by the tribulations of their Protestant co-religionists in those countries where many were victims of a vicious Catholic reaction. The Bishop of Llandaff, for example, protested that he could not seriously think of sending any money without prior and proper consultation with his diocese, while the Bishops of St David's, Bangor and St Asaph spoke vaguely of satisfying the demands of the Privy Council for donations at some indeterminate date.[53]

A little more interest in the cause of Czech Protestantism was shown in Pembrokeshire where, in 1620, a subscription was raised for the establishment of a church and college in Prague. The Mayor of Haverfordwest headed the list with 6d, and many aldermen and gentlemen followed his example; even the poorer members of the community gave what they could afford. The disaster of the battle of the White Mountain put an end to the project, and of the total sum of 12s and 1d, about half was paid to the ringers of Haverfordwest parish church, five shillings or so to one of the bailiffs of the town, but the remaining 4d was never accounted for.[54]

It is possible that the Bishops and many of their countrymen were hoping that Parliament, which was sitting at the time, would agree to vote money for the recovery of the Palatinate and so relieve them of any financial commitment in that respect. From now on, James and his son-in-law, the Elector Palatine, were dependent upon the generosity of the public. But the King was determined that if the public should fail to understand what was really meant by a benevolence or voluntary contribution to the Crown to further the policy of armed intervention, then they should accept the Bishop of London's definition of it. Preaching at St Paul's Cross, that prelate had told his listeners that 'what we have is not our

---

[52] *Acts of the Privy Council, 1621–23*, pp. 406–10.
[53] PRO State Papers Domestic, James I 1619–23, vol. 118, fols 64 and 82.
[54] Phillips, *The History of Pembrokeshire*, p. 481.

owne, and what we gave was but rendering and restoring'.[55] His audience's reaction to this brusque disposal of their money has not been recorded, but the repercussions of his sermon, at least on this specific point, were soon felt in Wales, where the name of Palatinate became synonymous with yet another financial exaction.

Under pressure from London, the tempo of contributions from the Principality quickened appreciably, and pleas for exemption were brushed aside. The first to realize the futility of further prevarications were the clergy, and by September 1622, the four Welsh dioceses between them had donated almost £7,000. Some resistance was put up by a few counties, notably Anglesey and Carmarthenshire. The inhabitants of the latter county woefully pleaded economic depression and instability, but were brusquely reminded that if they were in a position to pay subsidies to the King, as they undoubtedly were, they could also afford to furnish money for his son-in-law without undue hardship. No better luck attended the efforts of the men of Anglesey to be allowed to forget about the Palatinate. The Privy Council was notified that 'they alleadged theire povertie and want of money, beinge exceedinglie decaied in theire estate these last foure yeares for want of sale of cattle whereon theire whole estate dependeth'.[56] There is evidence that Anglesey and Caernarvonshire were affected by an agricultural slump, but this kind of argument was cold-shouldered by the Privy Council at a time when other Welsh shires, which had previously complained of an identical economic paralysis, were now keeping up a steady flow of cash to the Palatine Liberation Fund at the Exchequer. It is possible that this turn in the tide of Welsh contributions was caused by the Council's directive that the names of those who refused to donate money should be taken down and communicated to the Government.

It was Monmouthshire that was to be closely involved in the cause of the Palatinate. Initially, its inhabitants had been vociferous about their destitution; nevertheless, they had managed to collect and dispatch over £200 to London. Now the order arrived for the impressment of a number of men to serve in the expeditionary force which was to be commanded by

---

[55] McClure, *Letters of John Chamberlain*, vol. II, p. 443. Chamberlain to Sir Dudley Carleton, dated 1 July 1622.

[56] PRO State Papers Domestic, James I 1619–23, vol. 130, fol. 131 The Justices of the Peace of Anglesey to the Privy Council, dated 20 May 1622.

Count Mansfield. He was a German and a soldier of considerable experience, but, possibly to arouse the enthusiasm of the Monmouthshire contingent, they were placed in the charge of a Welshman, Sir Charles Williams, likewise a veteran who had seen active service in the Palatinate.[57]

After an initial period of training they were to march to Dover and, being able-bodied men, were expected to cover twelve miles a day in return for the ordinary soldier's pay of 8d daily. They did so, but it remains an open question whether they threw discipline to the wind and joined the 11,000 other soldiers mustered at Dover in January 1624, who created terror in that town and in Kent generally, and looted indiscriminately until martial law was declared and the entire unruly horde embarked for the continent.

---

[57] PRO State Papers Domestic, James I 1623–5, vol. 175, fol. 115. List of the Coronels and Captaines with the nombers of soldiers that are to serve under Count Mansfield. According to this list, only fifty men were levied in Monmouthshire.

Bibliography

Primary Sources

Public Record Office, London
Chancery Records
Chancery Proceedings, Series I (C 2)
Chancery Proceedings, Series II (C 3)
Country Depositions (C 21)
Town Depositions (C 24)
Exchequer Records
Various Accounts (E 101)
Depositions (E 134)
Informations (E 148)
Miscellanea (E 163)
Licences to pass beyond the seas (E 157)
Special Commissions (E 178)
Proceedings of the Court of Star Chamber (St. Ch. 8)
Proceedings of the Court of Requests (Requests 2)
Audit Office Various Accounts (AO 3)
Lowndes Papers (T 48)
Records of the High Court of Admiralty Oyer and Terminer (HCA 1)
Duchy of Lancaster Records
Rentals and Surveys (DL 43)
Special Commissions and Returns (DL 44)
Published Calendars
State Papers Domestic, James I (SP 14)
State Papers Domestic, James I – Addenda (SP 15)
State Papers Domestic, James I – Supplementary (SP 46)
State Papers Foreign, Flanders (SP 77)
State Papers Foreign, Holland (SP 84)
State Papers Foreign, Spain (SP 94)
State Papers Foreign, Venice (SP 99)

British Museum
Additional MSS 6178, 10609, 25244
Harleian MSS 280, 324, 368, 4220
Lansdowne MSS 153, 167
Cottonian Collection, Vatellius C 1

National Library of Wales
Wales 4 Gaol Files, Denbighshire 13/2

Cardiff Borough Records

Published Works

Acts of the Privy Council of England, 1613–1625.
Bradney, Sir J. A., *The Diary of Walter Powell, 1603–1654* (1907).
Bridges, John, *The History and Antiquities of Northamptonshire*, ed. Rev. Peter Whalley (Oxford, 1791).
Browne, James, *A History of the Highlands and of the Highland Clans* (Glasgow, 1845).
Calendar of Scottish Papers (1589–93).
Calendar of Wynn (of Gwydir) *Papers* (1515–1696) (Cardiff, 1926).
Carey, Robert, Earl of Monmouth, *Memoirs*, ed. John, Earl of Cork (London, 1759).
Charles, B. G., *Calendar of the Records of the Borough of Haverfordwest*, Board of Celtic Studies, University of Wales, no. 24 (Cardiff, 1967).
Corbet, William, *Parliamentary History of England* (1806).
Davies, Ceri, *Writers of Wales – Latin Writers of the Renaissance* (Cardiff, 1981).
Davies, D. J., *The Economic History of South Wales prior to 1800* (Cardiff, 1933).
Davies, R. R., *Lordship and Society in the March of Wales* (Oxford, 1978).
Devon, Frederick, *Issues of the Exchequer during the reign of James I* (London, 1836).
Dodd, A. H., *The Industrial Revolution in North Wales, Studies in Stuart Wales* (Cardiff, 1953).
_____'Wales and the Scottish Succession', *Transactions of the Cymmrodorion Society*, 1937, 201–25.
_____'North Wales and the Essex Revolt of 1601', *English Historical Review*, LIX, 1944, 363–4.

Edwards, Edward, *The Life of Sir Walter Ralegh* (London, 1868).

Fontblanque, E. Barrington de, *Annals of the House of Percy* (London, 1887)

Gardiner, S. R., *History of England from the Accession of James I to the Outbreak of Civil War, 1603–1642* (10 vols, London 1883–4, 1894–6).

Godfrey, Eleanor S., *The Development of English Glassmaking, 1560–1640* (Oxford, 1975).

Goodman, Godfrey,*The Court of King James the First* (London, 1839).

Gruffydd, Geraint, 'Bishop Francis Godwin's Instructions for the Diocese of Llandaff', *Journal of the Historical Society of the Church in Wales*, IV, 1954, 14–22.

Ham, R. H., 'The Four Shires Controversy', *Welsh Historical Review*, VIII, 1976–7, 381–99.

Historical Manuscripts Commission, *Calendar of Bath (Longleat) MSS*, vol. V.

_____*Calendar of Buccleuch and Queenberry MSS.*

_____*Calendar of Delisle and Dudley MSS*, vols V and VI.

_____*Calendar of Downshire MSS*, vols V and VI.

_____*Calendar of Gawdy MSS.*

_____*Calendar of Salisbury (Cecil) MSS*, vols XX–XXIV.

Howell, James, *Familiar Letters or Epistolae Hoelieniae* (1645).

Jasnowski, Jozef, *England and Poland in the XVI and XVII Centuries* (Oxford, 1948).

Jones, E. D., 'The Family of Nannau', *Journal of the Merioneth Historical and Record Society*, II, 1953–6, 5–13.

Jones, E. Gwynne, *Cymru a'r Hen Ffydd* (Cardiff, 1951).

_____'County Politics and Electioneering 1558–1625', *Caernarvonshire Historical Society Transactions*, 1939, 42–6.

Jones, Francis, 'The Old Families of South-West Wales', *Ceredigion, Journal of Cardiganshire Antiquarian Society*, IV, 1960–3, 15–16.

Jones, J. Gwynfor, 'The Welsh Poets and their Patrons', *Welsh Historical Review*, IX, 1978–9, 245–77.

Jones-Pierce, T. (ed.), *Clenennau Letters and Papers in the Brogyntyn Collection, National Library of Wales Journal Supplement* (1947).

Journals of the House of Commons, 81 vols (London, 1742–1826).

Journals of the House of Lords, 31 vols (London, 1767–77).

Lee, Sidney (ed.), *The Autobiography of Edward, Lord Herbert of Cherbury* (London, 1886).

Lloyd, Howell A., *The Gentry of South-West Wales, 1540–1640* (Cardiff, 1968).

Loomie, Albert J., *The Spanish Elizabethans* (New York, 1963).

_____'Spain and the Jacobean Catholics', *Catholic Record Society*, vols 64 (1973) and 69 (1978).

McClure, N. E., *The Letters of John Chamberlain* (Philadelphia, 1939).

Morgan, W. T., 'Disputes concerning seats in church before the Consistory Court of St. David's', *Journal of the Historical Society of the Church in Wales*, XI, 1961, 65–89.

Murray, J. Tucker, *English Dramatic Companies 1558–1642* (2 vols, London, 1910).

Notestein, W., Relf, F., and Simpson, H., (eds), *Commons Debates 1621* (Yale, 1971).

Parry, R., 'A Sixteenth Century Merioneth Ironworks', *Journal of the Merioneth Historical and Record Society*.

Phillimore, W. P. W., *An Index to the Signet Office Docquet Books, 1584–1624*, British Record Society, London, 1890.

Phillips, James, *History of Pembrokeshire* (London, 1909).

Prestwich, Menna, *Cranfield – Politics and Profits under the early Stuarts* (Oxford, 1966).

Proceedings and Debates of the House of Commons in 1620 and 1621 (Oxford, 1766).

Pugh, Frank H., 'Glamorgan Recusants, 1577–1611', *South Wales and Monmouthshire Record Society*, III, 1954, 49–62.

_____'Monmouthshire Recusants in the reigns of Elizabeth and James I', *Ibid*, IV, 1957, 57–110.

Rees, William, *South Wales and the March, 1284–1415* (London, 1924).

Roberts, Glyn, 'The Glynnes and Wynns of Glynllifon', *Transactions of the Caernarvonshire Historical Society*, IX, 1948, 25–40.

Roberts, Hywel, 'Noddi Beirdd yng Ngheredigion', *Ceredigion – Journal of Cardiganshire Antiquarian Society*, VII, 1972–5, 14–39.

Ruigh, Robert E., *The Parliament of 1625* (Cambridge, Massachusetts, 1973).

Sisson, C. J., *Thomas Lodge and other Elizabethans* (Harvard, 1933).

Skrene, W. F., *The Highlanders of Scotland* (Stirling, 1902)

Stafford, H. C., *James VI of Scotland and the throne of England* (London, 1940).

Strong, Roy, *Portraits of Queen Elizabeth* (Oxford, 1963).

Williams, Glanmor, *Religion, Language and Nationality in Wales* (Cardiff, 1979).

_____'The Diocese of St David's from the end of the Middle Ages to the Methodist Revival', *Journal of the Historical Society of the Church in Wales*, XXV, 1976.

Williams, Penry, *The Council in the Marches of Wales under Elizabeth I* (Cardiff, 1959).

_____'The Attack on the Council of the Marches', *Transactions of the Cymmrodorion Society*, 1961, pt 1, 1–22.

Wilson, D. H., *King James I and VI* (London, 1956).

Zeiler, Martin, *Itinerarii Galliae et Magnae Britanniae* (Strasbourg, 1634).

Journals and Transactions

Catholic Record Society
Ceredigion – Journal of the Cardiganshire Antiquarian Society
English Historical Review
Journal of the Historical Society of the Church of Wales
Merioneth Historical and Record Society
South Wales and Monmouthshire Record Society
Transactions of the Caernarvonshire Historical Society
Transactions of the Honourable Society of Cymmrodorion
Welsh Historical Review

Index

Chester, 106, 135, 143
Chichester, Sir Arthur, 129
Chichester, Francis Leigh, Lord, 143
Chirk (Chirkland), 77, 104, 105, 106
Christopher, Richard, 105
Cichocki, Caspar, Canon of
  Sandomir: his *Alloquia Osiacensa*, 98
Cilgerran (Pembrokeshire), 130, 177
Clarke, Reynold, of Church Stretton
  (Montgomeryshire), 86
Clenennau (Caernarvonshire), 46,
  48, 56, 57
Clennok *or* Clynog, —, Welsh priest,
  70
cloth trade: in North Wales, 133
coal, 123, 132, 147
Codnor Castle (Derbyshire), 135
Coed mab Paun *or* Paynswood
  (Monmouthshire), 124
Coed Morgan (Monmouthshire), 124
Coke, Sir Edward, 43
Cole, Edward, of Shropshire, 40, 41
Cole, John, of Shropshire, 40, 41
Commons, House of, 27, 28, 34, 41,
  43, 45, 46, 47, 57, 81, 108, 109,
  110, 132, 146, 152, 153, 154, 156,
  157, 159, 164; King's concession,
  35; failure of project for Anglo-
  Scottish union, 51
Comortha, *see* Cymortha
Compton, William, Earl of North-
  ampton, President of Council of
  Wales, 63, 182
Constantinople, 138
Conway (Flintshire), family of, 85
Conway, Sir John, sheriff of
  Flintshire, 85
Conway Castle, 66
Copley, Anthony, 71, 72
Corbyn, John, 40
Cork, 136
Cornwallis, Sir Thomas, 99, 100
Council of the North, 43, 51
Council of Wales *or* Court of the
  Welsh Marches, *passim*; defied by
  Farlie, 23, 24, 40; alleged popularity
  in four English shires, 39
Court, English, 16, 57, 112, 113, 153,
  156, 182; Spanish report on, 17
Court, Scottish, 1, 16
Court of Chancery, 12, 36
Court of Common Pleas, 23
Court of High Commission, 43
Court of King's Bench, 23, 40

Court of Requests, 43
Court of Star Chamber, 43 & n 62,
  156
Coventry, 37
Cowbridge (Glamorgan), 134
Coychurch (Glamorgan), 92
Creswell, Peter, English Catholic
  adventurer, 99, 100
Croft, Sir Herbert, of Croft Castle
  (Herefordshire), 28, 30, 31, 32, 33,
  34, 38, 39, 41, 42, 43, 44 & n 78
Cromwell, Sir Thomas, of Hereford-
  shire, 33
Crowther, Brian, of Radnorshire,
  165, 166
Cymortha (Comortha), 10, 18, 117 &
  n 13, 118, 167

Dale, William, of London, 142, 143
Danvers, Sir Henry, later Earl of
  Danby, 65
Darowen (Montgomeryshire), 68
Daugleddau (Pembrokeshire), 130
Denbigh, 65, 134
Denbighshire, 140, 164; recusants
  in, 10, 17, 104, 106
Derllys (Carmarthenshire), 130
Devereux, Sir George, of Ystrad Ffin
  (Carmarthenshire), 13
Devereux, Robert, Earl of Essex (*d*
  1601), 65
Devereux, Robert, Earl of Essex (*d*
  1646), 112
Dewisland (Pembrokeshire), 130
Digby, Sir Everard, 77
Digby, Sir John, later Earl of Bristol,
  172
Dinas (Breconshire), Lordship of,
  180
*Discription of Wales, see Historie of
  Cambria*
Dolben, William, of Denbigh, 65
Dolgellau, 178
Donne, Sir Daniel, 57
Dort, Synod of (1618), 51, 52
Dorset, Earl of, *see* Sackville,
  Thomas
Douai: Croft's death, 44; Welsh
  recusant students, 97
Dover, 187
Drinos (Monmouthshire), 123, 124
Dublin, 53, 135
Dudley, Robert, Earl of Leicester, 42
Dwyriw (Montgomeryshire), 176

Madock, John, sheriff of Breconshire, 85

Madona Island, eastern Mediterranean, 138

Madrid, 79, 99, 100

Main Plot, The (Catholic), 69, 70

Malines, Gerard, German mineralogist, 60

Mallaen (Carmarthenshire), 131

Manordeilo (Carmarthenshire), 131

Mansel or Mansell, Sir Francis, of Muddlescombe (Carmarthenshire), 132 n 57, 179, 180

Mansel or Mansell, Sir Robert, of Margam, 146, 147, 153

Mansfeld, Ernst, Count, 187

maps, 148, 149

Maria, Infanta of Spain, 79

Marloes (Pembrokeshire), 10

Marshalsea Prison, London, 108

Maskal, Bartholomew, 142

Mathew, Edmund, of Radyr (Glamorgan), 142

Mathew, Edward, of Radyr, 12, 13

Mathew, George, of Radyr, 12, 13

Maurice, Sir William, of Clenennau (Caernarvonshire), 158; supporter of Anglo-Scottish union, 46, 47, 48 & n 83; rivalry between Lord Eure and, 56–9

Maxwell, John, Lord, Scottish rebel, 53

measles: and Lord Zouche, 21

Mediterranean, 137, 138

Mendips (Somerset), 144

Mercurius Gallobelgicus, 149

Meredith, —, of Abergavenny, 70

Merionethshire, 14, 55, 56, 57, 59, 65, 81, 90, 119, 125, 128, 140, 142, 176, 177

Merrick, Francis, of Pembrokeshire, 140

Merthyr (Glamorgan), 14

Meyrick, Sir Gelly, 65

Middelburg, 145

Middlesex, 177

Middleton, Fulk, sheriff of Denbighshire, 105

Middleton, Sir Hugh, 144; New River Company in London, 154

Middleton (Mydleton), Sir Thomas (*d* 1631), 107

Middleton (Mydleton), Sir Thomas (*d* 1667), 107

Milan, 98

Milbourne, Richard, Bishop of St David's, 185

Milford (Milford Haven), 69, 70, 78, 81, 132, 135, 136, 147

Milford Lane, London, 126

millstones, 140

Minehead, 135

Mise, 164–7

Monmouth, 142

Monmouthshire, 14, 65, 123, 163, 165, 186, 187; recusants in, 67, 76, 82, 93, 102, 108, 110, 113

Montagu, Sir Walter, Deputy Constable of Forest of Dean, 148

Montgomery, 153, 176

Montgomeryshire, 66, 120, 125, 153, 176, 232; recusants in, 68

Mooney, Sir Patrick, of the King's Privy Chamber, 57 n 106

Morgan, Anastasia, 99

Morgan, Lady Anne, 147

Morgan, David, of Abergavenny, 108 & n 95

Morgan, Edward, of Flintshire, 97

Morgan, Edward, of Llantarnam, 67, 84, 103, 104, 125, 128

Morgan, Sir Edward, of Monmouthshire, 99

Morgan, Grace, 148

Morgan, John, of Pencoed (Monmouthshire), 147

Morgan, Sir Matthew, 99

Morgan, Sir William, 148

Morgan, Sir William, of Tredegar (Monmouthshire), 108

Morgan, Winifred, 85

Morgan, of Talyllyn (Merionethshire), family of, 119

mortgages, 125

Mostyn (Flintshire), 127

Mostyn, of Talacre (Flintshire), family of, 85

Mostyn, Sir Roger, of Mostyn Hall, (Flintshire), 63, 153

Mostyn, Thomas, of Talacre, 97

Mostyn, Sir Thomas, of Mostyn Hall, 153

Mumbles (near Swansea), 136

music and musicians, 37; virginals, 148 & n 98; harp, 148

Myles, Thomas, of New Radnor, 169

Powys (Powes land), 49
Prague, 184, 185
Presteigne (Radnorshire), 15, 155, 165
Price, Charles, of Pilleth
    (Radnorshire), 132
Price, Edward, of Merionethshire, 119
Price, Edward, of Newtown
    (Montgomeryshire), 67
Price, James, of Mynachty
    (Monaughty) (Radnorshire), 154,
    155, 156
Price, John, of Rhiwlas (Merioneth-
    shire, 126
Price, John, of Strata Florida, 13
Price, Richard, of Gogerddan, 159
Price, William, 97
Price, of Merionethshire, family of, 119
priests, seminary, 20, 82, 97, 110
Pritchard, Nicholas, of Monmouth-
    shire, 97
Privy Council, *passim*
Privy Seal, 163, 173
Prothero, John, of Hawksbrook
    (Carmarthenshire), 148
Prys, Thomas, of Plas Iolyn, 157
Prys, Thomas, son of the above, 11
    & n 5, 57
Pugh, F. H., 83 & n 39
Pugh, Robert, of Denbighshire, 17
Purchase: his *Pilgrimages*, 148
Pwllheli, 68, 98

Quaternity, 18, 22

Radnorshire, 14, 115, 120, 154, 164,
    165, 168, 171, 172, 176
Radyr, 12, 142
Raglan Castle, 110, 112
Raglorship (Rhaglaw), office of, 131
Ralegh, Sir Walter, 69; his *Chronicles*,
    148
Randolph, Sir Edward, 148
Rea, Thomas, sheriff of Radnorshire,
    154
recusants, *passim*. *See also* under
    names of shires
rents, leases, 121–3, 125
retainers, 116–18
Rhiwaedog (Rhiwadog) (Merioneth-
    shire), 119
Rhiwlas (Merionethshire), 126
Rhos (Pembrokeshire), 130
Rhydderch, Rice, of Laugharne
    (Carmarthenshire), 158

Rhymni (Monmouthshire), Lord-
    ship of, 165
Rice, Sir Walter, of Newton,
    Llandeilo (Carmarthenshire), 127
Roberts, John, of Trawsfynydd, 97
Roche (Pembrokeshire), 147
Rome, 79
Rosser, —, Welsh recusant
    composer of songs, 108 & n 95
Rowland, Henry, Bishop of Bangor,
    88, 170, 185
Rudd, Anthony, Bishop of St
    David's, 170
Rug (Merionethshire), 65
Russell, Thomas, 144

Sackeld, —, English pirate, 136
Sackville, Thomas, Earl of Dorset,
    Lord High Treasurer, 166, 178
Salusbury *or* Salisbury, Sir John, of
    Denbighshire, 99
Salusbury *or* Salisbury, Sir John, of
    Llewenni, 20, 53, 164
Salusbury *or* Salisbury, John, of
    Bachymbyd (Denbighshire), 158
Salusbury *or* Salisbury, John, of
    Rug, 65
Salusbury *or* Salisbury, Owen, of
    Rug, 65
Salop, *see* Shropshire
salt, manufacture of, 40
sanctuary, decline of respect for, 119
Scotland, 1, 29, 161, 182; projected
    union of England and, 44–51;
    Church of, 51
Scudamore, family of, 33
Semeyne, Peter, 133, 134
Senghennydd (Glamorgan), 129
Severn, river, 84, 132
Seville, 98
ships: *Anne*, 136; *Jane*, 137, 138
Shrewsbury, 40, 133
Shropshire (Salop), 23, 24, 40, 42,
    128; Welsh speaking minority in, 4
Sicily, 138
Sloughe, Philip, of Radnorshire, 15
Smith, John, of Newcastle under
    Lyme, ironmaster, 142, 143
Snowdon, Crown Forest of, 177
Somerset, Edward, Earl of
    Worcester, 63, 67 & n 8, 76, 92,
    100, 112, 113, 134, 170, 185
Somerset, Henry, Lord Herbert of
    Chepstow, son of preceding, 134

Somersetshire, 133, 144
sorcery: in Caernarvonshire, 51–2 &
    n 83
Sousse (Souza), Tunisia, 138
Spain, 11, 23, 69, 79, 111, 132, 133,
    134, 137, 138, 145; Infanta of, *see*
    Maria; king of, *see* Philip III
Speed, John, 149
Spiller, Sir Henry, 103, 104, 157
Spooneley, —, in Cole's service, 40
St Asaph: Bishopric of, 68, 89;
    Bishop of, *see* Parry
St David's: Bishopric of, 68; Bishop
    of, *see* Rudd; Milbourne
St David's Head, 136
St James, Court of, 156
St John, Sir William, of Glamorgan,
    136
St Paul's Cross, London, 183, 185
St Winifred's Well (Wenefrids Well),
    Flintshire, 10, 95
Staffordshire: hired labour in Wales,
    120
Stepneth or Stepney, Alban, of
    Prendergast, sheriff of Pembroke-
    shire, 75, 130
Stradling, Sir John, of St Donat's
    Glamorgan, 63
Strata Florida, 13
Stuart, Arabella, 69, 71
subsidies, 164, 166, 173, 186
Swansea, 98, 136, 157
Sychffynhonnau (Monmouthshire),
    124

Talacre (Flintshire), 97
Talyllyn (Merionethshire), 119
Tenby, 132, 136
Tenbury (Worcestershire), 36
tenures, 122
Thacker, Gilbert, 176
Thelwall, Sir Bevis, 144
Thomas, Hugh, 97
Thomas, John, of Caernarvonshire,
    151
Thurbridge (Turbridge), Robert, 114
Tintern: ironworks, 146
tithes, 91, 92, 93
tobacco, 135
Torture: Council of Wales authorised
    to use, 18; employed by brigands,
    120
Townshend, Sir Henry, Justice of
    Assize, 22, 39, 106, 107

Towy, river, 81
Trafford, Thomas, 35
Trawsfynydd, 97
Treasury, *see* Exchequer
Trefgrug (Monmouthshire), 124
Trefor *or* Trevor, Sir John, of Plas
    Teg (Flintshire), 156
Tregarnedd (Anglesey), 175
Tripoli, 138
Tunis, 138
Tyburn, London, 97

Ulster, 112
Usk (Monmouthshire), 76
Utrecht, 134

Valladolid: Welsh recusant students
    at, 97, 98
Vaughan, Edward, of
    Cardiganshire, 166
Vaughan, Fowke, 114
Vaughan, Henry, of Carmarthen-
    shire, 131
Vaughan, Sir John, of Golden Grove
    (Carmarthenshire), 71, 81; family
    of, 128
Vaughan, John, of Merionethshire,
    125
Vaughan, Richard, Bishop of
    Bangor, later of London, 88
Vaughan, Dr Richard, of Radnor-
    shire, 154, 155
Vaughan, Thomas, Captain, of
    Carmarthenshire, 71
Vaughan, Thomas, 114
Vaughan, William, of Llowes
    (Radnorshire), 154, 155, 156
Vaughan, William, of Radnorshire,
    115
Vaughan, of Bodrichwyn (Denbigh-
    shire), family of, 119
Vaughan, of Eyton (Denbighshire),
    family of, 119
Vaughan, of Glanllyntegid (Meri-
    onethshire), family of, 119
Vaughan, —, JP of Monmouthshire,
    72
Venice, 137, 138, 139
Vere, Sir Francis, 15 & n 16
Vienna, 183
Villiers, George, Earl, later Duke, of
    Buckingham, 63, 162
Virginia, 135; trading company of,
    146